OCEAN POLITICS
AND LAW

OCEAN POLITICS AND LAW

An Annotated Bibliography

JAMES C. F. WANG

Bibliographies and Indexes in Law and Political Science,
Number 16

GREENWOOD PRESS
New York • Westport, Connecticut • London

Library of Congress Cataloging-in-Publication Data

Wang, James C. F.
    Ocean politics and law : an annotated bibliography / James C. F.
Wang.
        p.   cm.—(Bibliographies and indexes in law and political
science, ISSN 0742-6909 ; no. 16)
    Includes indexes.
    ISBN 0-313-27925-X (alk. paper)
    1. Maritime law—Bibliography.   2. Marine resources conservation—
Law and legislation—Bibliography.   I. Title.   II. Series.
Z6464.M2W36   1991
[JX4411]
016.3414'5—dc20   91-30202

British Library Cataloguing in Publication Data is available.

Library of Congress Catalog Card Number: 91-30202
ISBN: 0-313-27925-X
ISSN: 0742-6909

First published in 1991

Greenwood Press, 88 Post Road West, Westport, CT 06881
An imprint of Greenwood Publishing Group, Inc.

Printed in the United States of America

The paper used in this book complies with the
Permanent Paper Standard issued by the National
Information Standards Organization (Z39.48-1984).

10 9 8 7 6 5 4 3 2 1

Contents

Preface

This bibliographic volume on the law and politics of the sea, with annotation for a selected number of entries, is the outgrowth of preparation for the <u>Handbook on Ocean Politics and Law</u> published by Greenwood Press.

This bibliography with selected annotation is arranged in twelve subject categories: physical features of the world's oceans; international conferences on the uses of the oceans; development of international principles; living resources disputes and management; mineral or non-living resources; deep seabed mining; marine environmental protection and pollution control; regional arrangements for marine environmental protection and cooperation; legality and prohibition of military use; navigation and shipping; marine scientific research; and major players and their positions on selected issues at the Third United Nations Conference on the Law of the Sea.

The selection for inclusion in the bibliography is based on these criteria: pertinency to the discussion in the text of the handbook, up-to-dateness, and significance of the work. The criteria for selecting the entries for annotation are based on the following: 1) the importance or significance of the topic in relation to ocean law and politics; 2) up-to-dateness; 3) a wider representation from different authors on similar topics; and 4) works which show different perceptions from authors on the topics over time.

One needs to keep in mind that a truly comprehensive bibliography on ocean affairs and the law of the sea would most likely run into volumes; such a goal is beyond the scope of this work. What is offered here in the bibliography is a selective listing of major works on the subjects considered in all respects most useful and sufficient enough to enable the readers and users to probe further or delve deeper. The bibliographies and guides to ocean affairs and law of the sea literature mentioned in the introduction are readily accessible and are provided as additional aids. Hopefully, in a sense, both the handbook about ocean law and politics and this bibliography will serve as ready references and convenient guides to the rapidly growing volume of literature concerning ocean affairs, law, and public policy.

Entries selected for annotation represent those works or studies which in the author's judgment (a subjective one at that) are considered either because of the importance of the topic discussed or the analytical significance, or simply because of the timeliness. On the whole, the anno- tated material should provide an adequate selection for a variety of topics on ocean law and politics that would be useful for library reference. In fact, the bibliographic volume is intended to make it convenient for libraries, ocean research organizations, foreign offices, university students, and the general public to access with minimum frustration the material that is available.

The preparation of this bibliography on ocean law and politics would not have been possible without the help of a number of persons. First, a word of gratitude to Catherine Tignac for her valuable assistance in compiling entries. Then, my appreciation to Edith Worsencroft for her help in editing and typing the camera-ready manuscript. Finally, to Mildred Vasan, a senior editor at Greenwood, for her guidance, patience and encouragement in making this production possible.

Introduction

Since the mid-1960s when the United Nations General Assembly began its seabed debate, there has been published a cascade of literature on the subject of ocean affairs reflecting multidisciplinary research and studies. The bulk of the literature appeared from the 1960s to the mid-1980s, with a somewhat declining rate of production after the signing of the Law of the Sea Convention in December 1982. Subjects for study and inquiry on ocean or marine affairs for the past two decades range from fishery conservation and management, marine environmental protection and pollution control, offshore mineral resource exploitation and exploration, to navigation, transportation, shipping and military or security uses. But they tend to revolve around the central issues of legal disputes and public policies among and between nations, as well as methods for achieving international cooperation. Thus, the term "ocean affairs studies" refers to not only fishery technology, ocean engineering, and oceanography, but the social sciences of law, politics and economics, as well.

Basic Information Sources

One of the very useful bibliographic guides was published in 1973 by the Law of the Sea Institute, now affiliated with the University of Hawaii: Ann L. Hollick's Maritime Policy, Law and Economics Bibliography. This bibliography is a lengthy annotation of major works in maritime law, economics and policy for the period 1970-1973. Two years later the Law of the Sea Institute published a second bibliographic guide of periodical literature on ocean affairs for the 1970s: Law of the Sea: A Bibliography of the Periodical Literature of the 1970s, edited by C. B. Ilana, John King Gamble, Jr. and C. Quinn. This bibliographic guide contains a comprehensive list of some two hundred journal articles published from 1970-1975, with brief annotation updating that compiled by Ann L. Hollick in 1973.

Then in 1987 Martinus Nijhoff, of the Netherlands, and Graham and Trotman, of London, published a comprehensive index to literature on marine law and policy: Marine Affairs Bibliography: A Comprehensive Index to Marine Law and Policy Literature Cumulation, 1980-1985, edited by Christian L. Wiktors and Leslie A. Foster. This is a massive cumulative index listing nine thousand entries of writings in many academic disciplines and published in six languages besides English and French. The index was compiled under the auspices of the Dalhousie Ocean Studies Programme, Dalhousie Law School and the International Institute for Transportation and Ocean Policy Studies. The indexes are arranged and divided into some thirty topics on ocean affairs and the law of the sea.

The United Nations has also published three separate volumes of selected bibliography on the law of the sea, the third one in 1989, under the auspices of the Office of the Special Representative of the Secretary-General for the Law of the Sea. The Law of the Sea: A Selected Bibliography is designed for use by those interested in law of the sea matter in general and the Law of the Sea Convention (1982) in particular. It is a selected list of books and articles published primarily in the English, French and Spanish languages. Entries are arranged in twenty-seven subject categories with an index arranged according to author. All cited references in the United Nations selected bibliography

are available   at the   three libraries of the United Nations
headquarters in New York: the Law   of the   Sea Library, the
Legal Library, and the Dag Hammarskjold Library.

For those who are not familiar with periodicals dealing
with ocean affairs, it is advisable   to consult   the article
by Judith B. Barnett, "A Guide to Periodicals for the Study
of Marine Affairs," <u>Ocean Development and International Law</u>,
vol. 10,   nos. 3-4,   1982, pp.   557-377.   Judith B. Barnett,
associated with the Graduate   School of   Oceanography at the
University of Rhode Island, has prepared a useful review and
guide to periodicals devoted   to the   study of international
marine affairs.   In   addition to   a description of selected
journals and periodicals on ocean affairs, she also provides
a valuable guide to the indexes to these periodicals.

The Council on Ocean Law, a Washington, D.C. based non-
profit corporation, founded in 1980 to   support the development of   international   laws   for the oceans, has published
periodically a bibliography of current material dealing with
international   ocean   law   and   policy.   It is arranged in
subject categories of general ocean law and policy, environment,   marine   scientific   research,   navigation, fisheries,
deep   seabed   mining,   boundaries,   minerals,   and security.
Unfortunately, the   Council on   Ocean Law   ceased to publish
such a bibliography for its members after the   February 1990
issue.   For   these   bibliographies,   consult   the Council on
Ocean Law's Bibliography issues of July   1988, October 1988,
January 1989, April 1989, July 1989, and February 1990.

Official Records and Documents to the Third United Nations
Conference on the Law of the Sea

The United Nations has   published seventeen   volumes of
Official   Records   and   Documents   of   Meetings of the Third
United Nations Conference on the Law of the   Sea, 1973-1982.
These are listed in the section on International Conferences
on the Uses of   the   Ocean   of   this   supplement.   For the
official text   and index   to the 1982 Convention see <u>The Law
of the Sea: United Nations Convention on the Law of   the Sea
with Index   and Final   Act of   the Third United Nations Conference on the Law of the Sea</u>, 1983.   This   volume contains
the basic texts and agreements of the Conference with useful
explanatory background materials.

The United Nations also   publishes a   volume which contains   a   bibliographic   listing   of   all   reports,   meeting
records and relevant official   documents   issued   during the
Conference   from   1973-1982: <u>Law   of   the   Sea: Master File
Containing References to   Official   Documents   of   the Third
United Nations Conference on the Law of the Sea</u>, 1985.   As a
useful supplement to this   listing, the   United Nations also
publishes <u>The Law of the Sea: Multilateral Treaties Relevant
to the United Nations Convention   on   the   Law   of   the Sea</u>,
1985.   This volume   contains a comprehensive list of multilateral treaties   and   instruments   of   global   and regional
character which are still in force and which are relevant to
the issues covered by the 1982 Convention.

The United Nations Office for Ocean Affairs and the Law
of the   Sea, in   New York,   has published   an updated volume

regarding ocean affairs since the signing of the 1982 Convention: Annual Review of Ocean Affairs: Law and Policy,
Main Documents, 1985-1987, vols. 1 and 2, November 1988.
From 1985 to December 1989, that office also published four-
teen issues of Law of the Sea Bulletin, which contains the
status of the 1982 LOS Convention (signatures and ratifications), legal information relevant to the 1982 LOS
Convention, development of the Preparatory Commission for
the International Seabed Authority, and other information on
the law of the sea.
    There are four other guides to the Third United Nations
Conference on the Law of the Sea which need to be noted
here. One is a United Nations publication regarding the
global negotiation process on the law of the sea, entitled
Crowded Agendas, Crowded Rooms, Institutional Arrangements
at UNCLOS III: Some Lessons in Global Negotiations, 1981. A
guide or a review of the 1982 Convention is contained in the
book by Rosenne Shabari and Louis B. Sohn: United Nations
Convention on the Law of the Sea, vols. I-V, 1981, Martinus
Nijhoff, publishers for the Center for Ocean Law and Policy,
University of Virginia. A massive collection of documents
on the Law of the Sea Conference is available in Renate
Platzoder: The Third United Nations Conference on the Law of
the Sea: Documents (18 volumes), Dobbs Ferry, NY: Oceana
Publications, Inc., 1989. And, finally, there is Bermaerts'
Guide to the Law of the Sea (1982 United Nations Conven-
tion), United Kingdom: Fairplay Publications, Ltd., 1989.

Selected Bibliographies, Guides, Indexes on Specific Topics
Related to the Law of the Sea

    There are a number of useful reference aids on specific
topics dealing with some of the provisions in the 1982 LOS
Convention. First, the Office of the Special Representative
of the Secretary-General (now the Office for Ocean Affairs
and the Law of the Sea) published The Law of the Sea: Rights
of Access of Land-Locked States to and from the Sea and the
Freedom of Transit, 1987. It is basically a legislative
history of Part X, Articles 124 and 132, of the 1982 LOS
Convention concerning access-to-the-seas rights of land-
locked states. A year earlier, Kluwer published Martin
Glassner's Bibliography on Land-Locked States, 2nd revised
edition, The Hague: Kluwer Publishers, 1986.
    On the subject of deep seabed mining, there is a Bibli-
ography and Index to the Literature on Manganese Nodules
(1961-1979), by the Department of Business and Economic
Development, State of Hawaii, January 1981. This is a
massive collection--more than five hundred pages of entries
concerning manganese nodules. Somewhat more selective is
the appendix of references on ferro-manganese in Marine
Mining: A New Beginning, Conference Proceedings, July 18-21,
1982 in Hilo, Hawaii, also published by the State of Hawaii,
in 1987. There is also a list of publications on ocean
mining entitled "Ocean Mining: Economic, Technical, Political, Legal and Environmental Aspects," International
Challenges, vol. 8, no. 1, July 1988.

There is an excellent collection of bibliographical entries on deep seabed resources in Volume III, Parts 1 & 2, of E. D. Brown's Seabed Energy and Mineral Resources and the Law of the Sea, published in 1986 by Graham and Trotman. It is a 39-page listing of books and articles on seabed energy and mineral resources. A very useful selected bibliography on the legal aspects of deep seabed mining can be found in Volume II, pp. 5-37, of Theodore G. Kronmiller's Lawfulness of Deep Seabed Mining, published in 1988 by Oceana Publications, Inc.

For assistance on marine scientific research, the bibliography to Alfred H. A. Soons' Marine Scientific Research and the Law of the Sea, Antwerp, Boston, London and Frankfurt: Kluwer Law and Taxation Publishers, 1982, is a very useful one. Also, the United Nations has compiled a volume on national legislation concerning marine scientific research: Law of the Sea: National Legislation, Regulation and Supplementary Documents on Marine Scientific Research in Areas under National Jurisdiction, 1989.

On marine environmental protection and pollution control, there are a number of bibliographic guides. First is the excellent selected bibliography on international environmental law by Blanka Kudej, published in Vol. 20, no. 3 (Spring 1988) of the Journal of International Law and Politics by New York University. It provides a list of reference aids, books and articles on international environmental law, divided and arranged according to the world's regions, as well as a list of complementary periodical literature on the subject. The United Nations Environmental Programme Office has published a guide to environmental information entitled "ACCIS Guide to United Nations Information Sources on the Environment," 1988.

Special mention must be made of the almost exhaustive listing of reference material on marine pollution in the four-volume work by John Warren Kindt: Marine Pollution and the Law of the Sea, Buffalo, NY: William S. Hein & Co., Inc., 1986. At the end of each of the thirty chapters, there is a detailed bibliography on the subjects discussed in the chapter, in addition to a listing of pertinent treaties, statutes and cases. On the subject of ocean dumping, the United Nations has published a legislative history on rules enforcement and standards entitled The Law of the Sea: Pollution by Dumping, 1985.

There are two bibliographic guides relating to the role of Third World nations at the Law of the Sea Conference. One is by Michael A. Morris and Penelope Simoes Ferreira: "Latin-America, Africa, and the Third United Nations Conference on the Law of the Sea: Annotated Bibliography," in Ocean Development and International Law, vol. 9, nos. 1-2, 1981, pp. 101-186. The other is by Alberto Szekely in his Bibliography on Latin America and the Law of the Sea, a comprehensive listing of Latin American and selected U.S. writings on the law of the sea published in 1976 by The Law of the Sea Institute, which is now affiliated with the University of Hawaii.

Also, there are two bibliographic guides to literature related to the Antarctic: James H. W. Hain, "A Reader's Guide to the Antarctic," Oceanus, vol. 31, no. 2, Summer 1988, pp. 2-4; and Orrego F. Vicuna's Antarctic

Bibliography, published by the Institute of International Studies, University of Chile, 1987.

Annual Special Publications Devoted to Ocean Affairs and the Law of the Sea

Three annual exclusive publications on ocean affairs are selected as good sources of reference to current writings and research by specialists in the ever expanding field of ocean studies. The listing of these annual events that culminated in publication does not detract in any way from the important role the numerous periodicals and journals on international law and ocean affairs have played in enriching mankind's knowledge and awareness about the oceans.

First is the Ocean Yearbook, now in its eighth volume, edited by Elisabeth Mann Borgese and Norton Ginsburg, and published by the University of Chicago Press, which began issuing its annual publication in 1978. Each volume of the Ocean Yearbook contains a rich source of material on the uses of the ocean and relevant facts and figures about these uses.

Then the Netherlands Institute for the Law of the Seas publishes yearly the International Organization and the Law of the Sea: Documentary Yearbook. The yearbook is intended to reproduce the most important documents about the law of the sea issued each year by international organizations. Some questions have been raised with respect to the criteria used for selecting the documents reproduced in the yearbook as provided by the various international organizations.

The Law of the Sea Institute, now Honolulu-based and affiliated with the University of Hawaii, convenes an annual conference on the law of the sea which is now in its twenty-fourth year. The annual conference is held in a different part of the world each year and is attended by leading ocean affairs experts from all over the world. The conference papers are edited and published in bound volumes. The annual conference concentrates on the latest developments in many aspects of ocean law and policy.

Since 1971 the San Diego Law Review has devoted one issue each year to the law of the sea; it is entitled "Law of the Sea I (1969) to XXII (1990)." There is as yet no cumulative index for the articles published in this special series. However, many of these articles have been cited or referred to as references in the chapters in this handbook.

OCEAN POLITICS
AND LAW

The World's Oceans and Their Physical and Geographic Features

1. "A Brief History of Antarctica." Oceanus, vol. 31, no. 2, Summer 1988, pp. 28-31. Academic American Encyclopedia. Princeton, NJ: Arete Publishing Co., Inc., 1981, vol. 2, pp. 104-106, 294-296; vol. 14, pp. 321, 325-333; vol. 15, pp. 5-8.

2. Anderson, A. T. "The Ocean Basins and Ocean Water." Elisabeth Mann Borgese and Norton Ginsburg, eds. Ocean Yearbook 3. Chicago and London: University of Chicago Press, 1982, pp. 135-156.

3. "Antarctica: Is Any Place Safe from Mankind?" TIME. January 1990, pp. 56-62.

4. "Antarctica Pact Eludes Talks." The New York Times. 22 October 1989, p. A-9.

5. Archer, Clive. "General Features of Political Development and Possibilities for Cooperation in the Arctic." Current Research on Peace and Violence. vol. xi, no. 4, 1988, pp. 137-446.

6. Armi, Laurence. "Mixing in the Deep Ocean: The Importance of Boundaries." Oceanus. vol. 21, no. 1, Winter 1978, pp. 14-19.

Armi discusses recent scientific study of the ocean bottom to show that mixing of water in the abyss is not due to uniform stirring, but it is the process dominated by near-bottom turbulence where water contacts topographic features.

7. Bencivenga, Jim. "Awesome 'Engine' of the Atlantic Ocean." The Christian Science Monitor. 8 August 1989, p. 13.

8. Bhatt, J. J. Oceanography: Exploring the Planet Ocean. New York: D.Van Nostrand Company, 1978.

For beginners in oceanography Bhatt's book is useful for acquiring basic background on some of the principles, concepts and processes of the oceans. These fundamental oceanographic principles and concepts are discussed in terms of contemporary problems on ocean resources, management and environmental pollution.

9.   Borgese, Elisabeth Mann. <u>The Mines of Neptune: Minerals and Metals from the Sea</u>. New York: Harry N. Abrams, Inc., 1985.

This is a work by a prominent writer on ocean affairs who sees the oceans as a laboratory wherein mankind can pursue new economic, political and social institutions.

10.   _____. <u>The Future of the Oceans: A Report to the Club of Rome</u>. Montreal: Harvest House, 1986.

11.   Brigham, Lawson. "Workshop on the Soviet Maritime Arctic." <u>Arctic Research of the United States</u>. vol. 2, Spring 1988.

12.   Burke, C. A. and C. L. Drake. <u>The Geology of Continental Margins</u>. New York: Springer-Verlag, 1974.

13.   <u>Chambers Encyclopedia</u>. Oxford: Pergamon Press, 1967, vol. 10, pp. 172-177.

14.   <u>Collier's Encyclopedia</u>. New York: MacMillan Educational Company, 1988, vol. 3, pp. 158-160; vol. 12, p. 638; vol. 18, pp. 58-63, 277-278.

15.   Conant, Melvin A. "The Call of the Arctic." <u>Oceanus</u>. vol. 25, no. 4, Winter 1982-83, pp. 51-57.

Urges a strong federal commitment to develop vast resources of the Arctic in an environmentally responsible way.

16.   Cousteau, Jacques Yves. <u>The Ocean World</u>. New York: Abradale Press/Harry N. Abrams, Inc., 1985.

This is perhaps one of the best and most comprehensive treatments of the oceans by the famed explorer. The book contains 18 lively chapters, enhanced by fabulous illustrations and marine photography.

17.   Cuyvers, Luc. <u>Ocean Uses and Their Regulation</u>. New York: John Wiley and Sons, Inc., 1984.

An excellent book for non-experts; it attempts to take an inventory of the uses of the sea and regulations governing those uses.

18.   Eckert, Ross. <u>The Enclosure of Ocean Resources: Economics and the Law of the Sea</u>. Stanford, CA: Hoover Institution Press, 1979.

19.   <u>The Encyclopedia Americana</u>. International ed. Danbury, CT: Grolier Inc., 1984, vol. 11, pp. 176-185; vol. 15, pp. 48-49; vol. 20, pp. 611-616.

20. Encyclopaedia Britannica.   Chicago: Encyclopaedia Bri-
     tannica, Inc., 1970, vol. 2, pp. 694-698; vol. 12, pp.
     113-114; vol. 17, pp. 14-18.

21. Gordon, Arnold L.   "The Southern Ocean and Global
     Climate." Oceanus. vol. 31, no. 2, Summer 1988, pp.
     39-46.

22. Hodgson, R. and L. Alexander. Towards an Objective
     Analysis of Special Circumstances: Bays, Rivers,
     Coastal and Oceanic Archipelagos and Atolls. Occa-
     sional Paper 13. Honolulu: Law of the Sea Institute,
     University of Hawaii, 1972.

This is a very comprehensive study of the major geographic
issues concerning bays, rivers, archipelagos and atolls that
the 1958 and 1962 Convention on the Territorial Sea failed
to reconcile.

23. Hollister, Charles D. "In Pursuit of Oceanography and
     a Better Life for All." Oceanus. vol. 26, no. 2,
     Summer 1983, pp. 10-16.

Discusses career opportunities in physical oceanography,
geological and geophysical oceanography, and ocean
engineering.

24. Huyghe, Patrick. "Oceans from Comets--New Evidence."
     Oceanus. vol. 21, no. 2, March-April 1988, pp. 8-11.

Provides some answers to the question, "Where does the ocean
get its water?"

25. Joyner, Christopher C. "Antarctica and the Indian
     Ocean States: The Interplay of Law, Interests, and
     Geopolitics." Ocean Development and International
     Law. vol. 21, no. 1, 1990, pp. 41-70.

26. _____. "Antarctica and the Law of the Sea: An
     Introductory Overview." Ocean Development and Inter-
     national Law. vol. 13, no. 3, 1983, pp. 277-290.

27. _____ and Sudhir K. Chopra. The Antarctic Legal
     Regime. Dordrecht, The Netherlands: Martinus Nijhoff
     Publishers, 1988.

This is an important study which examines major political,
economic and legal issues affecting the Antarctic regime.

28. _____ and Peter J. Lipperman. "Conflict Jurisdic-
     tion in the Southern Ocean: The Case of an Antarctic
     Regime." Virginia Journal of International Law. vol.
     27, no. 1, Fall 1986, pp. 1-38.

29. Kesteven, G. L. "The Southern Ocean." Elisabeth Mann
     Borgese and Norton Ginsburg, eds. Ocean Yearbook 1.
     Chicago and London: University of Chicago Press, 1978,
     pp. 467-499.

4 OCEAN POLITICS AND LAW

30. Kimball, Lee A. Southern Exposure: Deciding Antarctica's Future. Washington, DC: World Resources
Institute, 1990.

Deals with the need and means for improving the governance
system for protecting the southern ten percent of the Earth.
As scientific research activities and tourism increase, the
time has come for re-evaluating the existing management
system for Antarctica.

31. _____. "Antarctica: The Challenges that Lie
Ahead." Journal of Human Environment. vol. xviii, no.
1, 1989.

32. _____. "Antarctic Issues Today." Choon-ho Park
and Jae Kyu Park, eds. The Law of the Sea: Problems
from the East Asian Perspective. Honolulu: The Law of
the Sea Institute, University of Hawaii, 1987, pp. 524-
535.

33. Koroma, Abdul G. "Perspective of Non-Parties to the
Antarctic Treaty." Thomas A. Clingan, Jr., ed. The
Law of the Sea: What Lies Ahead? Honolulu: The Law of
the Sea Institute, University of Hawaii, 1988, pp. 380-
385.

34. Lamson, Cynthia and David Vander Zwaag. "Arctic Waters:
Needs and Options for Canadian-American Cooperation."
Ocean Development and International Law. vol. 18, no.
1, 1987, pp. 49-100.

35. Lemonick, Michael D. "Journey to the Earth's Core."
TIME. 13 June 1988, p. 57.

36. Lipperman, Peter J. "Conflicting Jurisdictions in the
Southern Ocean: The Case of an Antarctica Minerals
Regime." Virginia Journal of International Law. vol.
27, no. 1, Fall 1986, pp. 1-38.

37. May, John. Antarctica: A New View of the Seventh
Continent. Garden City, NY: Doubleday, 1989.

38. McCoy, Floyd W. and Philip D. Rabinowitz. "The Evolution of the South Atlantic." Oceanus. vol. 27, no. 1,
Fall 1986, pp. 1-38.

39. McGraw-Hill Encyclopedia of Ocean and Atmospheric
Sciences. New York: McGraw-Hill Book Company, 1977,
pp. 63-65, 103-104, 119-122, 139-144, 233-241, 327,
336-337, 387-390, 461-462.

40. Mitchell, Barbara. "The Southern Ocean in the 1980s."
Elisabeth Mann Borgese and Norton Ginsburg, eds. Ocean
Yearbook 3. Chicago and London: University of Chicago
Press, 1982, pp. 349-385.

41. Morris, Michael A. "South American Antarctic Policies."
Elisabeth Mann Borgese, Norton Ginsburg and Joseph R.

Morgan, eds. <u>Ocean Yearbook 7.</u>   Chicago and London: University of Chicago Press, 1988, pp. 356-371.

Discusses the politics of Antarctic claims by Argentinia and Chile.

42.   <u>The New Encyclopaedia Britannica.</u>   Macropaedia ed. Chicago: Encyclopaedia Britannica, Inc., 1984, vol. 7, pp. 112-113; vol. 13, pp. 482-484.

43.   <u>The New Encyclopaedia Britannica.</u>   Micropaedia ed. Chicago: Encyclopaedia Britannica, Inc., 1984, vol. i, pp. 41-42; vol. ii, pp. 470-471.

44.   Officer, Charles B.   "Physical Oceanography of Estuaries." <u>Oceanus.</u> vol. 19, no. 3, Spring 1976, pp. 3-9.

45.   _____.   <u>Physical Oceanography of Estuaries</u> (and Associated Coastal Waters). New York and London: John Wiley and Sons, 1976.

This is a technical book which attempts to provide a coherent treatment of the physical oceanography of estuaries and related bodies of water such as straits, bays and lagoons. It utilizes mathematical calculus and equations in its analysis and explanations.

46.   Parker, Henry S. <u>Exploring the Oceans: An Introduction for the Traveler and Amateur Naturalist.</u>   Englewood Cliffs, NJ: Prentice-Hall, Inc., 1985.

47.   Peterson, M. J. "Antarctic Implications of the New Law of the Sea." <u>Ocean Development and International Law.</u> vol. 16, no. 2, 1986, pp. 137-182.

48.   Pharand, Donat.   "Canada's Sovereignty over the Newly Enclosed Arctic Waters."   <u>The Canadian Yearbook of International Law.</u> 1987, pp. 325-341.

49.   Pichard, George L. and William J. Emery. <u>Descriptive Physical Oceanography: An Introduction.</u>   4th enl. ed. Oxford and New York: Pergamon Press, 1982.

This is an introductory text on the synoptic aspects of physical oceanography suitable   for   graduate students. Therefore, it is a technical text with numerous figures and technical formulae.

50.   Richardson, Jacques G., ed. <u>Managing the Ocean: Resources, Research, Law.</u> Mt. Airy, MD: Lomond Publications, Inc., 1985.

51.   Rodgers-Miller, Lynne and John E. Bardach, "In Face of a Rising Sea." Elisabeth Mann Borgese, Norton Ginsburg and Joseph R. Morgan, eds. <u>Ocean Yearbook 7.</u> Chicago and London: University of Chicago Press, 1988, pp. 177-190.

Discusses the changing interface of sea and shore, explains the causes of sea-level change and predicts the global sea-level rise.

52. Ross, David A. Introduction to Oceanography. 3rd ed. Englewood Cliffs, NJ: Prentice-Hall, Inc., 1982.

This is an updated basic introductory text on oceanography. The 15 chapters provide a wide range of coverage on the subject of the oceans.

53. _____. Opportunities and Uses of the Ocean. New York: Springer-Verlag, 1978.

A primer on ocean uses written by a leading ocean expert.

54. Rowe, Gilbert T., ed. Deep-Sea Biology. New York: John Wiley and Sons, 1983.

This is a volume of articles by an international panel of experts devoted to deep sea biology, motivated by the 1977 discovery of fauna around the deep Galapagos hydrothermal vents.

55. Schlee, John S., David W. Folger, William P. Dillon, Kim D. Klugord and John A. Grow. "The Continental Margins of the Western North Atlantic." Oceanus, vol. 22, no. 3, Fall 1979, pp. 40-47.

There are two reasons why this entry is annotated. One, the authors provide a good summary of the interpretation of earlier phases of the earth's history. Second, it points out that a study of the structural and sedimentary history of the United States continental margin improves chances for finding new hydrocarbon resources.

56. Scott, Ronald W. "Protecting United States Interest in Antarctica." San Diego Law Review, vol. 26, no. 3, August-September 1989, pp. 575-624.

57. Scovazzi, Tuillo. "Bays and Straight Baselines in the Mediterranean." Ocean Development and International Law, vol. 19, no. 5, 1988, pp. 401-420.

58. Shapiro, Harvey A. "The Landfilled Coast of Japan's Inland Sea." Elisabeth Mann Borgese, Norton Ginsburg and Joseph R. Morgan, eds. Ocean Yearbook 7. Chicago and London: University of Chicago Press, 1988, pp. 294-316.

59. Shusterich, Kurt M. "International Jurisdictional Issues in the Arctic Ocean." Ocean Development and International Law, vol. 14, no. 3, 1984, pp. 235-272.

60. Skinner, Brian J. and Karl K. Turekian. Man and the Ocean. Englewood Cliffs, NJ: Prentice-Hall, Inc., 1973.

61. Smith, Peyton L., Robert A. Ragotzkie, Anders W. Andren and Hallet J. Harris. "Estuary Rehabilitation: The

Green Bay Story." Oceanus. vol. 31, no. 3, Fall 1988, pp. 13-20.

62. Thurman, Harold V. Introductory Oceanography. 2nd ed. Columbus, OH: Charles E. Merrill Publishing Company, 1978.

63. Turekian, K. K. Oceans. 2nd ed. Englewood Cliffs, NJ: Prentice-Hall, Inc., 1976.

64. Vallega, Adalberto. "A Human Geographical Approach to Semi-enclosed Seas: The Mediterranean Case." Elisabeth Mann Borgese, Norton Ginsburg and Joseph R. Morgan, eds. Ocean Yearbook 7. Chicago and London: University of Chicago Press, 1988, pp. 372-393.

65. Whitaker, J. H. McD. Submarine Canyons and Deep Sea Fans: Modern and Ancient. Stroudsburg, PA: Dowden, Hutchinson and Ross, Inc., 1976.

A collection of articles by oceanography experts who were interested in, or have done work on, submarine canyons.

66. The World Book Encyclopedia. Chicago: World Book, Inc., 1988, pp. 656-673.

67. Young, Oran R. The Arctic in World Affairs. Seattle: Washington Sea Grant Program, University of Washington, 10 May 1988.

68. _____. "Arctic Waters." Ocean Development and International Law. vol. 18, no. 1, 1987, pp. 101-114.

69. Zacklin, R. and L. Caflisch. The Legal Regime of International Rivers and Lakes. London: Graham & Trotman, Ltd., 1981.

International Conferences
on the Uses of the Oceans

70. Agrait, Luis E. "The Third United Nations Conference on the Law of the Sea and Non-Independent States." Ocean Development and International Law. vol. 7, nos. 1-2, 1979, pp. 19-30.

71. Anand, R. P. "Odd Man Out: The United States and the UN Convention on the Law of the Sea." Jon M. Van Dyke, ed. Consensus and Confrontation: The United States and the Law of the Sea Convention. Honolulu: The Law of the Sea Institute, University of Hawaii, 1985, pp. 73-124.

72. Ball, Milner S. "Law of the Sea: Expression of Solidarity." San Diego Law Review. vol. 19, no. 3, April 1982, pp. 461-473.

73. Bandow, Doug. "UNCLOS III: A Flawed Treaty." San Diego Law Review. vol. 19, no. 3, April 1982, pp. 475-492.

This is a highly critical essay declaiming the 1982 Law of the Sea Convention as a flawed document contrary to American ocean interests.

74. Borgese, Elisabeth Mann, Mahinda Perera and Aldo Chircop. "The UN Convention on the Law of the Sea: The Cost of Ratification." Elisabeth Mann Borgese, Norton Ginsburg and Joseph R. Morgan, eds. Ocean Yearbook 8. Chicago and London: University of Chicago Press, 1989, pp. 1-17.

Discusses the reasons for the slow ratification rate of the 1982 Law of the Sea Convention. It also deals with the cost of ratification in terms of new responsibilities over the extended areas of jurisdiction together with the cost or payments for the establishment and administration of new institutions.

75. _____. "Implementing the Convention: Development in the Preparatory Commission." Elisabeth Mann Borgese, Norton Ginsburg and Joseph R. Morgan, eds.

Ocean Yearbook 7. London and Chicago: University of Chicago Press, 1987, pp. 1-13.

Discusses the work and negotiations at the 1986-87 Preparatory Commission on the ocean mining regime.

76. _____. "The Convention is Signed: What Does the Future Hold?" Elisabeth Mann Borgese and Norton Ginsburg, eds. Ocean Yearbook 4. Chicago and London: University of Chicago Press, 1983, pp. 1-14.

77. _____. "The Draft Convention." Elisabeth Mann Borgese and Norton Ginsburg, eds. Ocean Yearbook 3. Chicago and London: University of Chicago Press, 1982, pp. 1-12.

78. Brown, E. D. and R. R. Churchill. The UN Convention on the Law of the Sea: Impact and Implementation. Honolulu: The Law of the Sea Institute, University of Hawaii, 1987.

The 19th annual conference of the Law of the Sea Institute, held in 1985 at the University of Wales Institute of Science and Technology, produced a rich collection of some thirty articles dealing with a host of issues and problems related to the 1982 Law of the Sea Convention.

79. Brown, Heidi E. "Synopsis: Recent Developments in the Law of the Sea 1986." San Diego Law Review. vol. 24, no. 3, May-June 1987, pp. 701-726.

80. Brunn, Stanley D. and Gerald L. Ingalls. "Voting Patterns in the UN General Assembly on Uses of the Seas." Elisabeth Mann Borgese, Norton Ginsburg and Joseph R. Morgan, eds. Ocean Yearbook 7. Chicago and London: University of Chicago Press, 1988, pp. 42-64.

Identifies and analyzes 33 votes taken on law of the sea issues at the UN General Assembly during the period 1959-85.

81. Burke, William T. "Reviews of Restatement (Third) of the Foreign Relations Law of the United States: Customary Law of the Sea: Advocacy or Disinterested Scholarship?" Yale Journal of International Law. vol. 14, 1989, p. 508.

82. Buzan, Barry. "Negotiating by Consensus: Developments in Technique at the United Nations Conference on the Law of the Sea." American Journal of International Law. vol. 75, no. 2, April 1981, pp. 324-348.

83. _____. Seabed Politics. New York: Praeger Publishers, 1976.

For a comprehensive discussion on the questions of why and how the seabed issue became an international problem, this is the book. The book provides a blow-by-blow account of seabed politics in the UN General Assembly from 1966 to 1975.

84.   Clemons, John H. "Recent Developments in the Law of the Sea 1983-1984."   San Diego Law Review, vol. 22, no. 4, July-August 1985, pp. 801-838.

85.   Clingan, Thomas A. Jr. The Law of the Sea: What Lies Ahead? Honolulu: The Law of the Sea Institute, University of Hawaii, 1988.

This is a collection of 31 articles presented at the 20th annual conference of the Law of the Sea Institute held in Miami, Florida, 1986.

86.   Colson, David A. "The United States, the Law of the Sea, and the Pacific." Jon M. Van Dyke, ed. Consensus and Confrontation: The United States and the Law of the Sea Convention. Honolulu: The Law of the Sea Institute, University of Hawaii, 1985, pp. 36-49.

87.   Crosby, Donald B. "The UNCLOS III Definition of the Continental Shelf: Application to the Canadian Offshore." Douglas M. Johnston and Norman G. Letalik, eds. The Law of the Sea and Ocean Industry: New Opportunities and Restraints. Honolulu: The Law of the Sea Institute, University of Hawaii, 1984, pp. 473-486.

88.   D'Amato, Anthony. "The Enforcement of Norms and Rules with Respect to Non-parties." Jon M. Van Dyke, ed. Consensus and Confrontation: The United States and the Law of the Sea Convention. Honolulu: The Law of the Sea Institute, University of Hawaii, 1985, pp. 488-495.

89.   _____. "The Law-Generating Mechanisms of the Law of the Sea Conferences and Conventions." Jon M. Van Dyke, ed. Consensus and Confrontation: The United States and the Law of the Sea Convention. Honolulu: The Law of the Sea Institute, University of Hawaii, 1985, pp. 125-137.

90.   _____. "An Alternative to the Law of the Sea Convention." American Journal of International Law. vol. 77, no. 2, April 1983, pp. 281-284.

91.   Dean, Arthur H. "The Geneva Conference on the Law of the Sea: What was Accomplished?" American Journal of International Law. vol. 52, October 1958, pp. 608-621.

92.   "Development Relating to the UN Convention on the Law of the Sea: Status of the Convention." Law of the Sea, Report of the Secretary-General, United Nations General Assembly. (A/43/718), 20 October 1988.

93.   Djalal, Hasjim. "Developments in the Law of the Sea during the Next Decade." Jon M. Van Dyke, ed. Consensus and Confrontation: The United States and the Law of the Sea Convention. Honolulu: The Law of the Sea Institute, University of Hawaii, 1985, pp. 531-533.

94.   _____. "The Effects of the Law of the Sea Convention on the Norms that Now Govern Ocean Activities."

Jon M. Van Dyke, ed. <u>Consensus and Confrontation: The United States and the Law of the Sea Convention.</u> Honolulu: The Law of the Sea Institute, University of Hawaii, 1985, pp. 50-56.

95. Evenson, Jens. "The Effect of the Law of the Sea Conference upon the Process of the Formation of International Law: Rapprochement between Competing Points of View." Robert B. Krueger and Stefan Riesenfeld, eds. <u>The Developing Order of the Oceans.</u> Honolulu: The Law of the Sea Institute, University of Hawaii, 1985, pp. 23-40.

96. Friedheim, Robert L. "The Political, Economic and Legal Ocean." Robert L. Friedheim, ed. <u>Managing Ocean Resources: A Primer.</u> Boulder, CO: Westview Press, 1979, pp. 24-41.

97. _____ and Robert E. Bowen. "Neglected Issues at the Third United Nations Law of the Sea Conference." John King Gamble, Jr., ed. <u>Law of the Sea: Neglected Issues.</u> Honolulu: The Law of the Sea Institute, University of Hawaii, 1978, pp. 2-39.

98. Fry, Ellen Moffat. "Recent Developments in the Law of the Sea 1984-1985." <u>San Diego Law Review.</u> vol. 23, no. 3, May-June 1986, pp. 701-722.

99. Gamble, John King, Jr. "The 1982 UN Convention on the Law of the Sea: A Midstream Assessment of the Effectiveness of Article 309." <u>San Diego Law Review.</u> vol. 24, no. 3, May-June 1987, pp. 627-644.

Discusses the legislative history of Articles 309 and 310 in the 1982 Law of the Sea Convention, which deal with reservations, declarations and statements designed to exclude or modify the legal effect of the Convention.

100. _____ and Maria Frankowska. "The 1982 Convention and Customary Law of the Sea: Observations, a Framework, and a Warning." <u>San Diego Law Review.</u> vol. 21, no. 3, June 1984, pp. 491-511.

Explores the relationship between the 1982 Law of the Sea Convention and customary law of the sea. It also discusses the perceptions of and reflections from the 1982 Convention.

101. _____ and Maria Frankowska. "The Significance of Signature to the 1982 Montego Bay Convention on the Law of the Sea." <u>Ocean Development and International Law.</u> vol. 14, no. 2, 1984, pp. 121-160.

102. _____ and Maria Frankowska. "Where Trends the Law of the Sea?" <u>Ocean Development and International Law.</u> vol. 11, nos. 1-2, 1981, pp. 61-92.

103. Greiveldinger, Geoffrey. "Is the LOS Convention Addressing Today's Changing Marine Scientific, Technological, Economic, Legal and Political Issues?"

Proceedings of the Law of the Sea Institute Conference. University of Rhode Island, June 1988.

104. Grolin, Jesper. "The Future of the Law of the Sea: Consequences of a Non-Treaty or Non-Universal Treaty Situation." Ocean Development and International Law. vol. 13, no. 1, 1983, pp. 1-32.

105. Hafner, Gerard. Die Seerechtliche Verteilung von Nutzungsrechten: Rechte der Binenstaaten in der Ausschlie-Blichen Wirtschaftszone. Vienna and New York: Springer-Verlag, 1987.

A summary of the Austrian participant at the Law of the Sea Conference; thus represents the views of the land-locked states.

106. Hargrove, John Laurence. "New Concepts in the Law of the Sea." Ocean Development and International Law. vol. 1, no. 1, Spring 1973, pp. 5-12.

107. Hodgson, Robert D. and Robert W. Smith. "The Informal Single Negotiating Text (Committee II): A Geographical Perspective," Ocean Development and International Law, vol. 3, no. 3, 1976, pp. 225-260.

108. Hollick, Ann L. U. S. Foreign Policy and the Law of the Sea. Princeton, NJ: Princeton University Press, 1981.

This is a definitive study of the United States role in the evolution of the law of the seas dating from the Truman Proclamation of 1945 to the UN Third Conference on the Law of the Sea. This is a comprehensive record of the development of U. S. foreign policy concerning the law of the sea.

109. Hudson, Manley O. "The First Conference for the Codification of International Law." The American Journal of International Law. vol. 24, July 1930, pp. 449-466.

This was the unofficial account of events at the 1930 League of Nations Conference on Codification of International Law, written by the learned Harvard professor of international law.

110. "International Labour Conference: Conventions on Seafarer Health, Safety, Social Security and Repatriation, adopted at Its Seventy-Fourth (Maritime) Session, done at Geneva, 16 October 1987." International Legal Materials. vol. xxvii, no. 3, May 1988, pp. 631-667.

111. Jacobson, Jon L. "Law of the Sea--What Now?" Naval War College Review. vol. xxxvii, no. 2/sequence 302, March-April 1984, pp. 82-99.

112. Jagota, S. P. "Recent Developments in the Law of the Sea." Elisabeth Mann Borgese, Norton Ginsburg and

Joseph R. Morgan, eds. Ocean Yearbook 7. Chicago and London: University of Chicago Press, 1988, pp. 65-93.

Discusses current status and trends of the law of the sea for the five-year period from 1983-87.

113. _____. "The United Nations Convention on the Law of the Sea 1982." Elisabeth Mann Borgese and Norton Ginsburg, eds. Ocean Yearbook 5. Chicago and London: University of Chicago Press, 1985, pp. 10-28.

114. Juda, Lawrence. The United States without the Law of the Sea Treaty: Opportunities and Costs. Wakefield, RI: Times Press, Narragansett Graphics, Inc., 1983.

Consists of Proceedings of the 7th Annual Conference of the Center for Ocean Management Studies at the University of Rhode Island, 12-15 June 1983. Leading experts on ocean affairs offer their views of the possibilities open to the United States for further participation in the law of the sea developments.

115. Kiderien, Hans-Joachim. "Consolidating the Results of the Third UN Conference on the Law of the Sea by Pursuing the Process of the Conference." Robert B. Krueger and Stefan Riesenfeld, eds. The Developing Order of the Oceans. Honolulu: The Law of the Sea Institute, University of Hawaii, 985, pp. 50-54.

116. Kleid, Bernice R. "Recent Developments in the Law of the Sea 1980-1981." San Diego Law Review. vol. 19, no. 3, April 1982, pp. 631-658.

117. Koh, Tommy T. B. "The Origins of the 1982 Convention on the Law of the Sea." 29 Malaya Law Review. 1987, pp. 1-17.

118. Kolodkin, Anatoly and Anatoly Zakharov. "The UN Convention on the Law of the Sea and Customary Law." Jon M. Van Dyke, ed. Consensus and Confrontation: The United States and the Law of the Sea Convention. Honolulu: The Law of the Sea Institute, University of Hawaii, 1985, pp. 166-183.

119. Larson, David L. "When Will the UN Convention on the Law of the Sea Come into Effect?" Ocean Development and International Law. vol. 20, no. 2, 1989, pp. 175-202.

This is a study and analysis based on a recent questionnaire survey of some 89 signatory states to the 1982 Law of the Sea Convention concerning the status of ratification. It makes the prediction that the necessary number (60) of ratifications for the Convention to become effective could be achieved by January 1992.

120. _____. "The Reagan Rejection of the UN Convention." Ocean Development and International Law. vol. 14, no. 4, 1985, pp. 337-362.

121. The Law of the Sea: A Selected Bibliography, 1988.
     United Nations, 1989.

A rather comprehensive listing of literature on the law of
the sea topics and issues arranged under 22 subject
categories.

122. "Law of the Sea Debate in the United Nations General
     Assembly." Ocean Policy News. December 1989, pp. 1-6.

123. "The Law of the Sea: Multilateral Treaties Relevant to
     the United Nations Convention on the Law of the Sea."
     United Nations Publications, 1985.

A comprehensive list of multilateral treaties and instruments on marine affairs of global and regional character.

124. "Law of the Sea Treaty Ratifications." Ocean Policy
     News. April 1989, p. 1.

125. McDonald, Sally and Victor Prescott. "Baselines along
     Unstable Coasts: An Interpretation of Article 7(2)."
     Elisabeth Mann Borgese, Norton Ginsburg and Joseph R.
     Morgan, eds. Ocean Yearbook 8. Chicago and London:
     University of Chicago Press, 1989, pp. 70-89.

126. McDorman, Ted L. "Will Canada Ratify the Law of the
     Sea Convention?" San Diego Law Review. vol. 25, no. 3,
     1988, pp. 535-579.

This article examines Canada's role in the Law of the Sea
Conference negotiations and its specific interests on the
many issues. Then it examines the question of Canada's
ratification of the 1982 Convention as ocean policy,
economic and foreign policy issues.

127. Manley, Robert H. "Developing Nation Implications for
     a New Law of the Sea: UNCLOS I and III as Stages in the
     International Policy Process." Ocean Development and
     International Law. vol. 7, nos. 1-2, 1979, pp. 9-18.

128. Matte, Nicolas Mateesco. "The Law of the Sea and Outer
     Space: A Comparative Survey of Specific Issues."
     Elisabeth Mann Borgese and Norton Ginsburg, eds. Ocean
     Yearbook 3. Chicago and London: University of Chicago
     Press, 1982, pp. 13-37.

129. Miles, Edward L. "Preparation for UNCLOS IV?" Ocean
     Development and International Law. vol. 19, no. 5,
     1988, pp. 421-430.

This is an attempt to answer the question, "Is the world
community ready to call a 4th UN Conference on the Law of
the Sea?" aimed at obtaining accession by the United States
to the 1982 Convention.

130. _____. "An Interpretation of the Geneva Proceed-
     ings: Part I." Ocean Development and International
     Law. vol. 3, no. 3, 1976, pp. 187-224.

131. _____. "An Interpretation of the Geneva Proceedings: Part II." Ocean Development and International
Law, vol.3, no. 4, 1976, pp. 303-340.

132. Moore, John Norton. "Customary International Law after
the Convention." Robert B. Krueger and Stefan
Riesenfeld, eds. The Developing Order of the Oceans.
Honolulu: The Law of the Sea Institute, University of
Hawaii, 1985, pp. 41-49.

133. Nandan, Satya N. "The 1982 Convention on the Law of
the Sea: At a Crossroad." Ocean Development and
International Law, vol. 20, no. 5, 1989, pp. 515-518.

As the director for the Office of Ocean Affairs and the Law
of the Sea at the United Nations, Nandan projects the
possible ratification of the 60th instrument for accession
to the 1982 Convention within the next two to three years.
He points out the absurdity of the Convention coming into
force on the strength of small states.

134. _____. "The Law of the Sea Convention Today." Jon
M. Van Dyke, ed. Consensus and Confrontation: The
United States and the Law of the Sea Convention. Hono-
lulu: The Law of the Sea Institute, University of
Hawaii, 1985, pp. 28-31.

135. _____. "The UN and Peaceful Uses of the Ocean."
Robert B. Krueger and Stefan Riesenfeld, ed. The
Developing Order of the Oceans. Honolulu: The Law of
the Sea Institute, University of Hawaii, 1985, pp. 259-
263.

136. Nordquist, Myron H. United Nations Convention on the
Law of the Sea, 1982. Dordrecht, The Netherlands:
Martinus Nijhoff Publishers/Center for Ocean Law and
Policy, University of Virginia, 1990.

This multivolume work offers an insightful commentary on the
1982 Law of the Sea Convention. Taken as a whole, these
volumes represent an authoritative legislative history of
the Convention written by scholars and diplomats who
participated in the Third UN Conference on the Law of the
Sea, 1974-1982.

137. Oxman, Bernard H. "Summary of the Law of the Sea
Convention." Bernard H. Oxman, David Caron, Charles L.
O. Buderi, eds. Law of the Sea: U.S. Policy Dilemma.
San Francisco, CA: Institute for Contemporary Studies,
ICS Press, 1983, pp. 147-161.

Equally important and detailed is the legislative history of
negotiations on the drafting of the various articles in the
1982 Law of the Sea Convention. The history, written by
Bernard Oxman, a United States negotiator at the Conference,
is concise, comprehensive and revealing about the formal and
informal negotiations at the Conference from 1976 to 1981.

138. _____. "Introduction: On Evaluating the Draft Convention on the Law of the Sea." San Diego Law Review. vol. 19, no. 3, April 1982, pp. 453-460.

139. _____. "The Third United Nations Conference on the Law of the Sea: The Tenth Session (1981)." The American Journal of International Law. vol. 76, no. 1, January 1982, pp. 1-23.

140. _____. "The Third United Nations Conference on the Law of the Sea: The Ninth Session (1980)." The American Journal of International Law. vol. 75, no. 2, April 1981, pp. 211-255.

141. _____. "The Third United Nations Conference on the Law of the Sea: The Eighth Session (1979)." The American Journal of International Law. vol. 74, no. 1, January 1980, pp. 1-47.

142. _____. "The Third United Nations Conference on the Law of the Sea: The Seventh Session (1978)." The American Journal of International Law. vol. 73, no. 1, January 1979, pp. 1-41.

143. _____. "The Third United Nations Conference on the Law of the Sea: The 1977 New York Session." The American Journal of International Law. vol. 72, no. 1, January 1978, pp. 57-83.

144. _____. "The Third United Nations Conference on the Law of the Sea: The 1976 New York Sessions." The American Journal of International Law. vol. 71, no. 2, April 1977, pp. 247-269.

145. Pal, Mati L. "Recent Initiatives in Marine Development in the United Nations." Douglas M. Johnston and Norman G. Letalik, eds. The Law of the Sea and Ocean Industry: New Opportunities and Restraints. Honolulu: The Law of the Sea Institute, University of Hawaii, 1984, pp. 555-564.

146. Pardo, Arvid. "The Convention on the Law of the Sea: A Preliminary Appraisal." San Diego Law Review. vol. 20, no. 3, April 1983, pp. 489-503.

The author of the Maltese Resolution and a leading player at the 1966-70 UN seabed debates reviews in detail the 1982 Law of the Sea Convention. He points to the many areas of accommodation of competing interests in the drafting and negotiation of the various articles or issues.

147. _____. "The Evolving Law of the Sea: A Critique of the Informal Composite Negotiating Text (1977)." Elisabeth Mann Borgese and Norton Ginsburg, eds. Ocean Yearbook 1. Chicago and London: University of Chicago Press, 1978, pp. 9-37.

148. _____. "A Statement on the Future Law of the Sea In Light of Current Trends in Negotiation." Ocean

Development and International Law. vol. 1, no. 4, Winter 1973, pp. 315-336.

149. Park, Choon-ho and Jae Kyu Park. The Law of the Sea: Problems from the East-Asian Perspective. Honolulu: Law of the Sea Institute, University of Hawaii, 1987.

A rich collection of papers on law of the sea problems for East and Southeast Asia.

150. Polhamus, Jean E. "Recent Developments in the Law of the Sea 1982-1983." San Diego Law Review. vol. 21, no. 3, June 1984, pp. 769-791.

151. A Quiet Revolution: The United Nations Convention on the Law of the Sea. New York: United Nations, Department of Public Information, 1984, pp. 39-41.

152. Richardson, Elliot L. "The United States Posture toward the Law of the Sea Convention: Awkward but Not Irreparable." San Diego Law Review. vol. 20, no. 3, April 1983, pp. 505-520.

The importance of this entry is that the article is written by the chief United States negotiator at the Law of the Sea Conference. His conclusion is that the 1982 Convention is a political document and "package deal" of numerous political compromises.

153. _____. "The Politics of the Law of the Sea." Ocean Development and International Law. vol. 11, nos. 1-2, 1982, pp. 9-24.

154. _____. "Law of the Sea." Naval War College Review. vol. xxxii, no. 3/sequence 272, May-June 1979, pp. 3-10.

155. Robertson, B. David and Gaylene Vasaturo. "Recent Developments in the Law of the Sea 1981-1982." San Diego Law Review. vol. 20, no. 3, April 1983, pp. 679-711.

156. Rosenne, Shabtai and Louis B. Sohn. United Nations Convention on the Law of the Sea, 1982: A Commentary. Volume V. London: Graham & Trotman, Ltd., 1988.

A most useful reference work which contains commentaries on Parts XV, XVI and XVII (Articles 279-320) of the Law of the Sea Convention--dealing with the settlement of disputes, as well as some general provisions of the Convention.

157. Simonds, Kenneth. The UN Convention and the Law of the Sea. Dobbs Ferry, NY: Oceana Publications, 1983.

158. Synopsis. "Recent Developments in the Law of the Sea, 1979-1980." San Diego Law Review. vol. 18, no. 3, April 1981, pp. 533-581.

159. _____; "Recent Developments in the Law of the Sea, 1978-1979." San Diego Law Review. vol. 17, no. 3, April 1980, pp. 691-724.

160. _____; "Recent Developments in the Law of the Sea, 1977-1979." San Diego Law Review. vol. 16, no. 3, April 1979, pp. 705-733.

161. Triggs, Gillian. "The 1982 Convention on the Law of the Sea: A Legal Twilight Zone?" Maritime Studies 39. March-April 1988.

162. UN Document, Official Records. Third United Nations Conference on the Law of the Sea. vol. i-xvii.

The 17-volume official records and documents for the Third United Nations Conference on the Law of the Sea represent the complete and authoritative official version of the Conference deliberations and debate on the law of the sea.

163. UN Document, Official Records. Third United Nations Conference on the Law of the Sea. vol. xvii. "Summary Records of Meetings, Documents." Resumed Eleventh Session: New York, 22-24 September 1982. Final Part of Eleventh Session and Conclusion of Conference.

164. _____. Third United Nations Conference on the Law of the Sea. vol. xvi. "Summary Records of Meetings, Documents." Eleventh Session: New York, 8 March - 30 April 1982.

165. _____. Third United Nations Conference on the Law of the Sea. vol. xv. "Summary Records of Meetings, Documents." Tenth Session and Resumed Tenth Session: New York and Geneva, 9 March - 16 April 1981.

166. _____. Third United Nations Conference on the Law of the Sea. vol. xiv. "Summary Records of Meetings, Documents." Resumed Ninth Session: Geneva, 28 July-29 August 1980.

167. _____. Third United Nations Conference on the Law of the Sea. vol. xiii. "Summary Records of Meetings, Documents." Ninth Session: New York, 3 March - 4 April 1980.

168. _____. Third United Nations Conference on the Law of the Sea. vol. xii. "Summary Records of Meetings, Documents." Resumed Eighth Session: New York, 19 July-24 August 1979.

169. _____. Third United Nations Conference on the Law of the Sea. vol. xi. "Summary Records of Meetings, Documents." Eighth Session: Geneva, 19 March - 27 April 1979.

170. _____. Third United Nations Conference on the Law of the Sea. vol. x. "Reports of the Committees and Negotiating Groups." Seventh Session: Geneva, 21 March

- 19 May 1978; Resumed Seventh Session: New York, 21 August - 15 September 1978.

171. _____ . Third United Nations Conference on the Law of the Sea, vol. ix. "Summary Records of Meetings, Documents." Seventh Session: Geneva, 28 March - 19 May 1979; Resumed Seventh Session: New York, 21 August - 15 September 1978.

172. _____ . Third United Nations Conference on the Law of the Sea. vol. viii. "Informal Composite Negotiating Text (A/Conf. 62/WP.10/Rev. 1, 28 April 1979)." Eighth Session: Geneva, 19 March - 27 April 1979.

173. _____ . Third United Nations Conference on the Law of the Sea. vol. vii. "Summary Records of Meetings." Sixth Session: New York, 23 May - 15 July 1977.

174. _____ . Third United Nations Conference on the Law of the Sea. vol. vi. "Summary Records of Meetings, Documents." Fifth Session: New York, 2 August - 17 September 1976.

175. _____ . Third United Nations Conference on the Law of the Sea. vol. v. "Summary Records of Meetings, Documents."   Fourth Session: New York, 15 March - 7 May 1976.

176. _____ . Third United Nations Conference on the Law of the Sea. vol. iv. "Summary Records of Meetings, Documents." Third Session: Geneva, 17 March - 9 May 1975.

177. _____ . Third United Nations Conference on the Law of the Sea. vol. iii. "Documents of the Conference." First Session: New York, 3-15 December 1973; Second Session: Caracas, 20 June - 29 August 1974.

178. _____ . Third United Nations Conference on the Law of the Sea. vol. ii. "Summary Records of Meetings." Second Session: Caracas, 20 June - 29 August, 1974.

179. _____ . Third United Nations Conference on the Law of the Sea. vol. i. "Summary Records of Meetings." First Session: New York 3-15 December 1973; Second Session: Caracas, 20 June - 29 August 1974.

180. United Nations. Official Text of the United Nations Convention on the Law of the Sea with Annexes and Index. Annex III: Basic Conditions of Prospecting, Exploration and Exploitation. New York: St. Martins Press, 1983, pp. 113-130.

181. "The United States and the 1982 UN Convention on the Law of the Sea: A Synopsis of the Status of the Treaty and Its Expanded Role in the World Today." Council on Ocean Law. September 1989, pp. 1-9.

182. "The United States Position on the Law of the Sea."
Douglas M. Johnston and Norman G. Letalik, eds. The
Law of the Sea and Ocean Industry: New Opportunities
and Restraints. Honolulu: The Law of the Sea Institute,
University of Hawaii, 1984, pp. 103-126.

183. "Update on LOS Convention Ratifications." Ocean Policy
News. December 1989, p. 1.

184. Van Dyke, Jon M. "The Role of Islands in Delimiting
Maritime Zones: The Case of the Aegean Sea." Elisabeth
Mann Borgese, Norton Ginsburg and Joseph R. Morgan,
eds. Ocean Yearbook 8. Chicago and London: University
of Chicago Press, 1989, pp. 44-69.

185. _____, ed. Consensus and Confrontation: The
United States and the Law of the Sea Convention.
Honolulu: The Law of the Sea Institute, University of
Hawaii, 1985.

Some 37 participants--diplomats and representatives from the
United States and Asian-Pacific nations, as well as scholars
on ocean affairs--gathered at the annual meeting of the Law
of the Sea Institute in 1984 and produced a variety of views
and criticisms as to why the United States refused to sign
the 1982 Law of the Sea Convention.

186. Vicuna, Francisco Orrego. "The Law of the Sea
Experience and the Corpus of International Law: Effects
and Inter-relationships." Robert B. Krueger and Stefan
A. Riesenfeld, eds. The Developing Order of the Oceans.
Honolulu: The Law of the Sea Institute, University of
Hawaii, 1985.

187. Von Munch, Ingo. Internationales Seerecht. Heidel-
berg: R. V. Decker's Verlag, G. Schenck, 1985.

188. Wiktor, Christian L. and Leslie A. Foster. Marine
Affairs Bibliography: A Comprehensive Index to Marine
Law and Policy Literature, 1980-1985. London: Graham &
Trotman, Ltd., 1987.

An outstanding source of reference on marine policy for the
period.

189. Williamson, Hugh R. "International Maritime Arbitra-
tion: Dispute Settlement without Recourse to the
Courts." Elisabeth Mann Borgese, Norton Ginsburg and
Joseph R. Morgan, eds. Ocean Yearbook 7. Chicago and
London: University of Chicago Press, 1988, pp. 94-114.

Provides information on maritime arbitration organization
and explains why parties arbitrate.

190. Zuleta, Bernardo. "The Law of the Sea after Montego
Bay." San Diego Law Review. vol. 20, no. 3, April 1983,
pp. 475-488.

Points out that the United Nations can be an effective forum for negotiation of complex issues and that the Preparatory Commission would re-examine the positions of those states which refused to sign the treaty.

191. _____. "The Law of the Sea: Myths and Realities." Oceanus. vol. 25, no. 3, 1982, pp. 28-30.

Development of
International Principles

192. Allen, Craig H. "Doctrine of Hot Pursuit: A Functional Interpretation Adaptable to Emerging Maritime Law Enforcement Technologies and Practices." Ocean Development and International Law. vol. 20, no. 4, 1989, pp. 309-342.

This article examines the doctrine of hot pursuit and its development as a customary international law, particularly in the light of recent expanded coastal state jurisdiction.

193. Alexander, Lewis. "Rights to Oceanic Resources: Deciding and Drawing Maritime Boundaries." Marine Policy. vol. 12, no. 1, January 1988, pp. 70-73.

194. _____. "International Straits of the World." Ocean Development and International Law. vol. 13, no. 2, 1983, pp. 269-276.

195. _____. "The Ocean Enclosure Movement: Inventory and Prospect." San Diego Law Review. vol. 20, no. 3, April 1983, pp. 561-594.

This is a good summary of development of the establishment of ocean regimes since 1945.

196. _____. "Offshore Claims and Fisheries in Northwest Europe." The Yearbook of World Affairs. vol. 14, 1960, pp. 236-259.

197. _____ and Lynne Carter Hanson. "Regionalizing the U.S. EEZ." Oceans. vol. 27, no. 4, Winter 1984-85, pp. 7-12.

198. _____ and Robert D. Hodgson. "The Impact of the 200-Mile Economic Zone on the Law of the Sea." San Diego Law Review. vol. 12, no. 3, April 1975, pp. 569-599.

Importance of the article lies in a discussion about the impact of a new regime for ocean enclosure on traditional freedoms of the high seas, at the time when Law of the Sea Conference negotiators were about to decide on establishing an exclusive economic zone.

199. _____ and Virgie Norton. "The 200-Mile Limit III: Maritime Problems between the U.S. and Canada." Oceanus vol. 20, no. 3, Summer 1977, pp. 24-34.

200. Alexanderson, G. The Baltic Straits. The Hague, Netherlands: Martinus Nijhoff, and London: Graham & Trotman Ltd., 1982.

201. Alverez, Jose A. "Strategic Implications of Conti-nental Shelves." Richard B. Lillich and John Norton Moore, eds. U.S. Naval College International Law Studies, Readings in International Law from Naval War College Review 1974-1977. vol. 61. Newport, RI: Naval War College Press, 1980, pp. 404-424.

202. Alverson, Dayton L. "Fisheries Developments in the Northeast Pacific and the FCMA/MFCMA." John P. Craven, Jan Schneider and Carol Stimson, eds. The Inter-national Implications of Extended Maritime Jurisdiction in the Pacific. Honolulu: The Law of the Sea Instiute, University of Hawaii, 1989, pp. 170-182.

203. Amerasinghe, C. F. "The Problem of Archipelagos in the International Law of the Sea." International and Comparative Law Quarterly. vol. 23, 1974, pp. 539-575.

204. Anand, R. P. "Transit Passage and Overflight in Inter-national Straits." Jon M. Van Dyke, Lewis M. Alexander and Joseph R. Morgan, eds. International Navigation: Rocks and Shoals Ahead? Honolulu: The Law of the Sea Institute, University of Hawaii, 1988, pp. 125-154.

A most comprehensive study on the issue of freedom of passage through straits, including passage of warships and passage of submerged vessels--in the context of the new Law of the Sea Convention provisions.

205. _____. Origin and Development of the Law of the Sea: History of International Law. London: Graham & Trotman, Ltd., 1982.

A good introduction to the historical development of the law of the sea and the practice of Asian nations.

206. _____. "Mid-ocean Archipelagos in International Law: Theory and Practice." Indian Journal of Inter-national Law. 1979, pp. 228-256.

207. _____. "Equitable Use and Sharing of the Common Heritage of Mankind." Lewis M. Alexander, ed. The Law of the Sea: Needs and Interests of Developing Countries. Kingston, RI: University of Rhode Island, February 1973, pp. 70-85.

One of the earliest defenders in favor of sharing the ocean resources in the area beyond national jurisdiction under the new concept of common heritage.

208. Andrassy, Juraj. International Law and the Resources of the Sea. New York: Columbia University Press, 1970.

209. "The Antarctic Treaty (1959 Text--Ratified 1961)." Oceanus. vol. 31, no. 2, Summer 1988, pp. 11-13.

210. Antinori, Camille M.   "The Bering Sea: A Maritime Delimitation Dispute between the United States and Soviet Union."   Ocean Development and International Law. vol. 18, no. 1, 1987, pp. 1-48.

The article represents a more recent study of the maritime delimitation dispute concerning the Bering Sea.

211. "The Archipelagic Theory."   Statement by Dr. Jose D. Ingles, Philippines Delegation to the United Nations, 28 June 1973.

212. Archipelago Proposal   by Indonesia.   Third United Nations Conference on the Law of the Sea, Official Records, Second Session, Caracas, 20 June - 29 August 1974, vol. ii. New York: United Nations, 1975, p. 260.

213. Ashmore, Edward. "The Possible Effects on Maritime Operations of Any Future Convention of the Law of the Sea." Richard B. Lillich and John Norton Moore, eds. U. S. Naval College International Law Studies, Readings in International Law from Naval War College Review 1974-1977. vol. 61. Newport, RI: Naval War College Press, 1980, pp. 199-207.

214. Attard, David Joseph. The Exclusive Economic Zone in International Law.   Oxford: Clarendon Press; and New York: Oxford University Press, 1987.

215. Aune, Bjorn. "Piracy and Its Repression under the 1982 Law of the Sea Convention."   Elisabeth Mann Borgese, Norton Ginsburg and Joseph R. Morgan, eds. Ocean Yearbook 8.   Chicago and London: The University of Chicago Press, 1989, pp. 18-43.

This is a recent study of piracy today with reference to boat people piracy, yacht piracy and politically motivated piracy.

216. "Australian-Indonesia Zone of Cooperation in the Timor Gap," Oceans Policy News, May 1989, p. 2.

217. "Australian-Indonesia Zone of Cooperation in the Timor Gap." Maritime Studies. no. 44, January-February 1989, pp. 18-19.

218. Barston, R. P. and Patricia Birnie, eds. The Maritime Dimension. London: George Allen & Unwin, 1980, pp. 5-6.

219. Beauchamp, Kenneth P.   "The Management Function of Ocean Boundaries." San Diego Law Review. vol. 23, no. 3, May-June 1986, pp. 611-660.

Argues the need for a functional and managerial approach to the exploitation of offshore resources and other uses of the ocean.

220. Beeby, Christopher D. "Extended Maritime Jurisdiction: A South Pacific Perspective."   John P. Craven, Jan Schneider and Carol Stimson, eds.   The International Implications of Extended Maritime Jurisdiction in the Pacific. Honolulu: The Law of the Sea Institute, University of Hawaii, 1989, pp. 18-26.

221. "Behind Bumping of Two U.S. Warships in the Black Sea," The Honolulu Star-Bulletin, 13 February 1988, p. A-6.

222. Belsky, Martin H.   "The Marine Ecosystem Management Model and the Law of the Sea: Requirements for Assessment and Modeling." John P. Craven, Jan Schneider and Carol Stimson, eds. The International Implications of Extended Maritime Jurisdiction in the Pacific. Honolulu: The Law of the Sea Institute, University of Hawaii, 1989, pp. 236-262.

223. _____.   "A Strategy to Avoid EEZ Conflicts." Oceanus. vol. 27, no. 4, Winter 1984-85, pp. 19-22.

224. Birnie, P. W.   "Contemporary Legal Problems." R. P. Barston and Patricia Birnie, eds.   The Maritime Dimension. London: George Allen & Unwin, 1980, pp. 169-189.

225. _____.   "The Law of the Sea before and after UNCLOS I and UNCLOS II."   R. P. Barston and Patricia Birnie, eds. The Maritime Dimension. London: George Allen & Unwin, 1980, pp. 8-26.

226. Blecher, M. D. "Equitable Delimitation of the Continental Shelf." American Journal of InternationalLaw. vol. 73, no. 1, January 1979, pp. 60-88.

227. Boggs, S. Whittemore. "Delimitation of Seaward Areas under National Jurisdiction."   American Journal of International Law. vol. 48, 1961, pp. 240-266.

Writing as special adviser on geography for the U. S. Department of State, Boggs reflects the thinking of the United States government on the question of defining the precise seaward limits of ocean enclosurement.

228. _____.   "National Claims in Adjacent Seas." The Geographical Review. vol. 41, April 1951, pp. 185-209.

229. _____.   "Problems of Water-Boundary Definition: Median Lines and International Boundaries through Territorial Waters." The Geographical Review. vol. 27, July 1937, pp. 445-456.

230. Borgese, Elisabeth Mann.   "A Constitution for the Ocean." Elisabeth Mann Borgese and David Krieger, eds. Tides of Change, Peace, Pollution and Potential of the Oceans. New York: Mason/Charter, 1975, pp. 345-348.

231. Bowen, Robert E. and Timothy M. Hennessey. "Adjacent State Issues for the United States in Establishing an Exclusive Economic Zone: The Cases of Canada and Mexico." Ocean Development and International Law. vol. 15, nos. 3-4, 1985, pp. 355-376.

232. _____ and Timothy M. Hennessey.   "U.S.   EEZ Relations with Canada and Mexico." Oceanus. vol. 27, no. 4, Winter 1984-85, pp. 41-47.

233. Bravender-Coyle, Paul. "The Emerging Legal Principles and Equitable Criteria Governing the Delimitation of Maritime Boundaries between States." Ocean Development and International Law. vol. 19, no. 3, 1988, pp. 171-228.

234. Briscoe, John. "Islands in Maritime Boundary Delimitation. "Elisabeth Mann Borgese, Norton Ginsburg and Joseph R. Morgan, eds. Ocean Yearbook 7. Chicago and London: University of Chicago Press, 1988, pp. 14-41.

Discusses the islands for maritime boundary delimitation purposes and its use in recent court cases to delimit the territorial sea and the continental shelf.

235. Brock, John R.   "Archipelago Concept of Limits of Territorial Seas." Richard B. Lillich and John Norton Moore, eds. U.S. Naval College International Law Studies, Readings in International Law from Naval War College Review 1974-1977. vol. 61. Newport, RI: Naval War College Press, 1980, pp. 328-361.

One of the best background studies on the origin and development of the archipelago concept, accompanied by state practices.

236. Broder, Sherry and Jon M. Van Dyke.   "Ocean Boundaries in the South Pacific." University of Hawaii Law Review. vol. 4, no. 1, 1982, pp. 1-60.

237. Brown, E. D. "Freedom of the High Seas Versus the Common Heritage of Mankind: Fundamental Principles in Conflict," San Diego Law Review, vol. 20, no. 3, April 1983, pp. 521-560.

This article takes the position that, owing to the refusal of the United States and a number of other major industrial powers to sign the 1982 Law of the Sea Convention, seabed mining can proceed under the reciprocal state regime or the "Mini-Treaty."

238. _____. "The Anglo-French Continental Shelf Case." San Diego Law Review. vol. 16, no. 3, 1979, pp. 461-530.

239. Bullard, Sir Edward. "Continental Shelves: Their Nature and History." <u>Oceanus</u>. vol. 19, no. 1, Fall 1975, pp. 3-7.

This is a required understanding on the nature and geology of the continental shelves as offshore areas for resource utilization.

240. Burke, William T. "Customary Law as Reflected in the LOS Convention: A Clippery Formula." John P. Craven, Jan Schneider and Carol Stimson, eds. <u>The International Implications of Extended Maritime Jurisdiction in the Pacific</u>. Honolulu: The Law of the Sea Institute, University of Hawaii, 1989, pp. 402-409.

241. _____. "National Legislation on Ocean Authority Zones and the Contemporary Law of the Sea." <u>Ocean Development and International Law</u>, vol. 9, nos. 3-4, 1981, pp. 289-322.

242. Burmester, Henry. "Commentary: Federal State Issues Arising in a 200 Nautical Mile Exclusive Economic Zone: An Australian Perspective." John P. Craven, Jan Schneider and Carol Stimson, eds. <u>The International Implications of Extended Maritime Jurisdiction in the Pacific</u>. Honolulu: The Law of the Sea Institute, University of Hawaii, 1989, pp. 369-374.

243. Bustamente, Teodoro. "Ocean Law Developments in Ecuador." John P. Craven, Jan Schneider and Carol Stimson, eds. <u>The International Implications of Extended Maritime Jurisdiction in the Pacific</u>. Honolulu: The Law of the Sea Institute, University of Hawaii, 1989, pp. 230-235.

244. Butler, W. E. "The Law of the Sea and Anglo-Soviet Legal Relations." <u>Marine Policy</u>. vol. 14, no.2, March 1990, pp. 103-105.

245. _____. <u>Northeast Arctic Passage</u>. The Hague, Netherlands: Martinus Nijhoff, and London: Graham & Trotman, Ltd., 1978.

246. Caminos, Hugo and Michael R. Molitor. "Progressive Development of International Law and the Package Deal." <u>American Journal of International Law</u>. vol. 79, no. 4, October 1985, pp. 871-890.

247. Campbell, Douglas III. "The Continental Shelf." David L. Larson, ed. <u>Major Issues of the Law of the Sea</u>. Durham, NH: University of New Hampshire, 1976, pp. 52-66.

248. _____. "The High Seas and Selected Issues." David L. Larson, ed. <u>Major Issues of the Law of the Sea</u>. Durham, NH: University of New Hampshire, 1976, pp. 190-213.

249. _____. "Navigation." David L. Larson, ed. <u>Major</u>

Issues of the Law of the Sea. Durham, NH: University of New Hampshire, 1976, pp. 125-139.

250. "Canada-France Dispute." Oceans Policy News. May 1989, p. 1.

251. "Canada-United States: Agreement on Arctic Cooperation and Exchange of Notes Concerning Transit of Northwest Passage." International Legal Materials. vol. xxvii, no. 1, January 1989.

252. Charney, Jonathan I. "The Exclusive Economic Zone and Public International Law." Ocean Development and International Law. vol. 15, nos. 3-4, 1985, pp. 233-288.

253. _____. "Ocean Boundaries between Nations: A Theory for Progress," American Journal of International Law, vol. 78, no. 3, July 1984, pp. 582-606.

254. _____. "The Offshore Jurisdiction of the States of the United States and the Provinces of Canada: A Comparison," Ocean Development and International Law, vol. 12, nos. 3-4, 1982, pp. 301-336.

255. _____. "The Delimitation of Lateral Seaward Boundaries between States in a Domestic Context." American Journal of International Law. vol. 75, no. 1, January 1981, pp. 28-68.

256. _____. "Law of the Sea: Breaking the Deadlock." Foreign Affairs. vol. 55, no. 3, April 1977, pp. 598-629.

The importance of this article lies in the fact that the author, a member of the U. S. Public Advisory Committee on the Law of the Sea, at the time of a deadlock in negotiations pointed out reasonable grounds for compromise on three critical issues: the economic zone, deep seabed mining, and the rights of landlocked states.

257. Chee, Choung Il. "Problems of Maritime Delimitation." Choon-ho Park and Jae Kyu Park, eds. The Law of the Sea: Problems from the East Asian Perspective. Honolulu: The Law of the Sea Institute, University of Hawaii, 1987, pp. 81-91.

258. Chen, Zhizhong. "Chinese Legislation on the Law of the Sea." John P. Craven, Jan Schneider and Carol Stimson, eds. The International Implications of Extended Maritime Jurisdiction in the Pacific. Honolulu: The Law of the Sea Institute, University of Hawaii, 1989, pp. 83-89.

259. Chiu, Hungdah. "Some Problems Concerning the Delimitation of the Maritime Boundary between the Republic of China (Taiwan) and the Philippines." Ocean Development and International Law. vol. 14, no. 1, 1984, pp. 79-106.

260. _____ and Choon-ho Park. "Legal Status of the Paracel and Spratly Islands." Choon-ho Park and Jae Kyu Park. eds. The Law of the Sea: Problems from the East Asian Perspective. Honolulu: The Law of the Sea Institute, University of Hawaii, 1987, pp. 456-481.

261. _____ and Choon-ho Park. "Legal Status of the Paracel and Spratly Islands," Ocean Development and International Law, vol. 3, no. 1, 1975, pp. 1-28.

262. Christie, Donna R. "Georges Bank: Common Ground or Continued Battleground? Comparative Marine Resource Management and Environmental Assessment in the United States and Canada." San Diego Law Review. vol. 23, no. 3, May-June 1986, pp. 491-543.

The article makes a comparative analysis of environmental assessment in conjunction with fishery management and outer continental shelf development in the Gulf of Maine.

263. Chung, Le Kim. "The Socialist Republic of Viet Nam and Her Exclusive Economic Zone (EEZ) in Relations with the Neighboring Countries in Southeast Asia." John P. Craven, Jan Schneider and Carol Stimson, eds. The International Implications of Extended Maritime Jurisdiction in the Pacific. Honolulu: The Law of the Sea Institute, University of Hawaii, 1989, pp. 60-65.

264. Churchill, R. R. and A. V. Lowe. The Law of the Sea. Manchester, UK and Dover, NH: Manchester University Press, 1983.

This is considered to be a basic book on the development of maritime law and its usage.

265. Cicin-Sain, Biliana and Robert Knecht. "The Problem of Governance of U.S. Ocean Resources and the New Exclusive Economic Zone." Ocean Development and International Law. vol. 15, nos. 3-4, 1985, pp. 289-320.

266. Clingan, Thomas A., Jr. "Dispute Settlement among Non-Parties to the LOS Convention with Respect to the Outer Limits of the Continental Shelf." Thomas A. Clingan, Jr., ed. The Law of the Sea: What Lies Ahead? Honolulu: The Law of the Sea Institute, University of Hawaii, 1988, pp. 495-500.

267. _____, ed. Law of the Sea: State Practice in Zones of Special Jurisdiction. Honolulu: Law of the Sea Institute, University of Hawaii, 1982.

The proceedings of the Law of the Sea Institute's annual conference, held in Mexico City, focus on the implications of coastal state practices in the special zones of territorial sea, continental shelf and fishery zone.

268. _____. "Emerging Law of the Sea: The Economic Zone Dilemma." San Diego Law Review. vol. 14, no. 3, April 1977, pp. 530-547.

A well-documented study showing the origin of the development of the exclusive economic zone concept at the early sessions of the Law of the Sea Conferences.

269. Colson, David A. "The Maritime Boundaries of the United States: Where Are We Now?" Thomas A. Clingan, Jr., ed. The Law of the Sea: What Lies Ahead? Honolulu: The Law of the Sea Institutc, Univcrsity of Hawaii, 1988, pp. 464-471.

270. _____. "The United Kingdom-France Continental Shelf Arbitration: Interpretive Decision of March 1978." American Journal of International Law. vol. 73, no. 1, January 1979, pp. 112-119.

271. Conforti, Benedetto, Gramprero Francalance, Angelo Labella and Daniela Romano, eds. Atlas of the Seabed Boundaries. Milan: Dott A. Giaffre Editore, 1987.

272. "Congressman Lowry Introduced Legislation to Extend the U.S. Territorial Sea from 3 to 12 Miles and the Contiguous Zone from 12 to 24 Miles." Ocean Science News. vol. 30, no. 20, July 15, 1988.

273. Cooper, John. "Delimitation of the Maritime Boundary in the Gulf of Maine Area." Ocean Development and International Law. vol. 16, no. 1, 1986, pp. 59-90.

274. Council on Ocean Law and the Institute for Marine Studies, University of Washington. "Resources or Freedoms on the High Seas: Policing the Ocean Commons." Oceans Policy News. March 1990, pp. 1-3.

275. Craven, John P. "Arvid Pardo and the Law of the Sea." Choon-ho Park and Jaw Kyu Park, eds. The Law of the Sea: Problems from the East Asian Perspective. Honolulu: The Law of the Sea Institute, University of Hawaii, 1987, pp. 6-11.

276. _____, Jan Schneider and Carol Stimson, eds. The International Implications of Extended Maritime Jurisdiction in the Pacific. Honolulu: The Law of the Sea Institute, University of Hawaii, 1989.

This is a collection of panel papers by maritime experts and scholars from the Asian/Pacific region dealing with marine boundary conflicts in the Pacific.

277. Cuyvers, Luc. "The Law of the Sea," Ocean Uses and Their Regulation. New York: John Wiley and Sons, 1984, pp. 146-165.

278. _____. The Strait of Dover. The Hague, Netherlands: Martinus Nijhoff, and London: Graham & Trotman, Ltd., 1986.

279. Dallmeyer, Dorinda G. and Louis Devorsey, Jr. Rights to Oceanic Resources: Deciding and Drawing Maritime

Boundaries.   The Hague, Netherlands: Martinus Nijhoff, and London: Graham & Trotman, Ltd., 1989.

The book is a compilation of a multi-disciplinary range of experts attempting to find resolutions to maritime juris- dictional disputes at state, national and international levels.

280. Danzig, Aaron L., "A Funny Thing Happened to the Common Heritage on the Way to the Sea." San Diego Law Review. vol. 12, no. 3, April 1975, pp. 655-664.

As early as 1975 there was an article by an officer for the Seabed Committee of World Peace through Law Center who argued that the developing nations were "being taken" to expect some revenue sharing in deep seabed mining under the common heritage concept.

281. Darby, Joseph J. "The Soviet Doctrine of the Closed Sea." San Diego Law Review. vol. 23, no. 3, May-June 1986, pp. 685-699.

A very important analysis on the application of the Soviet doctrine of closing the peripheral and semi-enclosed seas such as the Black Sea to warships of all non-littoral states.

282. "Denmark Brings a Case against Norway." Law of the Sea Bulletin. no. 12.   United Nations: Office for Ocean Affairs and the Law of the Sea, December 1988, p. 76.

283. "The Developing Regime of the Sea in Law and State Practice." Sea Changes. no. 5, 1987.

284. Dickey, Margaret Lynch. "Freedom of the Seas and the Law of the Sea: Is What's New for Better or Worse?" Ocean Development and International Law. vol. 5, no. 1, 1978, pp. 23-26.

285. "Discussion: Challenging Nonconforming Coastal State Claims." Jon M. Van Dyke, Lewis M. Alexander and Joseph R. Morgan, Eds. International Navigation: Rocks and Shoals Ahead? Honolulu: The Law of the Sea Institute, University of Hawaii, 1988, pp. 337-341.

286. Drigot, Diane C., "Oil Interests and the Law of the Sea: The Case of the Philippines." East West Environ- ment and Policy Institute. Reprint No. 47.   Honolulu: East West Center, University of Hawaii, 1984, pp. 29- 32, 41-48.

A detailed study concerning Philippine claims to ocean resources in the disputed areas of the South China Sea based on the archipelago and continental shelf concepts (the Spratlys). An important background study on pending dis- putes in the South China Sea.

287. Driver, Paul A.   "International Fisheries."   R. P.

Barston and Patricia Birnie, eds. The Maritime Dimension. London: George Allen & Unwin, 1980, pp. 27-53.

288. Dunning, Nicholas P.   "Boundary Delimitation in the Gulf of Maine: Implications for the Future of a Resource Area." Elisabeth Mann Borgese and Norton Ginsburg, eds. Ocean Yearbook 6. Chicago and London: University of Chicago Press, 1986, pp. 390-398.

289. Dupuy, Rene-Jean. The Law of the Sea: Current Problems. Dobbs Ferry, NY: Oceania Publications, Inc., 1974, pp. 24-45.

290. "Dutch Exclusive Economic Zone."   Oceans Policy News. March 1989, p. 2.

291. Dzurek, Danice J.   "Boundary and Resource Disputes in the South China Sea."   Elisabeth Mann Borgese and Norton Ginsburg, eds. Ocean Yearbook 5. Chicago and London: University of Chicago Press, 1982, pp. 254-284.

292. "EEZ and Uninhabited Islands: Where to Draw the Line?" Centerviews. March-April 1989, pp. 1-2.

293. Ehler, Charles N., Daniel J. Basta, Thomas F. La Pointe and Maureen J. Warren.   "New Oceanic and Coastal Atlases: Focus on Potential EEZ Conflicts." Oceanus. vol. 29, no. 3, Fall 1986, pp. 42-51.

The authors were the NOAA group which presented its strategic assessment of conflicts over resources within the exclusive economic zones.   An important aspect as nations begin their exploration and exploitations of resources inside these special enclosed ocean regimes.

294. Emery, K. O. "Geological Limits of the Continental Shelf." Ocean Development and International Law. vol. 10, nos. 1-2, 1981, pp. 1-12.

295. "Extension of the U.S. Territorial Sea: Seminar of Center for Ocean Law and Policy, University of Virginia." Oceans Policy News. April 1989, pp. 5-6.

296. F. V. "The Beagle Channel Affair." American Journal of International Law. vol. 71, no. 4, October 1977, pp. 733-739.

297. Feldman, Mark B. "The Tunisia-Libya Continental Shelf Case: Geographic Justice or Judicial Compromise?" American Journal of International Law. vol. 77, no. 2, April 1983, pp. 219-238.

298. Fenn, Percy Thomas, Jr.   "Origins of the Theory of Territorial Waters." American Journal of International Law. vol. 20, July 1926, pp. 465-482.

A must reading on the modern legal theory of territorial waters by going back to the theory of the Glossators.

299. Fincham, Charles and William van Rensburg. <u>Bread upon the Waters: The Developing Law of the Sea</u>. Forest Grove, OR: Turtledove Publishing, 1980.

300. Flemming, Nicholas C. "Ice Age and Human Occupation of the Continental Shelf." <u>Oceanus</u>. vols. 28, no. 1, Spring 1985, pp. 18-26.

301. Franckl, Erik. "'New' Soviet Delimitation Agreement with Its Neighbors in the Baltic Sea." <u>Ocean Development and International Law</u>. vol. 19, no. 2, 1988, pp. 143-158.

302. Friedheim, Robert L. "The Regime of the Arctic: Distributional or Integrative Bargaining?" <u>Ocean Development and International Law</u>. vol. 19, no. 6, 1988, pp. 493-510.

303. _____. "Factor Analysis as a Tool in Studying the Law of the Sea." Lewis M. Alexander, ed. <u>The Law of the Sea: Offshore Boundaries and Zones</u>. Columbus, OH: Ohio State University Press, 1967, pp. 47-70.

304. Froman, F. David. "Uncharted Waters: Non-innocent Passage of Warships in the Territorial Sea." <u>San Diego Law Review</u>. vol. 21, no. 3, June 1984, pp. 625-689.

This article discusses the importance of innocent passage to modern naval mobility, the controversy concerning innocent passage of warships in the territorial sea, in particular the question of prior authorization for transit of foreign warships in the territorial sea, international straits, and within archepelagic waters.

305. Fu, Kuen-Chen. <u>Equitable Ocean Boundary Delimitation: On Equitable Principles and Ocean Boundary Delimitation</u>. Taipei, Taiwan: National Taiwan University, Law Books, July 1989.

306. Gault, Ian Townsend. "Offshore Boundary Delimitation in the Arabian/Persian Gulf." Douglas M. Johnston and Phillip M. Saunders, eds. <u>Ocean Boundary Making: Regional Issues and Developments</u>. New York: Croom Helm, 1988, pp. 204-228.

307. Gilmore, William C. "Hot Pursuit and Constructive Presence in Canadian Law Enforcement: A Case Note." <u>Marine Policy</u>. vol. 12, no. 2, April 1988, pp. 105-111.

308. Glassner, Martin Ira. "The Land-Locked States of South and Southeast Asia and the Exclusive Economic Zones of the Indian Ocean." John P. Craven, Jan Schneider and Carol Stimson, eds. <u>The International Implications of Extended Maritime Jurisdiction in the Pacific</u>. Honolulu: The Law of the Sea Institute, University of Hawaii, 1989, pp. 306-312.

309. _____ , "The Transit Problems of Landlocked States: The Cases of Bolivia and Paraguay." Elisabeth Mann Borgese and Norton Ginsburg, eds.   Ocean Yearbook 4.   Chicago and London: University of Chicago Press, 1983, pp. 366-389.

310. _____ and Michael Unger. "Israel's Maritime Boundaries." Ocean Development and International Law. vol. 1, no. 4, Winter 1974, pp. 303-314.

311. Glauberman, Stu.   "Pacific Isles Trying to Solve Economic Zone Puzzle."   The Sunday Honolulu Star-Bulletin and Advertiser. 14 January 1990, p. A-28.

312. Gold, Edgar.   "Mare Liberum?   Mare Clausem? Mare Nostrum? Can We Really Have It All?"   John P. Craven, Jan Schneider and Carols Stimson, eds. The International Implications of Extended Maritime Jurisdiction in the Pacific. Honolulu: The Law of the Sea Institute, University of Hawaii, 1989, pp. 447-450.

313. Gomane, Jean-Pierre. "A French Perspective."   John P. Craven, Jan Schneider and Carol Stimson, eds. The International Implications of Extended Maritime Jurisdiction in the Pacific.   Honolulu: The Law of the Sea Institute, University of Hawaii, 1989, pp. 139-144.

314. Gross, Leo. "The Dispute between Greece and Turkey Concerning the Continental Shelf in the Aegean." American Journal of International Law. vol. 71, no. 1, January 1977, pp. 31-59.

315. Guang, Jin Zu.   "Conflicts between Foreign Ships Innocent Passage and National Security of the Coastal States." Jon M. Van Dyke, Lewis M. Alexander and Joseph R. Morgan, eds.   International Navigation: Rocks and Shoals Ahead? Honolulu: The Law of the Sea Institute, University of Hawaii, 1988, pp. 111-117.

Explains why the People's Republic of China holds different views on the right of innocent passage for warships.

316. Haerr, Roger Cooling. "The Gulf of Sidra." San Diego Law Review. vol. 24, no. 3, 1987, pp. 751-767.

Conflict over the Gulf of Sidra as Libyan territory, or as part of international waters, raises the important issue of a unilateral claim over a large span of ocean space and whether the use of force to settle the claim is in violation of the UN Charter and customary international law.

317. Hamid, Jamshed A.   "Pakistan's Perceptons on South Asia's Outstanding EEZ Issues."   John P. Craven, Jan Schneider and Carol Stimson, eds.   The International Implications of Extended Maritime Jurisdiction in the Pacific. Honolulu: The Law of the Sea Institute, University of Hawaii, 1989, pp. 288-291.

318. Harlow, Bruce A. "UNCLOS III and Conflict Management in Straits." Ocean Development and International Law. vol. 15, no. 2, 1985, pp. 197-208.

The article examines the need for refinement in the 1982 Law of the Sea Convention provisions concerning the regime for international straits.

319. Hedberg, Hollis D. "A Critique of Boundary Provisions in the Law of the Sea." Ocean Development and International Law. vol. 12, nos. 3-4, 1983, pp. 337-342.

320. Hodgson, Robert D. and John Cooper. "The Technical Delimitation of a Modern Equidistant Boundary." Ocean Development and International Law. vol. 3, no. 4, 1976, pp. 361-388.

321. Hollick, Ann L. "A New Beginning: The U.S. Adopts an Ocean Policy," U.S. Foreign Policy and the Law of the Sea. Princeton, New Jersey: Princeton University Press, 1981.

322. _____. "The Origins of the 200-Mile Offshore Zones." The American Journal of International Law. vol. 71, no. 3, July 1977, pp. 494-500.

323. _____. "Internal Waters." Max Sorensen, ed. Manual of Public International Law. New York: Macmillan Publishing Co., Inc., 1968, pp. 332-335.

324. Holser, Alexander F. "Offshore Lands of the USA: The U.S. Exclusive Economic Zone, Continental Shelf and Outer Continental Shelf." Marine Policy. vol. 12, no. 1, January 1988, pp. 2-8.

325. Hotta, Kenji. "The Use of Ocean Space in Japan." Oceanus. vol. 30, no. 1, Spring 1987, pp. 66-70.

326. Hsu, Richard T. S. "A Rational Approach to Maritime Boundary Delimitation." Ocean Development and International Law. vol. 13, no. 1, 1983, pp. 103-114.

327. Hull, E. W. S. The International Law of the Sea: A Case for a Customary Approach. Honolulu: The Law of the Sea Institute, University of Hawaii, 1976.

328. Inouye, Daniel K. U.S. Senator. "Extended Maritime Jurisdiction: A United States Perspective." John P. Craven, Jan Schneider and Carol Stimson, eds. The International Implications of Extended Maritime Jurisdiction in the Pacific. Honolulu: The Law of the Sea Institute, University of Hawaii, 1989, pp. 10-17.

329. Irwin, Paul C. "Settlement of Maritime Boundary Disputes: An Analysis of the Law of the Sea Negotiations." Ocean Development and International Law. vol. 8, no. 2, 1980, pp. 105-139.

330. Jaafar, Abu Bakar. "The Changing Legal Status of the Malacca and Singapore Straits." Jon M. Van Dyke, ed. Consensus and Confrontation: The United States and the Law of the Sea Convention. Honolulu: The Law of the Sea Institute, University of Hawaii, 1985, pp. 285-291.

331. Jacobson, Jon L. "Governance of the U. S. Exclusive Economic Zone: A Challenge to the American Federation." John P. Craven, Jan Schneider and Carol Stimson, eds. The International Implications of Extended Maritime Jurisdiction in the Pacific. Honolulu: The Law of the Sea Institute, University of Hawaii, 1989, pp. 329-352.

332. Jaenicke, Guenther. "The Delimitation of the Continental Shelf on the Basis of the 'Natural Prolongation' Concept." Edward L. Miles and Scott Allen, eds. The Law of the Sea and Ocean Development Issues in the Pacific Basin. Honolulu: The Law of the Sea Institute, University of Hawaii, 1983, pp. 547-560.

333. Jagota, S. P. Maritime Boundary. The Hague, Netherlands: Martinus Nijhoff, and London: Graham & Trotman, Ltd., 1985.

334. Jessup, Philip C. "Jurisdiction." Richard B. Lillich and John Norton Moore, eds. U. S. Naval College International Law Studies, Readings in International Law from Naval War College Review 1974-1977. vol. 61. Newport, RI: Naval War College Press, 1980, pp. 303-318.

335. Johnston, Douglas M. The Theory and History of Ocean Boundary Making. Montreal: McGill-Queen's University Press, 1989.

One of the most comprehensive and definitive studies on the theory and history of maritime boundary making. It is rich in case illustration and contains a valuable background study of the complex process in ocean boundary making.

336. _____. "The Economic Zone in North America: Scenarios and Options." Ocean Development and International Law. vol. 3, no. 1, 1975, pp. 53-68.

337. _____ and E. Gold. The Economic Zone in the Law of the Sea Survey, Analysis, and Appraisal of Current Trends. Honolulu: Law of the Sea Institute, University of Hawaii, 1973.

Examines development of the economic zone concept and discusses the characteristics of the economic zone and the claim process.

338. _____ and Phillip M. Saunders, eds. "Introduction." Ocean Boundary Making: Regional Issues and Developments. New York: Croom Helm, 1988, pp. 1-15.

339. _____ and Phillip M. Saunders, eds. "Ocean Boundary Issues and Developments in Regional Perspective,"

Ocean Boundary Making: Regional Issues and Developments. New York: Croom Helm, 1988, pp. 313-349.

340. _____ and Phillip M. Saunders, eds. Ocean Boundary Making: Regional Issues and Developments. New York: Croom Helm, 1988.

The volume is a collection of seven studies by maritime experts dealing with ocean boundary-making issues in different areas of the world: in the Arctic region, East Asia, the Mediterranean, the Caribbean, the Persian Gulf, West Africa and the Southwest Pacific.

341. Joyner, Christopher. "The Antarctic Legal Regime and the Law of the Sea." Oceanus. vol. 31, no. 2, Summer 1988, pp. 22-27.

342. _____. "The Exclusive Economic Zone and Antarctica: The Dilemmas of Non-Sovereign Jurisdiction." Ocean Development and International Law. vol. 19, no. 6, 1988, pp. 469-492.

343. Juda, Lawrence. "Innocent Passage by Warships in the Territorial Sea of the Soviet Union: Changing Doctrine." Ocean Development and International Law. vol. 21, no. 1, 1990, pp. 111-116.

Examines recent change from past practice by the Soviet Union on the navigational rights of warships under the innocent passage concept.

344. _____. "The Exclusive Economic Zone: Non-Claimant States," Ocean Development and International Law, vol. 19, no. 6, 1988, pp. 431-444.

345. _____. "The Exclusive Economic Zone and Ocean Management." Ocean Development and International Law. vol. 18, no. 3, 1987, pp. 305-332.

346. _____. "The Exclusive Economic Zone: Compatibility of National Claims and the UN Convention on the Law of the Sea." Ocean Development and International Law. vol. 16, no. 1, 1986, pp. 1-58.

347. Kaczynski, Vladimir M. "200-Mile EEZ and Soviet Fisheries in the North Pacific Ocean: An Economic Assessment." John P. Craven, Jan Schneider and Carol Stimson, eds. The International Implications of Extended Maritime Jurisdiction in the Pacific. Honolulu: The Law of the Sea Institute, University of Hawaii, 1989, pp. 193-203.

348. Kantaatmadja, Komar. "Various Problems and Arrangements in the Malacca Straits (An Indonesian Perspective)." Jon M. Van Dyke, Lewis M. Alexander and Joseph R. Morgan, eds. International Navigation: Rocks and Shoals Ahead? Honolulu: The Law of the Sea Institute, University of Hawaii, 1988, pp. 165-171.

Discusses regional arrangements concerning the Malacca and Singapore Straits.

349. Karl, Donald E.   "Lands and the Delimitation of the Continental Shelf: A Framework for Analysis." American Journal of International Law. vol. 71, no. 4, October 1977, pp. 642-673.

350. Keith, Kent M.   "Laws Affecting the Development of Ocean Resources in Hawaii." University of Hawaii Law Review. vol. 4, no. 1, 1982, pp. 237-239, 240-244.

351. Kent, George.   "Harmonizing Extended Zone Legislation in Southeast Asia."   Ocean Development and Inter-national Law. vol. 13, no. 2, 1983, pp. 247-268.

352. Kent, H. S. K. "The Historical Origins of the Three-Mile Limit."   American Journal of International Law. vol. 48, October 1954, pp. 537-553.

353. Kewening, Wilheim A. "The Common Heritage of Mankind: A Political Slogan or a Key Concept of International Law?" Law and State. vol. 24, pp. 7-29.

A representative view from Kiel, West Germany calling for attention to the meaning and implications of the common heritage of mankind concept.

354. Kibola, Hamisi S. "A Note on Africa and the Exclusive Economic Zone." Ocean Development and International Law. vol. 16, no. 4, 1986, pp. 380-400.

355. Kildow, Judith T. "The Seas: Heritage for the Few, or Hope for the Many?" Lewis M. Alexander, ed. The Law of the Sea: Needs and Interests of Developing Countries. Kingston, RI: University of Rhode Island, 1973, pp. 59-63.

356. Kimball, Lee A. "International Law and Institutions: The Oceans and Beyond," Ocean Development and Inter-national Law, vol. 21, no. 2, 1990, p. 147-166.

The article argues for an evolving role of regional and global institutions in furthering international law develop-ment and ocean management.

357. Kimball, Lee A. "The Antarctic Treaty System." Oceanus. vol. 31, no. 2, Summer 1988, pp. 14-19.

358. Knauss, John A.   "Creeping Jurisdiction and Customary International Law."   Ocean Development and Inter-national Law. vol. 15, no. 2, 1985, pp. 209-216.

359. Knecht, Robert W. and Thomas R. Kitsoo. "Multiple-Use Management in the EEZ" Oceanus. vol. 27, no. 4, Winter 1984-85, pp. 13-18.

360. Knight, H. Gary.   "The Kiev and the Turkish Straits."

American Journal of International Law. vol. 71, no. 1, January 1977, pp. 130-132.

361. Koh, Tommy T. B. "The Exclusive Economic Zone." 30 _Malaya Law Review_. 1988, pp. 1-33.

362. _____. "The Territorial Sea, Contiguous Zone, Straits and Archipelagoes under the 1982 Convention on the Law of the Sea." 29 _Malay Law Review_, 1987, pp. 163-199.

363. Koroleva, N. D. "The Right of Pursuit from the Exclusive Economic Zone." _Marine Policy_. vol. 14, no. 2, March 1990, pp. 137-141.

364. Kotobalavu, Jiuji. "Extended Maritime Jurisdiction in the Pacific: Maximizing Benefits from Marine Resources." John P. Craven, Jan Schneider and Carol Stimson, eds. _The International Implications of Extended Maritime Jurisdiction in the Pacific_. Honolulu: The Law of the Sea Institute, University of Hawaii, 1989, pp. 132-135.

365. Krueger, Robert B. and Myron H. Nordquist. "The Evolution of the 200-Mile EEZ: State Practices in the Pacific Basin." _Virginia Journal of International Law_. vol. 19, no. 2, Winter 1979, pp. 321-400.

366. Kusumaatmadja, Mochtar. "The Legal Regime of the Archipelagoes: Problems and Issues." Lewis M. Alexander, ed. _The Law of the Sea, Needs and Interests of Developing Countries_. Kingston, RI: University of Rhode Island, 1973, pp. 166-177.

367. Kwaiatkowska, Barbara. _The 200-Mile Exclusive Economic Zone in the Law of the Sea_. Dordrecht, Netherlands: Martinus Nijhoff, and London: Graham & Trotman, Ltd., 1989.

This is a comprehensive study of the 200-mile exclusive economic zone and its operation.

368. Lagoni, Rainer. "Interim Measures Pending Maritime Delimitation Agreements." _American Journal of International Law_. vol. 78, no. 2, April 1984, pp. 345-368.

369. Langdon, J. B. R. L. "The Extent of Transit Passage: Some Practical Anomalies." _Maritime Policy_. vol. 14, no. 2, March 1990, pp. 130-136.

370. Lapidoth, Ruth. "The Strait of Tiran, the Gulf of Aqaba, and the 1979 Treaty of Peace between Egypt and Israel." _American Journal of International Law_. vol. 77, no. 1, January 1983, pp. 84-108.

371. Lapidoth-Eschelbacher, R. _The Red Sea and the Gulf of Aden_. The Hague, Netherlands: Martinus Nijhoff, and London: Graham & Trotman, Ltd., 1982.

372. Larson, David L. Major Issues of the Law of the Sea.
     Durham, NH: The University of New Hampshire, 1976.

This is a convenient simply designed booklet concerning some
of the major issues then facing the UN Third Conference on
the Law of the Sea.

373. Laursen, Finn, ed. "The Law of the Sea and Inter-
     national Security: Aspects of Superpower Policy."
     Toward a New International Marine Order. The Hague,
     Netherlands: Martinus Nijhoff Publishers, 1982, pp. 82-
     83.

374. The Law of the Sea: Maritime Boundary Agreements (1970-
     1984). United Nations: Office for Ocean Affairs and
     the Law of the Sea, 1988.

Contains the texts of 74 agreements up to 1984 with detailed
illustrated maps of the areas under discussion.

375. The Law of the Sea: National Legislation on the Exclu-
     sive Economic Zone, The Economic Zone and the Exclusive
     Fishery Zone. United Nations: Office for Ocean Affairs
     and the Law of the Sea, 1989.

Contains an analysis of the exclusive economic and fishery
zones based on the provisions adopted by the 1982 Law of the
Sea Convention.

376. The Law of the Sea: Official Text of the United Nations
     Convention on the Law of the Sea with Annexes and
     Index. New York: St. Martins Press, 1983.

377. The Law of the Sea: Regime of Islands. United Natons,
     1987.

A legislative and negotiation history on the regime of
islands at the 1958 and 1974-82 Law of the Sea Conferences.

378. Leanza, Umberto and Luigi Sico. Mediterranean Conti-
     nental Shelf: Delimitations and Regimes, International
     and National Legal Sources. Dobbs Ferry, NY: Oceana
     Publications, Inc., 1988.

These useful volumes will be helpful for Italian and English
speaking oil experts and lawyers to be familiar with the
legal regimes governing offshore hydrocarbon activities in
the Mediterranean.

379. Lee, Roy S. "The New Law of the Sea and the Pacific
     Basin." Ocean Development and International Law, vol.
     12, nos. 3-4, 1982, pp. 247-264.

380. Legault, L. H. and Blair Hankey. "From Sea to Seabed:
     The Single Maritime Boundary in the Gulf of Maine
     Case." The American Journal of International Law, vol.
     79, no. 4, October 1985, pp. 961-991.

The article deals with maritime boundary delimitation in the Gulf of Maine. It also addresses both of the continental shelf boundaries, as well as the exclusive economic zones, claimed by Canada and the United States.

381. Leifer, M. Malacca, Singapore and Indonesia. The Hague, Netherlands: Martinus Nijhoff, and London: Graham & Trotman, Ltd., 1978.

382. Leng, Lee Yong. "The Archipelagic Concept and the Impact on Southeast Asia." Singapore Journal of Tropical Geography. vol. 4, no. 1, 1983, pp. 34-39.

Presents the Indonesian and Philippine perceptions on the archipelagic principle and its impact on Southeast Asia in terms of baselines and navigational rights through and over enclosed archipelagic waters.

383. Leonhard, Alan T. "Ixtoc I: A Test for the Emerging Concept of the Patrimonial Sea." San Diego Law Review. vol. 17, no. 3, April 1980, pp. 617-627.

384. Letalik, Norman G. "Boundary Making in the Mediter-ranean." Douglas M. Johnston and Phillip M. Saunders, eds. Ocean Boundary Making: Regional Issues and Developments. New York: Croom Helm, 1988, pp. 109-141.

385. Lowry, Kem and H. J. M. Wickremeratne. "Coastal Area Management in Sri Lanka." Elisabeth Mann Borgese, Norton Ginsburg and Joseph R. Morgan, eds. Ocean Yearbook 7. Chicago and London: University of Chicago Press, 1988, pp. 263-293.

386. Luard, Evan. The Control of the Seabed: A New Inter-national Issue. London: Heineman, 1974.

A most readable book for general audiences on the UN seabed debates in 1967 which resulted in calling for the Third UN Conference on the Law of the Sea.

387. McCaffrey, Stephen C. "The Law of International Watercourses: Some Recent Developments and Unanswered Questions." Denver Journal of International Law and Policy. vol. 17, no. 3, Spring 1989, pp. 505-526.

388. MacChesney, Brunson. "Special Aspects of Jurisdiction at Sea." Richard B. Lillich and John Norton Moore, eds. U. S. Naval College International Law Studies, Readings in International Law from Naval War College Review 1974-1977. vol. 61. Newport, RI: Naval War College Press, 1980, pp. 319-327.

389. McDonald, Sally and Victor Prescott. "Baselines along Unstable Coasts: An Interpretation of Article 7(2)," Elisabeth Mann Borgese, Norton Ginsburg and Joseph R. Morgan, eds. Ocean Yearbook 8. Chicago and London: The University of Chicago Press, 1989, pp. 70-89.

Explores the premise that drawing straight baselines is
separate from indented coasts and coasts with fringed
islands. The paper examines the background and purpose of
Article 7(2) in the 1982 Law of the Sea convention.

390. McDougal, Myres S. "Internatonal Law and the Law of
the Sea." Lewis M. Alexander, ed. The Law of the Sea:
Offshore Boundaries and Zones. Columbus, OH: Ohio
State University Press, 1967, pp. 18-20.

391. _____ and William T. Burke. The Public Order of
the Oceans: A Contemporary International Law of the
Sea. New Haven, CT: New Haven Press, 1987.

This is the latest edition of a massive study of all aspects
of the law of the sea. Its coverage of the development of
maritime principles is most comprehensive.

392. McKelvey, V. E. "Interpretation of the UNCLOS III
Definition of the Continental Shelf." Douglas M.
Johnston and Norman B. Letalik, eds. The Law of the
Sea and Ocean Industry: New Opportunities and
Restraints. Honolulu: The Law of the Sea Institute,
University of Hawaii, 1983, pp. 465-472.

393. Maechling, Charles Jr. "Crisis at the Turkish
Straits." Proceedings. Annapolis, MD: U.S. Naval
Institute, August 1988, pp. 64-71.

394. Mahmoudi, Said. "Customary International Law and
Transit Passage." Ocean Development and International
Law. vol. 20, no. 2, 1989, pp. 157-174.

395. Mangone, Gerard J. The Elements of International Law:
A Casebook. Homewood, IL: The Dorsey Press, Inc.,
1963.

396. Mawdsley, Andres Aguilar. "The Law of the Sea: The
Latin American View." Giulio Pontecorvo, ed. The New
Order of the Oceans: The Advent of a Managed Environment. New York: Columbia University Press, 1986, pp.
158-198.

397. Mesznik, Roger. "Transit Fees for Ocean Straits and
Their Impact on Global Economic Welfare." Ocean
Development and International Law. vol. 8, no. 4, 1980,
pp. 337-354.

398. Mfodwo, S. K. B., B. M. Tsamenyi and S. K. N. Blay.
"The Exclusive Economic Zone: State Practice in the
African Atlantic Region." Ocean Development and
International Law. vol. 20, no. 5, 1989, pp. 445-500.

399. Miles, Edward and John King Gamble, Jr., eds. Law of
the Sea: Conference Outcomes and Problems of Implementation. Cambridge, MA: Ballinger Publishing Company,
1977.

400. Mitchell, James K. "Coastal Management Since 1980: The U.S. Experience and Its Relevance for Other Countries." Elisabeth Mann Borgese and Norton Ginsburg, eds. Ocean Yearbook 6. Chicago and London: University of Chicago Press, 1986, pp. 319-345.

401. Mizukami, Chiyuki. "The Relation between International Treaties and National Regulation in East Asia and International Cooperation in Marine Pollution: Japan." John P. Craven, Jan Schneider and Carol Stimson, eds. The International Implications of Extended Maritime Jurisdiction in the Pacific. Honolulu: The Law of the Sea Institute, University of Hawaii, 1989, pp. 90-93.

402. Molodtsov, Stepan. "The Exclusive Economic Zone: Legal Status and Regime of Navigation." Elisabeth Mann Borgese and Norton Ginsburg, eds. Ocean Yearbook 6. Chicago and London: University of Chicago Press, 1986, pp. 203-216.

Comments from an officer of the Ministry of Foreign Affairs, USSR, on the legal status of the exclusive economic zone after the adoption of the 1982 Law of the Sea Convention.

403. Monteiro, Pedro M. S. "Marion and Prince Edward Islands: The Legal Regime of the Adjacent Maritime Zones." Sea Changes. no. 5, 1987, pp. 63-109.

404. Moore, John Norton. "The Regime of Straits and the Third United Nations Conferences on the Law of the Sea." The American Journal of International Law. vol. 74, January 1980, pp. 77-121.

Makes a detailed study of the international regime for straits and presents arguments in defense of the draft on the strait regime negotiated at the Third UN Conference on the Law of the Sea.

405. Morgan, Joseph R. "Small Navies." Elisabeth Mann Borgese and Norton Ginsburg, eds. Ocean Yearbook 6. Chicago and London: University of Chicago, 1986, pp. 362-389.

406. Morris, Michael A. "EEZ Policy in South America's Southern Cross." Elisabeth Mann Borgese and Norton Ginsburg, eds. Ocean Yearbook 6. Chicago and London: University of Chicago Press, 1986, pp. 417-437.

407. Morrison, Charles E. "Critical Issues in Marine Policy." Asian Pacific Report: Trends, Issues, Challenges. Honolulu: East-West Center, University of Hawaii, 1986, pp. 45-88.

Discusses the changing law of the sea and the Asian-Pacific region in terms of maritime zones, boundary disputes, fisheries, pollution and navigation.

408. Mtango, E. D. and Friedl Weiss. "The Exclusive Economic Zone and Tanzania: Considerations of a

Developing Country." Ocean Development and International Law. vol. 14, no. 1, 1984, pp. 1-54.

409. Murphy, Cornelius F. "The Grotian Vision of World Order." American Journal of International Law. vol. 76, no. 3, July 1982, pp. 477-498.

410. Nakauchi, Kiyotuni. "Problems of Delimitation in the East China Sea and the Sea of Japan." Ocean Development and International Law. vol. 6, 1979, pp. 305-316.

411. Narokobi, Camillus S. N. "The Regime of Archipelagoes in International Law." Jon M. Van Dyke, Lewis M. Alexander and Joseph R. Morgan, eds. International Navigation: Rocks and Shoals Ahead? Honolulu: The Law of the Sea Institute, University of Hawaii, 1988, pp. 220-236.

A perspective on the regime of archipelagoes from Papua-New Guinea.

412. Neblett, William R. "The 1958 Conference on the Law of the Sea: What Was Accomplished?" Lewis M. Alexander, ed. The Law of the Sea: Offshore Boundaries and Zones. Columbus, OH: Ohio State University Press, 1967, pp. 39-42.

413. Nelson, L. Dolliver M. "The Delimitation of Maritime Boundaries in the Caribbean." Douglas M. Johnston and Phillip M. Saunders, eds. Ocean Boundary Making: Regional Issues and Developments. London and New York: Croom Helm, 1988, pp. 142-203.

414. Neubauer, Ronald D. "The Right of Innocent Passage for Warships in the Territorial Sea: A Response to the Soviet Union." Naval War College Review. vol. xli, no. 2-Sequence 322, Spring 1988, pp. 49-56.

415. Njenga, Frank X. "Historical Background of the Evolution of the Exclusive Economic Zone and the Contribution of Africa." Giulio Pontecorvo, ed. The New Order of the Oceans: The Advent of a Managed Environment. New York: Columbia University Press, 1986, pp. 125-157.

416. Nordquist, Myron H. "Existing Law and Legislative Proposals." John P. Craven, Jan Schneider and Carol Stimson, eds. The International Implications of Extended Maritime Jurisdiction in the Pacific. Honolulu: The Law of the Sea Institute, University of Hawaii, 1989, pp. 353-359.

417. _____. "The Innocent Passage Regime." Choon-ho Park and Jae Kyu Park, eds. The Law of the Sea: Problems from the East Asian Perspective. Honolulu: The Law of the Sea Institute, University of Hawaii, 1987, pp. 40-43.

418. Nweihed, Kaldone G.   "EZ (Uneasy)   Delimitation in the Semi-enclosed Caribbean Sea: Recent Agreements between Venezuela and Her Neighbors."   Ocean Development and International Law, vol. 8, no. 1, 1980, pp. 1-34.

419. Oda, Shigeru.   International Control of Sea Resources. The Hague, Netherlands: Martinus Nijhoff, and London: Graham & Trotman, Ltd., 1989.

420. _____.   The Law of the Sea in Our Time: New Developments, 1966-1975.   The Hague, Netherlands: Martinus Nijhoff, and London: Graham & Trotman Ltd., 1977.

421. Orlin, Hyman. "Offshore Boundaries: Engineering and Economic Aspects." Ocean Development and International Law. vol. 3, no. 1, 1975, pp. 87-96.

422. Oxman, Bernard H. "The High Seas and the International Seabed Area."   John P. Craven, Jan Schneider and Carol Stimson, eds.   The   International   Implications   of Extended Maritime Jurisdiction in the Pacific. Hono- lulu: The Law of the Sea Institute, University of Hawaii, 1989, pp. 410-424.

423. _____.   "The High Seas and the International Seabed Area," Michigan Journal of International Law, vol. 10, no. 2, Spring 1989, pp. 526-542.

424. _____.   "Customary International Law and the Ex- clusive Economic Zone."   Jon M. Van Dyke, ed. Con- sensus and Confrontation: The United States and the Law of the Sea Convention.   Honolulu: The Law of the Sea Institute, University of Hawaii, 1985, pp. 138-161.

425. Pabst, Richard W.   "The Economic Zone." David L. Larson, ed. Major Issues of the Law of the Sea. Durham, NH: University of New Hampshire, 1976, pp. 45-51.

426. _____.   "Islands and Archipelagos." David L. Larson, ed. Major Issues af the Law of the Sea. Durham, NH: University of New Hampshire, 1976, pp. 140-158.

427. Paik, Jin-Hyun.   "Some Legal Issues Relating to Maritime Jurisdictions of North Korea." John P. Craven, Jan Schneider and Carol Stimson, eds. The International Implications of Extended Maritime Juris- diction in the Pacific. Honolulu: The Law of the Sea Institute, University of Hawaii, 1989, pp. 94-113.

Discusses legal questions relating to various maritime jurisdictional claims by North Korea, including straight baselines, foreign warships in innocent passage and military boundary zones.

428. Pak, Chi Young.   The Korean Straits. Dordrecht, Boston, London: Martinus Nijhoff Publishers, 1988.

This is but one of many recent studies which illustrate the importance of ocean passages for commercial vessels and the naval forces.

429. _____. "The Continental Shelf between Korea, Japan and China." Marine Policy Reports. vol. 4, no. 5, June 1982.

430. Papadakis, N. The International Legal Regime of Artificial Islands. The Hague, Netherlands: Martinus Nijhoff, and London: Graham & Trotman, Ltd., 1977.

431. Park, Choon-ho. "South Korean Perspective." John P. Craven, Jan Schneider, and Carol Stimson, eds. The International Implications of Extended Maritime Juris-diction in the Pacific. Honolulu: The Law of the Sea Institute, University of Hawaii, 1989.

432. _____. "Dispute Settlement among Non-Parties to the LOS Convention with Respect to the Outer Limits of the Continental Shelf." Thomas A. Clingan, Jr., ed. The Law of the Sea: What Lies Ahead? Honolulu: The Law of the Sea Institute, University of Hawaii, 1988, pp. 494-515.

433. _____. "The Korea Strait." Jon M. Van Dyke, Lewis M. Alexander and Joseph R. Morgan, eds. Inter-national Navigation: Rocks and Shoals Ahead? Hono-lulu: The Law of the Sea Institute, University of Hawaii, 1988, pp. 173-188.

434. _____. "China and Maritime Jurisdiction: Some Boundary Issues." Choon-ho Park and Jae Kyu Park, eds. The Law of the Sea: Problems from the East Asian Per-spective. Honolulu: The Law of the Sea Institute, University of Hawaii, 1987, pp. 281-305.

435. _____. "The South China Sea Disputes: Who Owns the Islands and the Natural Resources?" Choon-ho Park and Jae Kyu Park, eds. The Law of the Sea: Problems from the East Asian Perspective. Honolulu: The Law of the Sea Institute, University of Hawaii, 1987, pp. 482-510.

436. _____. "The South China Sea Disputes: Who Owns the Islands and the Natural Resources?" Ocean Develop-ment and International Law, vol. 5, no. 1, 1978, pp. 27-60.

437. _____. Continental Shelf Issues in the Yellow Sea and the East China Sea. Honolulu: Law of the Sea Institute, University of Hawaii, 1972.

438. _____ and Jae Kyu Park, eds. The Law of the Sea: Problems from the East Asian Perspective. Honolulu: The Law of the Sea Institute, University of Hawaii, 1987.

439. Penick, F. V. W. "The Legal Character of the Right to Explore and Exploit the Natural Resources of the Continental Shelf." San Diego Law Review. vol. 22, no. 4, 1985, pp. 765-778.

440. Petit-Skinner, Solange. "Traditional Ownership of the Sea in Oceania." Elisabeth Mann Borgese and Norton Ginsburg, eds. Ocean Yearbook 4. Chicago and London: University of Chicago Press, 1983, pp. 308-318.

441. Pharand, D. Northwest Passage: Arctic Straits. The Hague, Netherlands: Martinus Nijhoff, and London: Graham & Trotman, Ltd., 1984.

442. Pirtle, Charles E. "Transit Rights and U.S. Security Interests in International Straits: The 'Straits Debate' Revisited." Ocean Development and International Law. vol. 5, no. 4, 1978, pp. 477-497.

443. Platzoeder, Renate. "The Regimes of the Territorial Sea of the Federal Republic of Germany and the German Democratic Republic." Jon M. Van Dyke, Lewis M. Alexander and Joseph R. Morgan, eds. International Navigation: Rocks and Shoals Ahead? Honolulu: The Law of the Sea Institute, University of Hawaii, 1988, pp. 102-105.

Provides discussion as to why the German Democratic Republic has extended its territorial sea and why the Federal Republic of Germany has not done so.

444. Pontecorvo, Giulio. "Contribution of the Ocean Sector to the United States Economy: Estimated Values for 1987: A Technical Note." Marine Technology Society Journal. vol. 23, no. 2, June 1989, pp. 7-14.

445. _____. "Existing and Potential Maritime Claims in the Southwest Pacific Ocean." Elisabeth Mann Borgese and Norton Ginsburg, eds. Ocean Yearbook 2. Chicago and London: University of Chicago Press, 1980, pp. 317-345.

446. _____. "Reflections on the Economics of the Common Heritage of Mankind: The Organization of the Deep-Sea Mining Industry and the Expected Benefits from Resource Exploitation." Ocean Development and International Law. vol. 2, no. 3, 1974, pp. 203-216.

447. Prescott, J. R. Victor. "Maritime Boundaries and Issues in Southwest Pacific Ocean." Douglas M. Johnston and Phillip M. Saunders, eds. Ocean Boundary Making: Regional Issues and Developments. New York: Croom Helm, 1988, pp. 268-312.

448. _____. "On the Resolution of Marine Boundary Conflicts." John P. Craven, Jan Schneider and Carol Stimson, eds. The International Implications of Extended Maritime Jurisdiction in the Pacific. Hono-

lulu: The Law of the   Sea   Institute,   University of Hawaii, 1987, pp. 33-40.

Discusses why boundary conflicts arise and the path leading to resolution of these disputes.

449. _____.   Political   Frontiers   and   Boundaries. London and Boston: Allen and Unwin, 1987.

450. _____.   The Maritime Political Boundaries of the World. London and New York: Methuen, 1985.

This is a practical book from a known political geographer with no attempt to develop any theory on maritime boundaries and claims. The book is a definitive study on the subject of maritime boundary-making as the result of political policies and strategies by governments.

451. _____. "International Maritime Boundaries in the Southwest Pacific Ocean."   Edward L. Miles and Scott Allen, eds. The Law of the Sea and Ocean Development Issues in the Pacific Basin. Honolulu: The Law of the Sea Institute, University of Hawaii, 1983, pp. 488-525.

452. _____. The Political Geography of the Oceans. New York: John Wiley and Sons, 1975.

453. "Presidential Proclamation on the Territorial Sea of the United States, December 27, 1988." International Legal Materials. vol. xxviii, no. 1, January 1989, p. 284.

454. "Protecting International Rights: Seminar of Center for Ocean Law and Policy, University of Virginia." Oceans Policy News. April 1989, p. 5.

455. Qader, Mohammed Afsarul.   "Extended Maritime Jurisdic- tion: A Case for Regional Cooperation in the Management of Fisheries Resources in the Bay of Bengal."   John P. Craven, Jan Schneider and Carol Stimson, eds. The International Implications of Extended Maritime Juris- diction in the Pacific. Honolulu: The Law of the Sea Institute, University of Hawaii, 1989, pp. 292-305.

456. Ramazani, R. K. The Persian Gulf and the Strait of Hormuz. The Hague, Netherlands: Martinus Nijhoff, and London: Graham & Trotman, Ltd., 1979.

457. Rao, P. C. and Bhimsen Rao.   "Implications of the Extended Maritime Jurisdiction: Outstanding Issues in South Asia Region." John P. Craven, Jan Schneider and Carol Stimson, eds. The International Implications of Extended Maritime Jurisdictions in the Pacific. Honolulu: The Law of the Sea Institute, University of Hawaii, 1989, pp. 281-286.

458. Rao, P. Sreenivasa.   The Public Order of Ocean Resources: A Critique of the Contemporary Law of the

Sea. Cambridge, MA: The MIT Press, 1975, pp. 124-135, 139-174.

459. Reblagliati, Orlando Ruben and David D. Carson. "Book Review: The Continental Platform and Its Outer Limit." American Journal of International Law. vol. 82, no. 2, 1988, pp. 403-405.

460. Regime of Islands: Legislative History of Part VIII (Article 121) of the United Nations Convention on the Law of the Sea. United Nations: Office for Ocean Affairs and the Law of the Sea, Februry 1988.

461. Reisman, Michael. "Regime of Straits and National Security: An Appraisal of International Lawmaking." The American Journal of International Law. vol. 74, January 1980, pp. 48-76.

This is an exhaustive study on the question of international straits in relation to national security.

462. Rhee, Sang-Myon. "Accommodating Conflicting Claims in the Northwest Pacific." Jon M. Van Dyke, Lewis M. Alexander and Joseph R. Morgan, eds. International Navigation: Rocks and Shoals Ahead? Honolulu: The Law of the Sea Institute, University of Hawaii, 1988, pp. 326-331.

463. _____. "The Boundary Delimitation between States before World War II." American Journal of International Law. vol. 76, no. 3, July 1982, pp. 555-588.

464. _____. "Equitable Solutions to the Maritime Boundary Dispute between the United States and Canada in the Gulf of Maine." American Journal of International Law. vol. 75, no. 3, July 1981, pp. 590-628.

465. _____ and James MacAulay. "Ocean Boundary Issues in East Asia: The Need for Practical Solutions." Douglas M. Johnston and Phillip M.Saunders, eds. Ocean Boundary Making: Regional Issues and Developments. New York: Croom Helm, 1988, pp. 74-108.

466. Robertson, Horace B. J. "The Effects of National Claims." Jon M. Van Dyke, Lewis M.Alexander and Joseph R. Morgan, eds. International Navigation: Rocks and Shoals Ahead? Honolulu: The Law of the Sea Institute, University of Hawaii, 1988, pp. 120-121.

467. _____. "The Straits Passage Regime." Choon-ho Park and Jae Kyu Park, eds. The Law of the Sea: Problems from the East Asian Perspective. Honolulu: The Law of the Sea Institute, University of Hawaii, 1987, pp. 44-48.

468. Roger, Kendrick F. "Japan's East China Sea Ocean Boundaries: What Solutions Can a Confused Legal Environment Provide in a Complex Boundary Dispute?"

Vanderbilt Journal of Transnational Law, vol. 22, no. 3, 1989, pp. 581-630.

Considered to be a definitive study on the ocean boundary delimitation conflict between Japan, China, Taiwan and South Korea in the East China Sea. Proposes alternatives to existing legal precedents for solving these disputes in the East China Sea.

469. Rolston, Susan J. and Ted L. McDorman. "Maritime Boundary Making in the Arctic Region." Douglas M. Johnston and Phillip M. Saunders, eds. _Ocean Boundary Making: Regional Issues and Developments_. New York: Croom Helm, 1988, pp. 16-73.

470. Rozakis, C. L. _The Greek-Turkish Dispute over the Aegean Continental Shelf_. Honolulu: The Law of the Sea Institute, University of Hawaii, 1975.

This is a comprehensive study about one of the oldest maritime boundary disputes in the world. It is detailed in legal arguments for both sides.

471. _____ and Petros N. Stagos. _The Turkish Straits_. The Hague, Netherlands: Martinus Nijhoff, and London: Graham & Trotman, Ltd., 1987.

Provides a detailed review of the legal regime of the Turkish Straits dating from the 1923 Lausanne Convention to the 1936 Montreux Convention.

472. Rubin, Alfred P. "The International Legal Effects of Unilateral Declarations." _American Journal of International Law_, vol. 71, no. 1, January 1977, pp. 1-32.

473. Ryan, Paul R. "The Exclusive Economic Zone." _Oceanus_, vol. 27, no. 4, Winter 1984-85, pp. 3-4.

474. St. John, Ronald Bruce. "The Boundary Dispute between Peru and Ecuador." _American Journal of International Law_, vol. 71, no. 2, April 1977, pp. 322-330.

475. Saman, Daniel Oscar. "A Comparison of the Law of the Sea Claims of Mexico and Brazil." _Ocean Development and International Law_. vol. 10, nos. 1-2, 1981, pp. 131-174.

476. Samuels, Marwyn S. _Contest for the South China Sea_. New York and London: Methuen, 1982.

477. Schachter, Oscar. "Concepts and Realities in the New Law of the Sea." Giulio Pontecorvo, ed. _The New Order of the Oceans: The Advent of a Managed Environment_. New York: Columbia University Press, 1986, pp. 29-59.

Thoughtful comments by a former legal advisor to the UN Secretariat's International Law Commission on the erosion of freedom in the oceans.

478. Schmidt, Markus G. _Common Heritage or Common Burden? The U.S. Position on the Development of a Regime for Deep Seabed Mining in the Law of the Sea Convention_. London: Oxford University Press, 1989.

479. Scovazzi, Tullio. "Bays and Straight Baselines in the Mediterranean." _Ocean Development and International Law_. vol. 19, no. 5, 1988, pp. 401-420.

480. _____. "Coastal State Practice in the Exclusive Economic Zone: The Right of Foreign States to Use This Zone." Thomas A. Clingan, Jr., ed. _The Law of the Sea: What Lies Ahead?_ Honolulu: The Law of the Sea Institute, University of Hawaii, 1988, pp. 310-328.

481. Selak, Charles B., Jr. "Recent Developments in High Seas Fisheries: Jurisdiction under the Presidential Proclamation of 1945." _The American Journal of International Law_. vol. 44, October 1950, pp. 670-681.

482. Shah, M. J. "Maritime Law and the Developing Countries: Attitudes and Trends." Elisabeth Mann Borgese and Norton Ginsburg, eds. _Ocean Yearbook 6_. Chicago and London: University of Chicago Press, 1986, pp. 107-138.

483. Shao, Jin. "The Question of Innocent Passage of Warships: After UNCLOS III." _Marine Policy_. vol. 13, no. 1, January 1989, pp. 56-67.

484. Shcherbina, Nickolai. "UN Convention on the Law of the Sea and USSR Economic Zone Legislation." John P. Craven, Jan Schneider and Carol Stimson, eds. _The International Implications of Extended Maritime Jurisdiction in the Pacific_. Honolulu: The Law of the Sea Institute, University of Hawaii, 1989, pp. 119-122.

485. Shyan, Marjula R. "Extended Maritime Jurisdiction and Its Impact on South Asia," _Ocean Development and International Law_, vol. 10, nos. 1-2, 1981, pp. 93-112.

486. Sinjela, A. Mpazi. "Land-Locked States Rights in the Exclusive Economic Zone from the Perspective of the UN Convention on the Law of the Sea." _Ocean Development and International Law_. vol. 20, no. 1, 1909, pp. 682.

Examines the extent of rights of landlocked states in the exploitation of resources in the exclusive economic zone, with the conclusion that the landlocked states lost their rights in the EEZ areas.

487. Skry, Mirjam. "The 1987 Law of Yugoslavia on the Coastal Sea and the Continental Shelf." _Ocean Development and International Law_. vol. 20, no. 5, 1989, pp. 501-514.

Analyzes the recent Yugoslavia national law on the regimes of the territorial sea and the continental shelf by pointing out the Yugoslavian law's concern for strengthening its national security interests in the territorial sea and the extension on the continental shelf of sovereign rights over historical objects.

488. Smith, Robert W. "Global Maritime Claims." Ocean Development and International Law. vol. 20, no. 1, 1989, pp. 83-104.

489. _____. Exclusive Economic Zone Claims: An Analysis and Primary Documents. Dordrecht, Boston, Lancaster: Martinus Nijhoff Publishers, 1986.

An invaluable reference book with documentary material concerning coastal states' claims to the 200-mile economic zone.

490. _____. "A Geographical Primer to Maritime Boundary-Making." Edward L. Miles and Scott Allen, eds. The Law of the Sea and Ocean Development Issues in the Pacific Basin. Honolulu: The Law of the Sea Institute, University of Hawaii, 1983, pp. 526-546.

491. _____. A Geographical Primer to Maritime Boundary-Making." Ocean Development and International Law. vol. 12, nos. 1-2, 1982, pp. 1-22.

492. Smyser, A. A. "Hawaii Could Lay Claim to Large Hunk of Pacific," The Honolulu Star-Bulletin, 11 April 1989, p. A-12.

493. Snow, Rodney A. "Extended Fishery Jurisdiction in Canada and the United States." Ocean Development and International Law. vol. 5, no. 2-3, 1978, pp. 291-344.

494. Society for Underwater Technology. Exclusive Economic Zones: Resources, Opportunities and the Legal Regime. The Hague, Netherlands: Martinus Nijhoff, and London: Graham & Trotman Ltd.,, 1986.

495. Soons, Alfred H. A. Artificial Islands and Installations in International Law. Honolulu: The Law of the Sea Institute, University of Hawaii, 1974.

496. Spinnato, John M. "Historic and Vital Bays: An Analysis of Libya's Claim to the Gulf of Sidra." Ocean Development and International Law. vol. 13, no. 1, 1983, pp. 65-86.

497. "State Practice and National Policy." Law of the Sea, Report of the Secretary-General, United Nations General Assembly (A/43/718) 20 October 1988.

498. "Straight Baselines Along Unstable Coasts." LOS Lieder, vol. 3, no. 3. Honolulu: The Law of the Sea Institute, University of Hawaii, December 1989, p. 1-2.

499. Swartztrauber, Sayre A. The Three-Mile Limit of Territorial Seas. Annapolis, MD: Naval Institute Press, 1972.

An excellent introductory book on the origin, development and historical practices of the three-mile territorial sea.

500. "Sweden-Union of Soviet Socialist Republics: Agreement on Principles for the Delimitation of Sea Areas in the Baltic Sea." International Legal Materials. vol. xxvii, no. 3, May 1988, pp. 695-697.

501. Symmons, Clive R. "The Maritime Zones and Falkland Islands." International and Comparative Law Quarterly. vol. 37, part 2, April 1988, pp. 283-324.

502. Symonides, Janusz. "Origin and Legal Essence of the Contiguous Zone." Ocean Development and International Law. vol. 20, no. 2, 1989, pp. 203-212.

Discusses the origin, development and changes in the concept of the contiguous zone since the adoption of the 1982 Law of the Sea Convention.

503. Szekely, Alberto. "Mexico Unilateral Claim to a 200-Mile Exclusive Economic Zone: Its International Significance." Ocean Development and International Law. vol. 4, no. 2, 1977, pp. 195-211.

504. Tangsubkul, Phiphat. "The New Zones of National Jurisdiction in the Law of the Sea: Developmental Implications for Southeast Asia." John P. Craven, Jan Schneider, Carol Stimson, eds. The International Implications of Extended Maritime Jurisdiction in thePacific. Honolulu: The Law of the Sea Institute, University of Hawaii, 1989, pp. 50-59.

Discusses the settlement of boundary delimitations, management of marine resources in the exclusive economic zones, and marine environmental protection for the region.

505. _____ and Daniel J. Dzurek. "The Emerging Concept of Midocean Archipelagos." Elisabeth Mann Borgese and Norton Ginsburg, eds. Ocean Yearbook 3. Chicago and London: University of Chicago Press, 1982, pp. 386-404.

506. "Territorial Sea Extension Hearing: U. S. Congress." Oceans Policy News. May 1989, pp. 4-5.

507. Truver, S. G. The Strait of Gibraltar and the Mediterranean. The Hague, Netherlands: Martinus Nijhoff, and London: Graham & Trotman, Ltd., 1980.

508. Tsarev, Victor F. "Confidence Measures: An Important Condition of Cooperation of States in the Asia and Pacific Region." John P. Craven, Jan Schneider and Carol Stimson, eds. The International Implications of Extended Maritime Jurisdiction in the Pacific. Honolulu: The Law of the Sea Institute, University of Hawaii, 1989, pp. 425-433.

509. Underwood, Peter C. "Ocean Boundaries and Resource Development in West Africa." Douglas M. Johnston and

Phillip M. Saunders, eds. <u>Ocean Boundary Making: Regional Issues and Developments</u>. New York: Croom Helm, 1988, pp. 229-267.

510. United Nations, Office for Ocean Affairs and the Law of the Sea. "Extent of National Claims over Maritime Zones." <u>Law of the Sea Bulletin</u>. no. 11, July 1988, pp. 46-56.

511. "U. S. Exclusive Economic Zone (EEZ)." <u>GIST</u>. Bureau of Public Affairs, Department of State, April 1983.

512. "U. S. Ocean Policy: EEZ Data Declassification." <u>Oceans Policy News</u>. May 1989, p. 2.

513. "U. S. Oceans Policy." President's statement, 10 March 1983. <u>Department of State Bulletin</u>. June 1983, p. 70-71

514. "U. S. Sets 200-mile Coastal Zone." <u>The New York Times</u>, 11 March 1983, p. A-4.

515. "U. S.-Soviet Statement on Innocent Passage." <u>Oceans Policy News</u>. September-October 1989, pp. 1-2.

516. Valencia, Mark J. "Seed of Conflict in the South China Sea." <u>Asian Wall Street Journal</u>. 13 July 1988, p. 8.

A more recent study on the Spratly Islands as seeds of international conflict. Advocates joint development of resources as the only alternative to no development or to confrontation.

517. _____ and David Vander Zwaag. "Maritime Claims and Management Rights of Indigenous Peoples: Rising Tides in the Pacific and Northern Waters." <u>Journal of Ocean and Shoreline Management</u>. vol. 12, no. 2, 1989, pp. 125-167.

518. Vallejo, Stella Maris A. "Development and Management of Coastal and Marine Areas: An International Perspective." Elisabeth Mann Borgese, Norton Ginsburg and Joseph R. Morgan, eds. <u>Ocean Yearbook 7</u>. Chicago and London: University of Chicago Press, 1988, pp. 205-222.

519. Van Dyke, Jon M. "The Role of Islands in Delimiting Maritime Zones: The Case of the Aegean Sea." Elisabeth Mann Borgese, Norton Ginsburg and Joseph R. Morgan, eds. <u>Ocean Yearbook 8</u>. Chicago and London: The University of Chicago Press, 1989, pp. 44-69.

This represents one of the most recent studies concerning the problem of delimiting the continental shelf between Turkey and Greece.

520. _____ and Robert A. Brooks. "Uninhabited Islands: The Impact on the Ownership of the Oceans' Resources." <u>Ocean Development and International Law</u>. vol. 12, nos. 3-4, 1982, pp. 265-300.

521. _____, Joseph R. Morgan and Jonathan Garish. "The Exclusive Economic Zone of the Northwestern Hawaiian Islands: When Do Uninhabited Islands Generate an EEZ?" San Diego Law Review. vol. 25, no. 3, 1988, pp. 425-494.

Argues that it is not a good policy for the United States to claim exclusive rights to resources around some of the small uninhabited islets or rocks northeast of the main Hawaiian islands--they should remain as wildlife preservation areas for endangered species.

522. _____, Ted N. Pellit, Jennifer Cook Clark and Allen T. Clark. "The Legal Status of Johnston Atoll and Its Exclusive Economic Zone." University of Hawaii Law Review. vol. 10, no. 1, Summer 1988, pp. 183-190.

523. _____ and Christopher Yuen. "'Common Heritage' v. 'Freedom of the High Seas': Which Governs the Seabed?" East-West Environment and Policy Institute. Reprint No. 31. Honolulu: East-West Center, 1982.

524. _____ and Christopher Yuen. "'Common Heritage' v. 'Freedom of the High Seas': Which Governs the Seabed?" San Diego Law Review, vol. 19, no. 3, April 1982, pp. 493-551.

Thoroughly examines the legal principles governing seabed exploration and exploitation.

525. Vargas, Jorge A. "Latin America and Its Contribution to the Law of the Sea." Finn Laursen, ed. Toward a New International Marine Order. The Hague: Martinus Nijhoff, 1982, pp. 62-64.

526. Varghese, Peter. Law Enforcement Capabilities in EEZs: Australia and the South Pacific Island States. Washington, DC: Embassy of Australia, 1988.

527. Vicuna, Francisco Orrego. "International Ocean Developments in the Southeast Pacific: The Case of Chile." John P. Craven, Jan Schneider and Carol Stimson, eds. The International Implications of Extended Maritime Jurisdiction in the Pacific. Honolulu: The Law of the Sea Institute, University of Hawaii, 1989, pp. 217-229.

528. Walker, Peter B. "What is Innocent Passage?" Richard B. Lillich and John Norton Moore, eds. U. S. Naval College International Law Studies, Readings in International Law from Naval War College Review 1974-1977. vol. 61. Newport, RI: Naval War College Press, 1980, pp. 365-387.

A most succinct study of the meaning and implications of the innocent passage concept.

529. Walker, Wyndham L. "Territorial Waters: The Cannon

Shot Rule." British Journal of International Law. vol. 22, 1945, pp. 210-231.

An earlier, but an important, discourse on the origin and development of the cannon shot rule for delimitation of the territorial sea in customary international law.

530. Walz, Jonathan A. "Baselines." David L. Larson, ed. Major Issues of the Law of the Sea. Durham, NH: University of New Hampshire, 1976, pp. 15-27.

531. _____. "The Contiguous Zone." David L. Larson, ed. Major Issues of the Law of the Sea. Durham, NH: University of New Hampshire, 1976, pp. 38-44.

532. _____. "The Territorial Sea." David L. Larson, ed. Major Issues of the Law of the Sea. Durham, NH: University of New Hampshire, 1976, pp. 28-37.

533. Walz, Kathleen L. and L. Poe Leggette. "United States Jurisdiction over the 200-Mile Maritime Zone." San Diego Law Review. vol. 23, no. 3, May-June 1986, pp. 545-582.

This article examines the extent of United States jurisdiction and control over continental shelf resources in customary international law and the development of legal concepts relating to continental shelf resources in terms of state practice.

534. Weil, Robert. The Law of Delimitation: Reflections. Trans. from the French by Maureen MacGlashan. Cambridge: Grotius Publications, 1989.

Deals with the whole range of issues and problems relating to delimitation of maritime boundaries in terms of title, nature and legal concepts.

535. Westerman, Gayl. The Juridical Bay. New York: Oxford University Press, 1987.

This is a major work dealing with interpretations of Article 7 of the 1958 Convention on the Territorial Sea, plus current state practices based on the United State Supreme Court decisions in the American Submerged Lands Cases.

536. Wigg, David G. "Ocean Policy in the Pacific." John P. Craven, Jan Schneider and Carol Stimson, eds. The International Implications of Extended Maritime Jurisdiction in the Pacific. Honolulu: The Law of the Sea Institute, University of Hawaii, 1989, pp. 123-129.

537. Wilkinson, John. "The First Declaration of the Freedom of the Seas: The Rhodian Sea Law." Elisabeth Mann Borgese and Norton Ginsburg, eds. Ocean Yearbook 2. Chicago and London: University of Chicago Press, 1980 pp. 89-93.

538. Willis, L. A.   "From Precedent to Precedent: The Triumph of Pragmatism in the Law of Maritime Boundaries." <u>The Canadian Yearbook of International Law</u>. 1986, pp. 3-59.

539. Wisnumurti, Nugroho.   "Some Impacts of the 1982 Convention on the Law of the Sea on Maritime Jurisdiction: An Indonesian Perspective."   John P. Craven, Jan Schneider and Carol Stimson, eds. <u>The International Implications of Extended Maritime Jurisdiction in the Pacific.</u> Honolulu: The Law of the Sea Institute, University of Hawaii, 1989, pp. 43-49.

540. _____.   "Archipelagic Waters and Archipelagic Sea Lanes."   Jon M. Van Dyke, Lewis M. Alexander and Joseph R. Morgan, eds.   <u>International Navigation: Rocks and Shoals Ahead?</u> Honolulu: The Law of the Sea Institute, University of Hawaii, 1988, pp. 198-209.

Discusses the legal status of archipelagic waters and sealanes.

541. Wolfe, Edward E.   "The International Implications of Extended Maritime Jurisdiction in the Pacific." <u>The International Implications of Extended Maritime Jurisdiction in the Pacific.</u>   Honolulu: The Law of the Sea Institute, University of Hawaii, 1989, pp. 145-149.

542. Wolfrum, R. "China's Jurisdiction over Its Offshore Petroleum Resources."   <u>Ocean Development and International Law</u>. vol. 12, nos. 3-4, 1982, pp. 191-208.

543. _____.   "The Emerging Customary Law of Marine Zones: State Practice and the Convention on the Law of the Sea." <u>Netherlands Yearbook of International Law</u>. vol. xviii, 1987, pp. 121-144.

544. Yonezawa, Kunio.   "Japanese North Pacific Fishery at the Crossroads." John P. Craven, Jan Schneider and Carol Stimson, eds. <u>The International Implications of Extended Maritime Jurisdiction in the Pacific.</u>   Honolulu: The Law of the Sea Institute, University of Hawaii, 1989, pp. 183-192.

545. Zackling, R. and L. Caflisch, eds. <u>The Legal Regime of International Rivers and Lakes</u>. The Hague, Netherlands: Martinus Nijhoff, and London: Graham & Trotman, Ltd., 1981.

546. Zimmerman, James Michael.   Comments: "The Doctrine of Historic Bays: Applying an Anachronism in the Alabama and Mississippi Boundary Case." <u>San Diego Law Review</u>. vol. 23, no. 3, 1986, pp. 763-790.

Questions the soundness of recent U.S. court decisions concerning the ownership of title to the Mississippi Sound based on the controversial doctrine of historic bays for settling numerous disputes between the federal government and coastal states.

Living Resources: Access, EFZ, Disputes, Regional Fishery Commissions, Marine Mammal Protection and Species Approach

547. Allen, K. Radway. <u>Conservation and Management of Whales</u>. Seattle: A Washington Sea Grant Publication, University of Washington Press, 1980.

548. Alexander, Lewis M. "The Ocean Enclosure Movement: Inventory and Prospect." <u>San Diego Law Review</u>. vol. 20, no. 3, April 1983, pp. 561-594.

This study traces the ocean enclosure movement dating back to at least the days of Grotius. It points out that many coastal claims and disputes have concerned fishing rights.

549. _____ and Virgil Norton. "The 200-Mile Limit III: Maritime Problems between the U. S. and Canada." <u>Oceanus</u>. vol. 20, no. 3, Summer 1977, pp. 24-34.

550. Alverson, Dayton L. "Fisheries Developments in the Northeast Pacific and the FCMA/MFCMA." John P. Craven, Jan Schneider and Carol Stimson, eds. <u>The International Implications of Extended Maritime Jurisdiction in the Pacific</u>. Honolulu: The Law of the Sea Institute, University of Hawaii, 1989, pp. 170-182.

551. _____. "Tug-of-War for the Antarctic Krill." <u>Ocean Development and International Law</u>. vol. 8, no. 2, 1980, pp. 171-182.

552. _____. "The 200-Mile Limit II: The North Pacific Fishery Management Council." <u>Oceanus</u>. vol. 20, no. 3, Summer 1977, pp. 18-23.

553. _____. "Management of the Ocean's Living Resources: An Essay Review." <u>Ocean Development and International Law</u>. vol. 3, no. 2, 1975, pp. 99-126.

554. Andresen, Steinar. "Science and Politics in the International Management of Whales." <u>Marine Policy</u>. vol. 13, no. 2, April 1989, pp. 99-117.

555. Anderson, Lee G. "A Classification of Fishery Management Problems to Aid in the Analysis and Proper Formu-
lation of Management Problems." Ocean Development and
International Law. vol. 4, no. 2, 1977, pp. 113-120.

556. Apollonio, Spencer. "Fisheries Management." Oceanus.
vol. 25, no. 4, Winter 1982/83, pp. 29-38.

557. Archer, Jack H.   "The Proposed Flower Garden Bank
Marine Sanctuary: Protecting Marine Resources under
International Law." Oceanus. vol. 31, no. 1, Spring
1988, pp. 54-58.

558. Bardach, John E. "Fish Far Away: Comments on Antarctic
Fisheries." Elisabeth Mann Borgese and Norton Ginsburg,
eds. Ocean Yearbook 6. Chicago and London: University
of Chicago Press, 1986, pp. 38-54.

559. _____ and Penelope J. Ridings. "Pacific Tuna:
Biology, Economics and Politics."   Elisabeth Mann
Borgese and Norton Ginsburg, eds. Ocean Yearbook 5.
Chicago and London: University of Chicago Press, 1985,
pp. 29-57.

560. Barston, R. P. and Hjalmar W. Hannesson. "The Anglo-
Icelandic Fisheries Dispute." International Relations.
vol. 4, no. 6, November 1974, pp. 559-584.

This is a detailed study of the 1971-73 North Atlantic
fishery dispute between Britain and Iceland.   The paper
discusses the reasons for the dispute and provides an
analysis of the stages in the conflict.

561. Beach, Douglas W. and Mason T. Weinrich. "Watching the
Whales: Is an Educational Adventure for Humans Turning
out to be Another Threat for Endangered Species?"
Oceanus. vol. 32, no. 1, Spring 1989, pp. 84-88.

562. Belsky, Martin. "The Marine Ecosystem Management Model
and the Law of the Sea: Requirements for Assessment and
Monitoring."   John P. Craven, Jan Schneider and Carol
Stimson, eds. The International Implications of Extended Maritime Jurisdictions in the Pacific. Honolulu:
The Law of the Sea Institute, University of Hawaii,
1989, pp. 236-262.

563. Berger, Tina.   "Bowhead Estimates Revised Upward: Hunt
Issues Ease." Oceanus. vol. 29, no. 1, September 1986,
pp. 81-84.

564. Birnie, Patricia W.   "Conference Reports: Whaling
Negotiations and Hardcore Issues, Fortieth Meeting of
the International Whaling Commission." Marine Policy.
vol. 13, no. 1, January 1989, p. 68.

565. _____ . "Contemporary Legal Problems."   R. P.
Barston and Patricia Birnie, eds. The Maritime Dimension. London: George Allen and Unwin, 1980, pp. 179-
181.

566. Bonker, Don. "U. S. Policy and Strategy in the International Whaling Commission: Sinking or Swimming?" Ocean Development and International Law. vol. 10, nos. 1-2, 1981, pp. 41-59.

A U.S. representative's criticism of United States performance at the International Whaling Commission proceedings; offers a reassessment of American cetacean policy.

567. Booth, William. "Unraveling the Dolphin Soap Opera." Oceanus. vol. 32, no. 1, Spring 1989, pp. 76-78.

568. Braham, Howard W. "Eskimos, Yankees and Bowheads." Oceanus. vol. 32, no. 1, Spring 1989, pp. 54-62.

569. Brill, E. J. The World of the Whales. New York: Spencer W. Tinker, 1988.

570. Brinkley, Marian. "Nova Scotian Offshore Groundfish Fishermen: Effects of the Enterprise Allocation and Drive for Quality, Marine Policy." The International Journal of Ocean Affairs. vol. 13, no. 4, October 1989, pp. 274-284.

571. Brittin, Burdick H. "The United States-Canada Fisheries Dispute." Douglas M. Johnston and Norman G. Letalik, eds. The Law of the Sea and Ocean Industry: New Opportunities and Restraints. Honolulu: The Law of the Sea Institute, University of Hawaii, 1983, pp. 326-329.

572. Broadus, James M. "The Galapagos Marine Resources Reserve and Tourism Development." Oceanus. vol. 30, no. 2, Summer 1987, pp. 9-15.

573. Brownell, Robert L., Jr., Katherine Ralls and William F. Perrin. "The Plight of the 'Forgotten' Whales." Oceanus. vol. 32, no. 1, Spring 1989, pp. 5-13.

A good summary of the plight of some species of the whale, including a quick reference chart with names, population estimates, and status of the whales.

574. Burke, William T. "Fishing in the Bering Sea Donut: Straddling Stocks and the New International Law of Fisheries." Ecology Law Quarterly. vol. 16, no. 1, 1989, pp. 285-310.

575. _____. "Coastal State Fishery Regulation under International Law: A Comment on the LaBretange Award of July 17, 1986; The Arbitration between Canada and France." San Diego Law Review. vol. 25, no. 3, August-September 1988, pp. 495-533.

The article comments on fishery jurisdiction disputes between Canada and France over two French islands off the coast of southern Newfoundland. The author argues that the prohibition of filleting by freeze trawlers issued by the arbitration tribunal was unwarranted, and that the catch quota set by Canada would be discriminatory against French freezer trawlers permitted to fish in the Gulf of Maine.

576. _____. "The Law of the Sea Convention and Fishing Practices of Non-Signatories with Special Reference to the United States." John M. Van Dyke, ed. Consensus and Confrontation: The United States and the Law of the Sea Convention. Honolulu: The Law of the Sea Institute, University of Hawaii, 1985, pp. 314-382.

577. _____. "Highly Migratory Species in the New Law of the Sea." Ocean Development and International Law. vol. 14, no. 3, 1984, pp. 273-314.

Discussion centers on the requirements of Article 64 relating to the meaning and consequence of failure to cooperate and the application of the treaty to enclosures of the high seas.

578. _____. "Exclusive Fisheries Zones and Freedom of Navigation." San Diego Law Review. vol. 20, no. 3, April 1983, pp. 595-623.

Suggests that only limited authority to affect navigation be recognized in the fisheries zones for the developing states and for their economic development.

579. _____. "U. S. Fishery Management and the Law of the Sea." American Journal of International Law. vol. 76, no. 1, January 1982, pp. 24-55.

580. _____. Some Thoughts on Fisheries and a New Con- ference on the Law of the Sea. Honolulu: The Law of the Sea Institute, University of Hawaii, 1971.

This is a volume which will provide many insights revealed by marine experts about the pending UN conference on the law of the sea regarding fisheries. In 1971, they explored the objectives for a new international conference in relation to fisheries.

581. Burton, Steven J. "The 1976 Amendments to the Fisher- men's Protection Act."   American Journal of Inter- national Law. vol. 71, no. 4, October 1977, pp. 740- 743.

582. Butler, Michael J. A.   "Plight of the Bluefin Tuna." National Geographic. vol. 162, no. 2, August 1982, pp. 220-239.

A fascinating study, with illustrations and charts--the life and behavior of bluefin tuna in the Atlantic.

583. Carlson, Cynthia E. . "The International Regulation of Small Cetaceans." San Diego Law Review. vol. 21, no. 3, June 1984, pp. 577-623.

There are about 60 species of small cetaceans or, whales, less than 30 feet in length which are assumed not to be regulated by the International Whaling Commission. This article points out the lack of definition for the term "whale" in any international conventions.

584. _____. "The Management of The Living Resources in the Baltic Sea and the Belts." Ocean Development and International Law. vol. 4, no. 3, 1977, pp. 213-232.

585. _____ and M. J. Savini. "The New International Law of Fisheries Emerging from Bilateral Agreements." Marine Policy. April 1979, pp. 79-98.

Based on the UN Food and Agriculture studies, this article provides an analysis of the various types of bilateral fisheries agreements concluded by coastal states from 1975-1978. It summarizes the terms and conditions of access for fishing concluded by these bilateral agreements.

586. Carroz, J. E. "Institutional Aspects of Fishery Management under the New Regime of the Oceans." San Diego Law Review. vol. 21, no.3, August 1984, pp. 531-540.

This article discusses the effect of the formation of exclusive economic zones on institutional arrangements, the regional fishery commissions, in the promotion of international cooperation for fishery management.

587. Chapman, Douglas G. "Whales," Oceanus. vol. 31, no. 2, Summer 1988, pp. 64-70.

588. Chopra, Sudhir K. "Whales: Towards a Developing Right of Survival as a Part of an Ecosystem." Denver Journal of International Law and Policy. vol. 17, no. 2, Winter 1989, pp. 255-270.

589. Christrup, Judy. "Second Second Chance." Greenpeace. vol. 14, no. 6, November-December 1989, pp. 14-15.

590. Christy, Francis T., Jr. "The Fishery Conservation and Management Act of 1976: Management Objectives and the Distribution of Benefits and Costs." Washington Law Review. vol. 52, 1977, pp. 657-680.

An authoritative analysis and some criticism of the 1976 Magnuson Act on fishery conservation and management.

591. _____. "Disparate Fisheries: Problems for the Law of the Sea Conference and Beyond." Ocean Development and International Law. vol. 1, no. 4, Winter 1973, pp. 337-354.

592. _____. Fisherman Quotas: A Tentative Suggestion for Domestic Management. Honolulu: The Law of the Sea Institute, University of Hawaii, 1973.

593. _____. "Northeast Atlantic Fisheries Agreement: A Test of the Species Approach." Ocean Development and

International Law. vol. 1, no. 1, Spring 1973, pp. 65-92.

594. Churchill, R. R. EEC Fisheries Law. Dordrecht, Boston, Lancaster: Martinus Nijhoff, 1987.

595. _____. "Falklands Fishing Zone: Legal Aspects." Marine Policy. vol. 12, no. 4, October 1988, pp. 343-360.

The book, written by a marine expert from the University of Wales, contains a critical analysis of the fisheries laws adopted by the European Economic Community (EEC).

596. "Coastal Area Development and Management, and Marine and Coastal Technology." Elisabeth Mann Borgese and Norton Ginsburg, eds. Ocean Yearbook 1. Chicago and London: University of Chicago Press, 1978, pp. 350-375.

597. Colson, David A. "Transboundary Fishery Stocks in the EEZ." Oceanus. vol. 27, no. 4, Winter 1984-85, pp. 48-51.

598. "Conservation and Management of Fisheries; Law of the Sea Debate in the United Nations General Assembly." Oceans Policy News. December 1989, p. 2.

599. Cook, B. A. and Richard L. McGow. "Interdependence in the Bay of Fundy Herring Fishery." Ocean Development and International Law. vol. 19, no. 5, 1988, pp. 367-380.

600. Cooper, John. "Delimitation of the Maritime Boundary in the Gulf of Maine Area." Ocean Development and International Law. vol. 16, no. 1, 1986, pp. 59-90.

601. Copes, Parzival. "The Law of the Sea and Management of Anadromous Fish Stocks." Ocean Development and International Law. vol. 4, no. 3, 1977, pp. 233-260.

602. _____. "Marine Fisheries Management in Canada: Policy Objectives and Development Constraints." Center for Ocean Management Studies, University of Rhode Island. Comparative Marine Policy--Perspectives from Europe, Scandinavia, Canada and the United States. Brooklyn, NY: J. F. Bergin Publishers, Inc., 1981, pp. 135-136.

603. Costa, Daniel. "The Sea Otter: Its Interaction with Man." Oceanus. vol. 21, no. 2, Spring 1978, pp. 24-30.

604. Coull, James R. "The North Sea Herring Fishery in the Twentieth Century." Elisabeth Mann Borgese, Norton Ginsburg and Joseph R. Morgan, eds. Ocean Yearbook 7. Chicago and London: University of Chicago Press, 1988, pp. 115-131.

Explains the development of monitoring and management for

North Sea herring, including catching methods, overfishing and allocation of national quotas.

605. Craven, John P. <u>The Management of Pacific Marine Re-</u><u>sources: Present Problems and Future Trends</u>. Boulder, CO: Westview Press, 1982.

606. Cross, Melvin L. "The Behavior of Licensed Fishing Firms: A Contrast with Sole Ownership." <u>Ocean Develop-</u><u>ment and International Law</u>. vol. 8, no. 3, 1980, pp. 201-223.

607. Cushing, D. H. "The Atlantic Fisheries Commissions." <u>Marine Policy</u>, vol. 1, no. 3, 1977, pp. 230-236.

608. Dahl, Christopher. "Traditional Marine Tenure: A Basis for Artisanal Fisheries Management." <u>Marine Policy</u>. vol. 12, no. 1, January 1988.

609. Dahmani, M. <u>The Fisheries Regime of the Exclusive</u> <u>Economic Zone</u>. Dordrecht, Boston, Lancaster: Martinus Nijhoff, 1987.

The book first examines the content and operation of the 200 nautical mile exclusive economic zone (EEZ).   Having pro- vided the necessary background on the genesis and develop- ment of the EEZ concept, the book then proceeds with an extensive discussion on coastal state fisheries management within the zonal arrangement.

610. Day, David.   <u>The Whale War</u>. San Francisco, CA: Sierra Club Books, 1987.

This is a book devoted exclusively to the changing role of the International Whaling Commission in its efforts to im- pose a whaling moratorium worldwide.

611. Devine, D. J. "Authorization of Foreign Fishing in the South African Fishing Zone: Some Anomalies and Uncer- tainties." <u>Sea Changes</u>. no. 7, 1988, pp. 79-88.

612. Donaldson, John and Giulio Pontecorvo. "Economic Rationalization of Fisheries: The Problem of Con- flicting National Interests on Georges Bank." <u>Ocean</u> <u>Development and International Law</u>. vol. 8, no. 2, 1980, pp. 149-170.

613. Doubleday, Nancy C. "Aboriginal Subsistence Whaling: The Right of Inuit to Hunt Whales and Implications for International Environmental Law." <u>Denver Journal of</u> <u>International Law and Policy</u>. vol. 17, no. 2, Winter 1989, pp. 373-394.

614. Doulman, David J. "In Pursuit of Fisheries Coopera- tion: The South Pacific Forum Fisheries Agency." <u>University of Hawaii Law Review</u>. vol. 10, no. 1, Summer 1988, pp. 137-150.

This is a detailed study which reviews the activities of the South Pacific Forum Fisheries Agency since 1980. It explains why the Agency is successful and why it has achieved international recognition and respect.

615. _____, ed. _Tuna Issues and Perspectives in the Pacific Islands Region_. Honolulu: East-West Center, University of Hawaii Press, 1987.

616. Driver, Paul A. "International Fisheries."   R. P. Barston and Patricia Birnie, eds. _The Maritime Dimension_. London: George Allen & Unwin, 1980, pp. 27-53.

617. Dunning, Nicholas P. "Boundary Delimitation in the Gulf of Maine: Implications for the Future of a Resource Area." Elisabeth Mann Borgese and Norton Ginsburg, eds. _Ocean Yearbook 6_. Chicago and London: University of Chicago Press, 1986, pp. 390-398.

618. Dwivedi, S. N. "Progress and Potential of Aquaculture: A Note on Development in India." Elisabeth Mann Borgese and Norton Ginsburg, eds. _Ocean Yearbook 4_. Chicago and London: University of Chicago Press, 1983, pp. 60-74.

619. "Eastern Pacific Ocean Tuna Fishing Agreement." Letter of Submittal, U. S. Department of State, 8 April 1983. Washington, DC: U. S. Government Printing Office, 1983.

620. Epler, Bruce C. "Ocean Enclosures: A Better Way to Manage Marine Resources."   Robert L. Friedheim, ed. _Managing Ocean Resources: A Primer_. Boulder, CO: Westview Press, 1979, pp. 91-100.

621. _____. "Whales, Whales and Tortoises." _Oceanus_. vol. 30, no. 2, Summer 1987, pp. 86-92.

622. Evans, Charles D. and Larry S. Underwood. "How Many Bowheads?" _Oceanus_. vol. 21, no. 2, Spring 1978, pp. 17-23.

623. Evans, William E. "Dolphins and Their Mysterious Sixth Sense." _Oceanus_. vol. 23, no. 3, Fall 1980, pp. 69-72.

624. Falk, Richard. "Introduction: Preserving Whales in a World of Sovereign States." _Denver Journal of International Law and Policy_. vol. 17, no. 2, Winter 1989, pp. 249-254.

625. Farnell, John. "EEC Fisheries Management Policy." Center for Ocean Management Studies, University of Rhode Island. _Comparative Marine Policy: Perspectives from Europe, Scandinavia, Canada and the United States_. Brooklyn, NY: J. F. Bergin Publishers, Inc., 1981, pp. 137-144.

626. Finn, Daniel P. "Georges Bank: The Legal Issues." _Oceanus_. vol. 23, no. 2, Summer 1980, pp. 28-38.

627. "Fishing on the High Seas: A Moribund Freedom." LOS Lieder. vol. 3, no. 2. Honolulu: The Law of the Sea Institute, University of Hawaii, October 1989, pp. 6-7.

628. Fitzpatrick, John. "Fishing Technology." Elisabeth Mann Borgese, Norton Ginsburg and Joseph R. Morgan, eds. Ocean Yearbook 8. Chicago and London: University of Chicago Press, 1989, pp. 90-116.

Discusses technological development for fishing and future action on fishing gear and vessel design.

629. Fluharty, David and Christine Dawson. "Management of Living Resources in the Northeast Pacific and the Unilateral Extension of the 200-Mile Fisheries Zone." Ocean Development and International Law. vol. 6, no. 1, 1979, pp. 1-72.

630. Foster, Nancy M. and Jack H. Archer. "The National Marine Sanctuary Program: Policy, Education and Research." Oceanus. vol. 31, no. 1, Spring 1988, pp. 5-17.

631. Frank, Donald. "The Convention on the Conservation of Antarctic Marine Living Resources." Ocean Development and International Law. vol. 13, no. 3, 1983, pp. 291-346.

632. Fujii, Takeji. "The Salmon Fishery." Oceanus. vol. 30, no. 1, Spring, 1987, pp. 16-18.

633. Fye, Paul M. Arthur E. Maxwell, Kenneth O. Emery and Bostwick H. Ketchum. "Ocean Science and Marine Resources." Edmund A. Gullion, ed. Uses of the Seas. Englewood Cliffs, NJ: Prentice-Hall, 1968, pp. 51-68.

634. Gaither, Normand and Ivan Strand. "The Fishery Conservation and Management Act of 1976: Economic Issues Associated with Foreign Fishing Fees and Foreign Allocation." Ocean Development and International Law. vol. 5, nos. 2-5, 1978, pp. 135-152.

635. Geraci, Joseph. "The Enigma of Marine Mammals Strandings." Oceanus. vol. 21, no. 2, Spring 1978, pp. 38-47.

636. Gerritsen, Rolf. "Collective Action Problems in the Regulation of Australia's Northern Prawn Fishery." Maritime Studies. vol. 37, November-December 1987.

637. Glantz, Michael H. "Man, State and Fisheries: An Inquiry into Some Societal Constraints that Affect Fisheries Management." Ocean Development and International Law. vol. 17, nos. 1-3, 1986, pp. 191-270.

638. _____. "El Niño: Lessons for Coastal Fisheries in Africa?" Oceanus. vol. 23, no. 2, Summer 1980, pp. 9-17.

639. Glass, Kathy and Kirsten Englund. "Why the Japanese Are So Stubborn about Whaling." Oceanus. vol. 32, no. 1, Spring 1989, pp. 45-51.

640. Glauberman, Stu. "Fisheries Hearing Looks at the Big Picture." The Honolulu Advertiser. 9 January 1990, p. A-3.

641. _____. "Six States, Including Isles, Urge U. S. and Canada to End Drift-netting." The Honolulu Advertiser. 7 November 1989, p. A-3.

642. Goodall, R. Natalie. "The Lost Whales of Tierra del Fuego." Oceanus. vol. 32, no. 1, Spring 1989, pp. 89-95.

643. Goodwin, Mel. "Changing Times for Caribbean Fisheries." Oceanus. vol. 30, no. 4, Winter 1987-88, pp. 57-64.

644. Gordon, William G. "Management of Living Marine Resources: Challenge of the Future." Center for Ocean Management Studies, University of Rhode Island. Comparative Marine Policy: Perspectives from Europe, Scandinavia, Canada and the United States. Brooklyn, NY: J. F. Bergin Publishers, Inc., 1981, pp. 145-167.

645. _____ and Richard Cutting. "The Coastal Fishing Industry and the EEZ." Oceanus. vol. 27, no. 4, Winter 1984-85, pp. 35-40.

646. Grassle, J. Federick. "Animals in the Soft Sediments Near the Hydrothermal Vents." Oceanus. vol. 27, no. 3, Fall 1984, pp. 63-66.

647. Graves, Howard. "U. S Decides to Endorse a Ban on Drift Netting in South Pacific." Associated Press, as reprinted in The Honolulu Advertiser, 13 October 1989, p. F-3.

648. Gulland, John. "Billfish Management." Marine Policy. vol. 13, no. 1, January 1989, pp. 73-74.

649. _____. "Policy Notes: Tuna and International Institutions." Marine Policy. vol. 12, no. 4, October 1988, p. 408.

650. Haedrich, R. L. and C. A. S. Hall. "Fishes and Estuaries." Oceanus. vol. 19, no. 3, Spring 1976, pp. 55-63.

651. Hajost, Scott A. "Authority to Manage Fisheries and Mineral Resources of the Southern Ocean: The Perspective of Non-Claimant Parties to the Antarctic Treaty." Thomas A. Clingan, Jr., ed. The Law of the Sea: What Lies Ahead? Honolulu: The Law of the Sea Institute, University of Hawaii, 1988, pp. 369-379.

652. Hanson, Arthur J.   "East Coast Canadian Fisheries and the 200-Mile Zone." Douglas M. Johnston and Norman Letalik, eds. The Law of the Sea and Ocean Industry: New Opportunities and Restraints. Honolulu: The Law of the Sea Institute, University of Hawaii, 1984, pp. 318-325.

Provides a broad analysis of Canada's east coast fisheries since its declaration of the 200-mile fishing zone.

653. Hawley, T. M.   "The Whale, A Large Figure in the Collective Unconscious." Oceanus. vol. 32, no. 1, Spring 1989, pp. 112-120.

654. Hilborn, Ray and John Sibert.   "Is International Management of Tuna Necessary?" Marine Policy. vol. 12, no. 1, January 1988, pp. 31-39.

655. Hinman, Ken.   "Bluefin Tuna: Politics over Biology." Nexus. vol. 10, no. 2, Spring 1988.

656. Hofman, Robert J. "The Marine Mammal Protection Act: A First of Its Kind Anywhere." Oceanus. vol. 32, no. 1, Spring 1989, pp. 21-25.

657. Hollick, Ann L. "The Roots of U. S. Fisheries Policy." Ocean Development and International Law, vol. 5, no. 1, 1978, pp. 61-105.

Discusses the roots of U.S. fisheries policy and the 200-mile zone to the 1958 UN Conference on the Law of the Sea by focusing on geographic concerns of U.S. fishing interests.

658. Holt, Sidney J. "Commentary: Changing Attitude toward Marine Mammals." Oceanus. vol. 21, no. 2, Spring 1978, pp. 2-8.

659. _____. "The Food Resources of the Ocean." Scientific American. vol. 221, no. 3, September 1969, pp. 178-194.

This is a concise essay, not only about the rate of fishery harvest and its potential yield to 200 million tons if it is well managed, but also a background view on the future expectation of the ocean as a major source of protein, analyzed in terms of fishing stock biology--growth, mortality and recruitment.

660. _____.   "Marine Fisheries."   Elisabeth Mann Borgese and Norton Ginsburg, eds. Ocean Yearbook 1. Chicago and London: University of Chicago Press, 1978, pp. 38-83.

661. _____ and C. Vanderbilt.   "Marine Fisheries." Elisabeth Mann Borgese and Norman Ginsburg, eds. Ocean Yearbook 2. Chicago and London: University of Chicago Press, 1980, pp. 9-56.

A comprehensive survey of marine fisheries by catch, weight, economic groups, catch values and other basic data on the world's marine fisheries for the 1970s.

662. Howard, Mathew. "The Convention on the Conservation of Antarctic Marine Living Resources: A Five-Year Review." International and Comparative Law Quarterly. vol. 38, pt. 1, January 1989, pp. 104-149.

A most updated review on the regime established by the 1980 Convention on Antarctic Marine Living Resources, an extension of the Antarctic Treaty System. Points out the problems of implementing the objectives, among them the secondary priority treaty members placed on conservation as a primary objective.

663. Hudson, Carolyn. "Fishery and Economic Zones as Customary International Law." San Diego Law Review. vol. 17, no. 3, April 1980, pp. 661-689.

664. Huh, Hyung-tack. "Korea's Distant-Water Fisheries." Choon-ho Park and Jaw Kyu Park, eds. The Law of the Sea: Problems from the East Asian Perspective. Honolulu: The Law of the Sea Institute, University of Hawaii, 1987, pp. 564-573.

665. Hyde, Laurel Lee. "Dolphin Conservation in the Tuna Industry: The United States' Role in an International Problem." San Diego Law Review. vol. 16, no. 3, April 1979, pp. 665-704.

666. "Illegal High Seas Salmon Interception." Oceans Policy News. March 1990, p. 4.

667. "Implementing the U. S.-Canada Pacific Salmon Treaty: Two Perspectives." Anadromous Fish Law Memo. Issue 47, December 1988.

668. "Indian Ocean Tuna Commission." Oceans Policy News. September-October 1989, p. 2.

669. Jacobson, Jon L. "Future Fishing Technology and Its Impact on the Law of the Sea." Francis T. Christy, Jr., Thomas A. Clingan, John King Gamble, H. Gary Knight, and Edward Miles, eds. Law of the Sea: Caracas and Beyond. Cambridge, MA: Ballinger Publishing Co., 1975, pp. 237-246.

Contains a good summary of fishing methods and technology and their implications for the law of the sea.

670. Jannasch, Halger W. "Chemosynthesis: The Nutritional Basis for Life at Deep-Sea Vents." Oceanus. vol. 27, no. 3, Summer 1984, pp. 73-78.

671. "Japanese Fishing Permit." Oceans Policy News. February 1989, pp. 3-4.

672. "Japan Pays Higher Fees to Fish in Soviet Waters." Asahi News Service, as reprinted in The Honolulu Star-Bulletin. 13 December 1988, p. A-9.

673. Johnson, Barbara and Frank Langdon. "Two Hundred Mile Zones: The Politics of North Pacific Fisheries." Pacific Affairs, vol. 49, no. 1, Spring 1976, pp. 5-27.

Analyzes the radical change that took place concerning the right to fish caused by the extension of control over the vast ocean space by major coastal states in Canada and the U.S. in the North Pacific--a fertile world fishing ground.

674. _____ and D. Middlemiss. "Canada's 200-Mile Fishery Zone: The Problem of Compliance." Ocean Development and International Law. vol. 4, no. 1, 1977, pp. 67-110.

675. Johnston, Douglas M. "The Driftnetting Problem in the Pacific Ocean: Legal Considerations and Diplomatic Options." Ocean Development and International Law. vol. 21, no. I, 1990, pp. 5-40.

A most up-to-date analysis of the use of driftnets in the Pacific, which presents a serious environmental threat to the utilization of living resources in that region. Douglas Johnston proposes solutions to the problem by the use of leverage and guideline diplomacy.

676. _____. The International Law of Fisheries: A Framework for Policy-Oriented Inquiries. Hingham, MA: Kluber Academic Publishers and New Haven Press, 1987.

The author takes the position that traditional maritime law or legal concepts are not adequate for dealing with contemporary needs and demands in exploiting fisheries resources. Specifically, the book discusses the process of use, claim and decision-making leading up to a model of shared exploitation authority for the conservation and management of fisheries resources.

677. Joseph, James. "Management of Tuna Fisheries in the Eastern Pacific Ocean." Edward L. Miles and Scott Allen, eds. The Law of the Sea and Ocean Development Issues in the Pacific Basin. Honolulu: The Law of the Sea Institute, University of Hawaii, 1983, pp. 145-157.

Deals with various aspects of the tuna fishery in the eastern Pacific Ocean by focusing on the work of the Inter-American Tropical Tuna Commission (IATTC).

678. _____ and Joseph W. Greenough. International Management of Tuna, Porpoise and Billfish: Biological, Legal and Political Aspects. Seattle and London: University of Washington Press, 1979.

679. _____ and Witold L. Klawe. "The Living Pelagic Resources of the Americas." Ocean Development and

International Law. vol. 2, no. 1, Spring 1974, pp. 37-64.

680. Juda, Lawrence. "The Exclusive Economic Zone and Ocean Management." Ocean Development and International Law. vol. 18, no. 3, 1987, pp. 305-331.

This is a study of requirements, opportunities and problems of fisheries management in the exclusive economic zones. The article points out the crucial importance of fisheries management in the context of increased pressure on ocean resources and their expanded uses.

681. Kaczynski, Vladimir M. "Foreign Fishing Fleets in the Sub-Sahara West African EEZ: The Coastal State Perspective." Marine Policy. vol. 13, no. 1, January 1989.

682. _____. "200-Mile EEZ and Soviet Fisheries in the North Pacific Ocean: An Economic Assessment." John P. Craven, Jan Schneider and Carol Stimson, eds. The International Implications of Extended Maritime Jurisdiction in the Pacific. Honolulu: The Law of the Sea Institute, University of Hawaii, 1989, pp. 193-203.

683. _____. "International Joint Ventures in the North Pacific Fisheries." Edward L. Miles and Scott Allen, eds. The Law of the Sea and Ocean Development Issues in the Pacific Basin. Honolulu: The Law of the Sea Institute, University of Hawaii, 1983, pp. 103-140.

684. _____. Distant Water Fisheries after 200-Mile Economic Zone. Seattle: Institute for Marine Studies, University of Washington, March 1982.

A most thorough study about distant water fishing by leading fishing nations in the northeast Pacific of the United States, the Gulf of Alaska, the northeast Bering Sea and the Aleutians.

685. _____. "Alternatives Facing Distant-Water Fishing States in the Northeast Pacific Ocean." Ocean Development and International Law. vol. 6, no. 2, 1978, pp. 73-102.

686. _____. "Controversies in Strategy of Marine Fisheries Development between Eastern and Western Countries." Ocean Development and International Law. vol. 4, no. 4, 1976, pp. 399-408.

687. Kask, J. L. Tuna: A World Resource. Honolulu: The Law of the Sea Institute, University of Hawaii, 1969.

688. Kawamura, Akito. "Whaling and Research." Oceanus. vol. 30, no. 1, Spring 1987, pp. 23-26.

689. Kaza, Stephanie. "Community Involvement in Marine Protected Areas." Oceanus. vol. 3, no. 1, Spring 1988, pp. 75-86.

690. Kearney, R. E. "The Development of Tuna Fisheries and the Future for Their Management in Tropical, Central and Western Pacific." Edward L. Miles and Scott Allen, eds. The Law of the Sea and Ocean Development Issues in the Pacific Basin. Honolulu: The Law of the Sea Institute, University of Hawaii, 1983, pp. 158-179.

691. _____. "The Law of the Sea and Regional Fisheries Policy," Ocean Development and International Law, vol. 5, nos. 2-3, 1978, pp. 249-286.

692. Keith-Reid, Robert. "Tuna at the Crossroads." Islands Business. June 1984, pp. 10-13.

693. Kent, George. "Fisheries Politics in the South Pacific." Elisabeth Mann Borgese and Norton Ginsburg, eds. Ocean Yearbook 2. Chicago and London: University of Chicago Press, 1980, pp. 346-381.

694. _____. The Politics of Pacific Island Fisheries. Boulder, CO: Westview Press, 1980.

695. Kesteven, G. L. "Latin American Fisheries." Elisabeth Mann Borgese and Norton Ginsburg, eds. Ocean Yearbook 4 Chicago and London: The University of Chicago Press, 1983, pp. 50-59.

696. Klinowska, Margaret. "How Brainy Are Cetaceans?" Oceanus. vol. 32, no. 1, Spring 1989, pp. 19-20.

697. Knight, H. Gary. Managing the Sea's Living Resources: Legal and Political Aspects of High Seas Fisheries. Lexington, MA: Lexington Books, 1977.

698. Kreuzer, Rudolf. "The Cradle of Sea Fisheries." Elisabeth Mann Borgese and Norton Ginsburg, eds. Ocean Yearbook 1. Chicago and London: University of Chicago Press, 1978, pp. 102-113.

699. Kury, Channing R. "The Application of a Market Theory to the Regulation of International Fisheries." Ocean Development and International Law. vol. 1, no. 4, Winter 1973, pp. 355-368.

700. Kwiatkowska, Barbara. "Conservation and Optimum Utilization of Living Resources." Thomas A. Clingan, Jr., ed. The Law of the Sea: What Lies Ahead? Honolulu: The Law of the Sea Institute, University of Hawaii, 1988, pp. 245-275.

701. Laist, David and John T. Epting. "Perspectives on an Ocean Management System." Ocean Development and International Law. vol. 7, nos. 3-4, 1979, pp. 257-298.

702. Laursen, Finn. Superpower at Sea: U. S. Ocean Policy. New York: Praeger Publishers, 1983.

703. Legault, L. H. and Blair Hankey. "From Sea to Seabed: The Single Maritime Boundary in the Gulf of Maine

LIVING RESOURCES   73

Case."   The American Journal of Internatonal Law. vol.
79, no. 4, October 1985, pp. 961-991.

A most comprehensive study of the judicial decision on the
maritime boundary that divides jurisdiction over both the
continental shelf and the exclusive fishery zones of Canada
and the United States in the Georges Bank area of the
Atlantic Ocean centering around the Gulf of Maine.

704. "A Liability Enforcement Program to Discourage Fishing
Gear Loss." LOS Lieder. vol. 3, no. 3. Honolulu: The
Law of the Sea Institute, University of Hawaii, Decem-
ber 1989, pp. 4-6.

705. Lipton, Josh. "Fisheries Trade in the Northwest
Atlantic: Duty Bound?" Nexus. vol. 10, no. 2, Spring
1988.

706. Liston, John and Smith Lynwood. "Fishing and the
Fishing Industry: An Account with Comments on Overseas
Technology Transfer." Ocean Development and Inter-
national Law. vol. 2, no. 3, Fall 1974, pp. 285-312.

707. "Living Resources: Law of the Sea Institute's 23rd
Annual Meeting." Oceans Policy News. June 1989, p. 3-4

708. Logan, Roderick MacKenzie. "Geography and Salmon: The
Noyes Island Conflict, 1957-1967." Journal of the
West. vol. 8, July 1969, pp. 438-446.

709. Lones, Laura. "The Marine Mammal Protection Act and
International Protection of Cetaceans: A Unilateral
Attempt to Effectuate Transnational Conservation."
Vanderbilt Journal of Transnational Law. vol. 22, no.
4, 1989, pp. 997-1028.

This article examines how the United States has used its
1972 Marine Mammal Protection Act to extend protection to
cetaceans such as dolphins, porpoises and whales.

710. Lucas, C. E. International Fishery Bodies in the North
Atlantic. Honolulu: The Law of the Sea Institute,
University of Hawaii, 1970.

711. Lucas, Kenneth C. and Tony Loftas. "FAO's EEZ Program:
Helping to Build the Fisheries of the Future." Elisa-
beth Mann Borgese and Norton Ginsburg, eds. Ocean
Yearbook 3. Chicago and London: University of Chicago
Press, 1982, pp. 38-76.

Describes and analyzes the worldwide fishery management
program for developing nations of the Food and Agricultural
Organization that stresses self-reliance, technological
transfer and regional cooperation.

712. Lyman, Henry. "The 200-Mile Limit I: The New England
Regional Fishery Management Council." Oceanus. vol.
20, no. 3, Summer 1977, pp. 7-17.

713. McCloskey, William, Jr. "The 200-Mile Fishing Limit." Jonathan Bartlett, ed. The Ocean Environment. vol. 48, no. 6 of The Reference Shelf, pp. 188-199. New York: The H. W. Wilson Company, 1977.

714. McDorman, Ted L. "Thailand's Fisheries: A Victim of 200-Mile Zones." Ocean Development and International Law. vol. 16, no. 2, 1986, pp. 183-210.

715. McElroy, James Kevin. "Indonesia's Tuna Fisheries: Past, Present and Future Prospects." Marine Policy. vol. 13, no. 4, October 1989, pp. 285-308.

716. McHugh, J. L. "The Whale Problem: A Status Report (A Book Review and Perspective)." Ocean Development and International Law. vol. 3, no. 4, 1976, pp. 389-412.

717. McHugh, Paul D. "International Law: Delimitation of Maritime Boundaries." Natural Resources Journal. vol. 25, no. 4, October 1985, pp. 1025-1038.

718. McNeil, William J. Salmon Production, Management and Allocation: Biological, Economic and Policy Issues. Corvalis, OR: Oregon State University Press, 1988.

719. _____. "Salmon Ranching: A Growing Industry in the North Pacific." Oceanus. vol. 27, no. 1, Spring 1984, pp. 27-31.

720. "Magnuson Act Amendments and Reauthorization," (on drift-net ban, high seas salmon interception, tuna inclusion, enforcement of international agreements, and Atlantic Tuna Convention authorization). Oceans Policy News. September-October 1989, pp. 3-4.

721. "Magnuson Act Reauthorization." Oceans Policy News. March 1990, p. 4.

722. Marshall, L. "Regional Implementation of Alternative Entry Control Policies and Their Role in Fisheries Management." Ocean Development and International Law. vol. 5, nos. 2-3, 1978, pp. 345-382.

723. Martin, Gene S., Jr. and James W. Brennan. "Enforcing the International Convention for the Regulation of Whaling: The Pelly and Packwood-Magnuson Amendments." Denver Journal of International Law and Policy. vol. 17, no. 2, Winter 1989, pp. 293-316.

724. Mate, Bruce R. "Watching Habits and Habitats from Earth Satellites." Oceanus. vol. 3, no. 1, Spring 1989, pp. 14-18.

725. Miles, Edward L. "Concepts, Approaches and Applications in Sea Use Planning and Management." Ocean Development and International Law. vol. 20, no. 3, 1989, pp. 213-238.

726. _____.   "The Future of Distant-Water Fishing."
Choon-ho Park and Jae Kyu Park, eds. The Law of the
Sea: Problems from the East Asian Perspective. Hono-
lulu: The Law of the Sea Institute, University of
Hawaii, 1987, pp. 18-25.

A leading expert gives his view of the future for distant-
water fishing.

727. _____.   "Changes in the Law of the Sea: Impact on
International Fisheries Organizations." Ocean Development and International Law. vol. 4, no. 4, 1977, pp.
409-444.

728. _____ and William T. Burke.   "Pressure on the
United Nations Convention on the Law of the Sea of 1982
Arising from New Fisheries Conflicts: The Problem of
Straddling Stocks." Ocean Development and International
Law. vol. 20, no. 4, 1989, pp. 343-358.

This article deals with the question of what to do with
those fishery stocks that are in and adjacent to the
exclusive economic zone. It is the contention of these two
marine experts that the 1982 Law of the Sea Convention
failed to provide adequate provisions for the straddling
stocks.

729. Miller, Marc L. and Charles F. Broches. "U. S. Fishery
Negotiations with Canada and Mexico." Ocean Development and International Law. vol. 14, no. 4, 1985, pp.
417-432.

Provides information for a general model of the bi-national
negotiation process by using U.S.-Canada and U.S.-Mexico
cases as examples.

730. Minghi, Julian V.   "The Conflict of Salmon Fishing
Policies in the North Pacific."   Pacific Viewpoint.
vol. 2, 1961, pp. 59-86.

731. Miovski, Laurene.   "Solutions in the Convention on the
Law of the Sea to the Problem of Overfishing in the
Central Bering Sea: Analysis of the Convention High-
lighting the Provisions Concerning Fisheries and
Enclosed and Semi-Enclosed Seas." San Diego Law Review.
vol. 26, no. 3, August-September 1989, pp. 525-574.

The dramatic increase in large-scale fishing in the Central
Bering Sea, from 15,000 metric tons of pollock in 1980 to a
harvest of one million metric tons in 1986, has raised legal
questions about 1982 Law of the Sea Convention provisions as
applicable to overfishing.

732. Moore, Gerald K.   Coastal State Requirements for
Foreign Fishing.   Rome: Legal Office, Fisheries
Legislation Section, FAO, 1985.

Contains comprehensive, state-by-state, coastal state
requirements for foreign fishing that includes access

agreements, licensing regulations and analysis of coastal state policies on foreign fishing.

733. "Moscow's South Pacific Fishing Fleet Is Much More than It Seems." <u>Backgrounder</u> (The Heritage Foundation). no. 80, 6 September 1988.

734. Mylonas-Widdall, Michael. "Aboriginal Fishing Rights in New Zealand." <u>International and Comparative Law Quarterly</u>. vol. 37, part 2, April 1988, pp. 386-390.

735. Nafziger, James A. R. "Global Conservation and Management of Marine Mammals." <u>San Diego Law Review</u>. vol. 17, no. 3, April 1980, pp. 591-615.

Examines pluralistic efforts to manage marine mammals, proposing greater reliance on the UN framework and provisions of the law of the sea draft being negotiated.

736. Namaliu, Rabbie. "The U. S. Position on Tuna and the Pacific Island Nations." Jon M. Van Dyke, ed. <u>Consensus and Confrontation: The United States and the Law of the Sea Convention</u>. Honolulu: The Law of the Sea Institute, University of Hawaii, 1985, pp. 376-382.

737. Nandan, Satya. "Implementing the Fisheries Provisions of the Convention." Jon M. Van Dyke, ed. <u>Consensus and Confrontation: The United States and the Law of the Sea Convention</u>. Honolulu: The Law of the Sea Institute, University of Hawaii, 1985, pp. 383-388.

738. Narakobi, Camillus. "The Tuna Issue, the South Pacific and the United States." Jon M. Van Dyke, ed. <u>Consensus and Confrontation: The United States and the Law of the Sea Convention</u>. Honolulu: The Law of the Sea Institute, University of Hawaii, 1985, pp. 370-375.

739. "Native Fishing Rights and Environmental Protection in North America and New Zealand: A Comparative Analysis." <u>Anadromous Fish Law Memo</u>. Issue 48, January 1989.

740. Nied, G. David. "International Adjudication: Settlement of the United States-Canada Maritime Boundary Dispute." <u>Harvard International Law Journal</u>. vol. 23, no. 2, Spring 1982, pp. 138-143.

741. Oda, Shigeru. "Fisheries under the United Nations Convention on the Law of the Sea." <u>The American Journal of International Law</u>. vol. 77, no. 4, October 1983, pp. 739-755.

742. Pabst, Richard W. "Fisheries." David L. Larson, ed. <u>Major Issues of the Law of the Sea</u>. Durham, NH: The University of New Hampshire, 1976, pp. 84-106.

743. Pariser, E. R. "Reducing Post-harvest Losses of Fish in the Third World." <u>Oceanus</u>. vol. 22, no. 1, Spring 1979, pp. 47-53.

744. Park, Choon-ho. "The Sino-Japanese-Korean Resources Controversy and the Hypothesis of a 200-Mile Economic Zone." Harvard International Law Journal, vol. 16, Winter 1975, pp. 27-40.

Discusses the immediate impact of a 200-mile economic zone on East Asian states in the East China Sea which have coasts opposite each other within 400 miles and which have no continental shelf boundary agreements.

745. _____. "Fishing under Troubled Waters: The Northeast Asia Fisheries Controversy." Ocean Development and International Law. vol. 2, no. 2, Summer 1974, pp. 93-136.

746. _____. Fisheries Issues in the Yellow Sea and the East China Sea. Honolulu: The Law of the Sea Institute, University of Hawaii, 1973.

747. Pauly, Daniel. "Problems of Tropical Inshore Fisheries: Fishery Research on Tropical Soft-Bottom Communities and the Evolution of Its conceptual Base." Elisabeth Mann Borgese and Norton Ginsburg, eds. Ocean Yearbook 6. Chicago and London: University of Chicago Press, 1986, pp. 29-37.

748. Perez, Efrain and Kilaparti Ramakrishna. "Two Legal Opinions on the Galapagos Marine Reserve: Ecuadorian Law." Oceanus. vol. 30, no. 2, Summer 1987, pp. 17-19.

749. Peterson, Curt D., La Verne D. Kulm, Paul D. Komar and Margaret S. Mumford. "Marine Placer Studies in the Pacific Northwest." Oceanus. vol. 31, no. 3, Fall 1988, pp. 21-28.

750. Pillay, T. V. R. "Progress of Aquaculture." Elisabeth Mann Borgese and Norton Ginsburg, eds. Ocean Yearbook 1 Chicago and London: University of Chicago Press, 1978, pp. 84-101.

751. Pinkerton, Evelyn, ed. Cooperative Management of Local Fisheries: New Directions for Improved Management and Community Development. Vancouver, BC: University of British Columbia, 1989.

752. Pinto, M. C. W. "Authority to Manage Fisheries and Mineral Resources of the Southern Ocean: Objectives of Management." Thomas A. Clingan, Jr., ed. The Law of the Sea: What Lies Ahead? Honolulu: The Law of the Sea Institute, University of Hawaii, 1988, pp. 343-365.

753. Polachek, Tom. "Harbor Porpoises and the Gillnet Fishery." Oceanus. vol. 32, no. 1, Spring 1989, pp. 63-70.

754. Pollnac, Richard B. and Susan Jacke Littlefield. "Socio-cultural Aspects of Fisheries Management." Ocean Development and International Law. vol. 12, nos. 3-4, 1982, pp. 209-246.

755. Pontecorvo, Giulio. "The Enclosure of the Marine
     Commons: Adjustment   and   Redistribution   in World
     Fisheries." Marine Policy. vol. 12, no. 4, October
     1988, pp. 343-360.

756. _____, ed. "Division of the Spoils: Hydrocarbons
     and Living Resources."   The New Order of the Oceans:
     The Advent of a Managed Environment. New York: Columbia
     University Press, 1986, pp. 16-21.

A most thoughtful and insightful essay on the concept of
ocean resources as common property and the biological limits
for full utilization of living resources.

757. _____. "From Cornucopia to Scarcity: The Current
     Status in Ocean Resource Use." Ocean Development and
     International Law. vol. 5, nos. 2-3, 1978, pp. 383-396.

758. Procida, Mary Angela. "International Agreements: Ter-
     mination of United States-Mexico Fisheries Agreements."
     Harvard International Law Journal. vol. 23, no. 1,
     Spring 1982, pp. 143-147.

759. "Proposals to Modify the Pelly Amendment." Oceans
     Policy News. December 1989, p. 4.

760. Pryor, Karen and Kenneth S. Norris. "The Tuna/Porpoise
     Problem: Behavioral Aspects." Oceanus. vol. 21, no. 2,
     Spring 1978, pp. 31-37.

761. Qader, Mohammed Afsural. "Extended Maritime Jurisdic-
     tion: A Case for Regional Cooperation for the Manage-
     ment of Fisheries Resources in the Bay of Bengal."
     John P. Craven, Jan Schneider, Carol Stimson, eds. The
     International Implications of Extended Maritime Juris-
     diction in the Pacific. Honolulu: The Law of the Sea
     Institute, University of Hawaii, 1989, pp. 292-305.

762. Queivolo, Lewis E. and Richard S. Johnston. "Distant
     Water Fishing Nations and Extended Fisheries Jurisdic-
     tion." Marine Policy. vol. 13, no. 1, January 1989, pp.
     16-21.

763. Rhee, Sang-Myon. "The Application of Equitable Prin-
     ciples to Resolve the United States-Canada Dispute over
     East Coast Fishery." Harvard International Law Journal.
     vol. 21, no. 3, Fall 1980, pp. 667-83.

764. Robinson, Davis R., David A. Colson and Bruce C.
     Rashkow. "Some Perspectives on Adjudicating before the
     World Court: The Gulf of Maine Case." The American
     Journal of International Law. vol. 79, no. 3, July
     1985, pp. 578-597.

765. Rocque, Arthur J., Jr. "Can Coastal Programs Survive?
     A Case for Revenue Sharing." Oceans. vol. 15, no. 2,
     March 1982, pp. 67-68.

766. Rosenne, Shabtai. "Settlement of Fiseries Disputes in the Exclusive Economic Zone," American Journal of International Law. vol. 73, no. 1, January 1979, pp. 89-103.

767. Rothschild, Brian. "Global Fisheries Management: The New Challenge." Douglas Johnston and Norman Letalik, eds. The Law of the Sea and Ocean Industry: New Opportunities and Restraints. Honolulu: The Law of the Sea Institute, University of Hawaii, 1983, pp. 330-344.

768. Ryan, Paul R. "Marine Mammals: A Guide for Readers." Oceanus. vol. 21, no. 2, 1978, pp. 9-16.

769. Saetersdal, Gunnar. "Problems of Managing and Sharing of Living Resources under the New Ocean Regime." Elisabeth Mann Borgese and Norton Ginsburg, eds. Ocean Yearbook 4. Chicago and London: University of Chicago Press, 1983, pp. 45-49.

770. Sanger, David E. "Japan to Limit Ships with Huge Fish Nets in the South Pacific." The New York Times. 20 September 1989, p. A-1.

771. Santa Cruz, Ambassador Fernando Zegers. "Authority to Manage Fisheries and Mineral Resources of the Southern Ocean." Thomas A. Clingan, Jr., ed. The Law of the Sea: What Lies Ahead? Honolulu: The Law of the Sea Institute, University of Hawaii, 1988, pp. 366-368.

772. Sato, Osamu. "The Japanese Fisheries System." Oceanus. vol. 30, no. 1, Spring 1987, pp. 9-15.

773. Scharfe, Joachim. "Fishing Technology for Developing Countries." Oceanus. vol. 22, no. 1, Spring 1979, pp. 54-59.

774. _____. "Interrelations between Fishing Technology and the Coming International Fishery Regime." Francis T. Christy, Jr., Thomas A. Clingan, Jr., John King Gamble, Jr., H. Gary Knight and Edward L. Miles, eds. The Sea: Caracas and Beyond. Cambridge, MA: Ballinger Publishing Co., 1975, pp. 259-264.

775. Scheffer, Victor B. "How Much Is a Whale's Life Worth, Anyway?" Oceanus. vol. 22, no. 1, Spring 1979, pp. 109-111.

776. Schneider, Jan. "The First ICJ Chamber Experiment: The Gulf of Maine Case; The Nature of an Equitable Result." The American Journal of International Law. vol. 79, no. 3, July 1985, pp. 573-577.

777. Scott, David Clark. "Tuna Controversy: Japan Casts Nets in Troubled Waters." The Christian Science Monitor. 24 April 1989, p. 3.

778. "Settlement Reached in Canada-France Fisheries and

Boundary Disputes." Government of Canada News Release. 31 March 1989.

779. Shabecoff, Philip. "Pact Reached to Monitor Japan's Fishery Practices." The New York Times. 18 May 1989, p. A-1.

780. Sherman, Kenneth. "Biomass Yields of Large Marine Ecosystems." Elisabeth Mann Borgese, Norton Ginsburg and Joseph R. Morgan, eds. Ocean Yearbook 8. Chicago and London: University of Chicago Press, 1989, pp. 117-137.

Discusses the stress imposed by the formation of exclusive economic zones on large marine ecosystems.

781. _____and Alan F. Ryan. "Antarctic Marine Living Resources." Oceanus. vol. 31, no. 2, Summer 1988, pp. 59-63.

782. Shyam, Manjula. "The Emerging Fisheries Regime: Implications for India." Ocean Development and International Law. vol. 8, no. 1, 1980, pp. 35-56.

783. Sigurjonsson, Johann. "To Icelanders, Whaling Is a Godsend." Oceanus. vol. 32, no. 1, Spring 1989, pp. 29-36.

784. Simons, Marlise. "Fish Nets Trap Dolphins in the Mediterranean, too." The New York Times. 6 September 1989, p. A-1.

785. Siniff, Donald B. "Seals." Oceanus. vol. 31, no. 2, Summer 1988, pp. 71-74.

786. Skud, Bernard Einar. "Jurisdictional and Administrative Limitations Affecting Management of the Halibut Fishery." Ocean Development and International Law. vol. 4, no. 2, 1977, pp. 121-142.

787. Slade, David C. "Back to the Drawing Board: Fourth Amendment Rights and the Marine Mammal Protection Act." Ocean Development and International Law. vol. 16, no. 1, 1986, pp. 91-102.

788. Smith, Courtland L. "Fishing Success in a Regulated Commons." Ocean Development and International Law. vol. 1, no. 4, Winter 1973, pp. 369-382.

789. Somero, George N. "Physiology and Biochemistry of the Hydrothermal Vent Animals." Oceanus. vol. 27, no. 3, Fall 1984, pp. 67-72.

790. "South Pacific Fisheries Declaration." Oceans Policy News. September-October 1989, p. 2.

791. Steele, John H. "Patterns in Plankton." Oceanus. vol. 23, no. 2, Summer 1980, pp. 2-7.

792. Stokes, Robert L., "Straddling Stocks in the Bering Sea." _Ocean Science News_, vol. 30, no. 11, 15 April 1988.

793. _____, "U. S. Policy toward Foreign Fisheries: An Economic Review of the Alaska Groundfish Case." Edward L. Miles and Scott Allen, eds. _The Law of the Sea and Ocean Development Issues in the Pacific Basin_. Honolulu: The Law of the Sea Institute, University of Hawaii, 1983, pp. 83-102.

794. _____ and Brian A. Offord. "Alaska Groundfish: A Financial Feasibility Analysis." _Ocean Development and International Law_, vol. 9, nos. 1-2, 1981, pp. 61-76.

795. Sullivan, Jeremiah J. _Pacific Basin Enterprise and the Changing Law of the Sea_. Lexington, MA: D. C. Heath and Company, 1977.

796. Sullivan, Karl W. "Conflict in the Management of a Northwest Atlantic Transboundary Cod Stock." _Marine Policy_, vol. 13, no. 2, April 1989, pp. 118-136.

797. Sullivan, William L., Jr. "Freedom of Fisheries Research in the U. S. in the Best Interest of the United States." _San Diego Law Review_, vol. 22, no. 4, July-August 1985, pp. 793-799.

Discusses the issue of whether the latitude granted marine researchers has resulted in damage to fisheries resources of the United States; examines how informal procedures for illegal fishing are minimized.

798. Suman, Daniel O. "Intermediate Technologies for Small-Scale Fishermen in the Caribbean." _Oceanus_, vol. 30, no. 4, Winter 1987-88, pp. 65-68.

799. Sumi, Kazuo. "The 'Whale War' between Japan and the United States: Problems and Prospects." _Denver Journal of International Law and Policy_, vol. 17, no. 2, Winter 1989, pp. 317-372.

800. Swan, Judith. "Tuna Management in the South Pacific." Thomas A. Clingan, Jr., ed. _The Law of the Sea: What Lies Ahead?_ Honolulu: The Law of the Sea Institute, University of Hawaii, 1988, pp. 184-192.

801. "Symposium. Whales and Whaling: Current Problems and Future Prospects." _Denver Journal of International Law and Policy_, vol. 17, no. 2, Winter 1989, pp. 249-394.

802. Szekely, Alberto. "Tuna in the Eastern Tropical Pacific." Thomas A. Clingan, Jr., ed. _The Law of the Sea: What Lies Ahead?_ Honolulu: The Law of the Sea Institute, University of Hawaii, 1988, pp. 177-183.

803. Tanaka, Shoichi. "Japanese Fisheries and Fishery Resources in the Northwest Pacific." _Ocean Development_

and International Law. vol. 6, no. 4, 1979, pp. 163-236.

804. Tanaka, Syoiti. "Japan's Fisheries and International Relations Surrounding Them under the Regime of 200-Mile Exclusive Fisheries Zone." Edward L. Miles and Scott Allen, eds. The Law of the Sea and Ocean Development Issues in the Pacific Basin. Honolulu: The Law of the Sea Institute, University of Hawaii, 1983, pp. 55-82.

805. Thomas, William J. "Fagatele Bay: A Sanctuary in Samoa." Oceanus. vol. 31, no. 1, Spring 1988, pp. 18-24

806. Thurker, David. "Asians Feel Put upon in Fishing Ground War." Associated Press release as reprinted in The Honolulu Star-Bulletin. 25 December 1989, p. B-14.

807. Tinker, Spencer Wilkie. The World of Whales. New York: E. J. Brill, 1988.

808. Torell, Magnus. "Thailand's Fishing Industry: Future Prospects." Elisabeth Mann Borgese, Norton Ginsburg and Joseph R. Morgan, eds. Ocean Yearbook 7. Chicago and London: University of Chicago Press, 1988, pp. 132-144.

809. "Trinidad and Tobago Developing a Fisheries Management Information System (FISMIS)." Ocean Science News. vol. 31, no. 16, 6 June 1989.

810. Truver, Scott C. and David E. Little. "U.S.-Flag Fish Processing Plantships for the Alaskan Groundfish Fishery." Ocean Development and International Law. vol. 13, no. 1, 1983, pp. 87-102.

811. Turner, R. D. and R. A. Latz. "Growth and Distribution of Mollusks at Deep-Sea Vents and Seeps." Oceanus. vol. 27, no. 3, Fall 1984, pp. 54-62.

812. Twitchell, Marlyn. "Implementing the U.S.-Canada Pacific Salmon Treaty: The Struggle to Move from 'Fish Wars' to Cooperative Fishery Management." Ocean Development and International Law. vol. 20, no. 4, 1989, pp. 409-428.

Status report on the implementation of the 1985 Pacific Salmon Treaty. The treaty provides a means to manage, conserve and rebuild stocks of five salmon species inhabiting the coastal waters of Oregon, Washington, Alaska and Canada's British Columbia. Gives a full background of problems of interception, overfishing, and habitat destruction which eventually led to the call for joint management.

813. Tyack, Peter L. and Laela S. Sayigh. "Those Dolphins Aren't Just Whistling in the Dark." Oceanus. vol. 32, no. 1, Spring 1989, pp. 80-83.

814. "U. S. Action against Taiwan Salmon Interception." Oceans Policy News, August 1989, pp. 1-2.

815. "U. S.-Canada Fisheries Enforcement." Oceans Policy News. August 1989, p. 1.

816. "U. S. Tuna Policy Hearings." Oceans Policy News. August 1989, pp. 3-4.

817. Valencia, J. "The Yellow Sea: Transnational Marine Resource Management Issues." Marine Policy. vol. 12, no. 4, October 1988, pp. 382-395.

818. Vander Zwaag, David. "Canadian Fisheries Management: A Legal and Administrative Overview." Ocean Development and International Law. vol. 13, no. 2, 1983, pp. 171-212.

819. Van Dyke, Jon and Susan Heftel. "Tuna Management in the Pacific: An Analysis of the South Pacific Forum Fisheries Agency." University of Hawaii Law Review. vol. 3, no. 1, 1986, pp. 1-66.

820. Wade, Susan O'Malley. "A Proposal to Include Tunas in U. S. Fishery Jurisdiction." Ocean Development and International Law. vol. 16, no. 3, 1986, pp. 255-304.

821. Wagner, Peter. "Waihee Pleads for Better Control over Hawaii's Ocean Resources." The Honolulu Star-Bulletin. 9 January 1990, p. A-5.

822. Waite, David. "Expedition to Oppose Driftnets." The Sunday Honolulu Star-Bulletin and Advertiser. 26 November 1989, p. A-3.

823. Walsh, Don, ed. The Law of the Sea: Issues in Ocean Resources Management. New York and London: Praeger Publishers, 1977.

824. Walz, Kathleen L. and L. Poe Leggette. "United States Jurisdiction over the 200-Mile Maritime Zone." San Diego Law Review. vol. 23, no. 3, May-June 1986, pp. 545-581.

825. Watkins, William A. "A Radio Tag for Big Whales." Oceanus. vol. 21, no. 2, Spring 1978, pp. 48-54.

826. Weil, Jeffrey G. "Law of the Sea: Exclusive Economic Zone." Harvard International Law Journal. vol. 16, Spring 1975, pp. 474-490.

Discusses background of the 1974 case before the International Court of Justice concerning the fishery dispute between the United Kingdom and Iceland.

827. Weld, Christopher M. "Critical Evaluation of Existing Mechanisms for Managing Highly Migratory Pelagic Species in the Atlantic Ocean." Ocean Development and International Law. vol. 20, no. 3, 1989, pp. 285-296.

828. "Whither the Whales." Oceanus. vol. 32, no. 1, Spring 1989, pp. 3-120.

829. Whitmarsh, David.   "Technological Change and Marine Fisheries Development." Marine Policy. vol. 14, no. 1, January 1990, pp. 15-22.

830. Whitworth, Thomas III. "The Antarctic Circumpolar Current." Oceanus. vol. 31, no. 2, Summer 1988, pp. 53-58.

831. Wilkinson, Dean W. "The Use of Domestic Measure to Enforce International Whaling Agreements: A Critical Perspective." Denver Journal of International Law and Policy. vol. 17, no. 2, Winter 1989, pp. 271-292.

832. Winkler, Michele, Shari E. Sitko and Paul N. Sund. "Tunas: Nomads of the Sea." Sea Frontiers. vol. 29, January-February 1983, pp. 51-56.

833. Wolfe, Edward E.   "U. S. Responsibilities in International Fisheries Matters." Current Policy. no. 1172, Bureau of Public Affairs, U. S. Department of State, 2 March 1989.

834. Wolff, T. Peruvian-United States Relations over Maritime Fishing: 1945-1969. Honolulu: The Law of the Sea Institute, University of Hawaii, 1970.

835. Woodworth, Donald C.   "U. S. Tuna: A Proposal for Resource Management in the American Pacific Islands." University of Hawaii Law Review. vol. 10, no. 1, Summer 1988, pp. 151-182.

A definitive study of the South Pacific Tuna Treaty. Detailed discussion is provided concerning recognition of coastal state tuna sovereignty, access to the treaty and licensing areas, and enforcement.

836. "World Court Panel Sets Boundary Line for Canada-United States Fishing Zones." UN Chronicle. vol. xxi, nos. 10-11, 1984, pp. 37-39.

837. Wursig, Bernd, Melany Wursig and Frank Cipriano. "Dolphins in Different Worlds." Oceanus. vol. 32, no. 1, Spring 1989, pp. 71-75.

838. Young, Oran R. "Fishing by Permit: Restricted Common Property in Practice." Ocean Development and International Law. vol. 13, no. 2, 1983, pp. 121-170.

839. _____. "The Political Economy of Fish: The Fishery Conservation and Management Act of 1976." Ocean Development and International Law. vol. 10, nos. 3-4, 1982, pp. 199-274.

840. Yonezawa, Kunio. "Japanese North Pacific Fishery at the Crossroads." John P. Craven, Jan Schneider and Carol Stimson, eds. The International Implications of Extended Maritime Jurisdiction in the Pacific. Honolulu: The Law of the Sea Institute, University of Hawaii, 1989, pp. 183-192.

Non-Living Resources: Offshore
Oil and Strategic Minerals

841. Albers, John P. "Offshore Petroleum: Its Geography and Technology." John King Gamble, Jr. and Giulio Pontecorvo, eds. Law of the Sea: The Emerging Regime of the Oceans. Cambridge, MA:: Ballinger Publishing Company, 1974, pp. 293-310.

842. Almond, Harry H., Jr. "Development of the Ocean Resource Industry: The Impact of UNCLOS III." Douglas M. Johnston and Norman G. Letalik, ed. The Law of the Sea and Ocean Industry: New Opportunities and Restraints. Honolulu: The Law of the Sea Institute, University of Hawaii, 1984, pp. 20-23.

843. Asante, Samuel K. B. "Restructuring Transnational Mineral Agreements." American Journal of International Law, vol. 73, no. 3, July 1979, pp. 335-371.

844. Auburn, F. M. "Legal Implications of Petroleum Resources of the Antarctic Continental Shelf." Elisabeth Mann Borgese and Norton Ginsburg, eds. Ocean Yearbook 1 Chicago and London: University of Chicago Press, 1978, pp. 500-515.

845. Baird, Irene M. "Planning for Offshore Petroleum Development in Newfoundland." Elisabeth Mann Borgese, Norton Ginsburg and Joseph R. Morgan, eds. Ocean Yearbook 8. Chicago and London: University of Chicago Press, 1989, pp. 138-157.

Discusses planning effort made over offshore resource ownership, control and managment of natural resources in Newfoundland.

846. Baram, Michael S., David Rice and William Lee. Marine Mining of the Continental Shelf: Legal, Technical and Environmental Considerations. Cambridge, MA: Ballinger Publishing Company, 1978.

847. Biggs, Robert B. "Offshore Industrial-Port Islands." Oceanus, vol. 19, no. 1, Fall 1975, pp. 56-66.

848. Blissenbach, Erich and Zohair Nawab. "Metalliferous Sediments of the Seabed: The Atlantis II: Deep Deposits of the Red Sea." Elisabeth Mann Borgese and Norton Ginsburg, eds. Ocean Yearbook 3. Chicago and London: University of Chicago Press, 1982, pp. 77-104.

849. Briscoe, John and Jo Lynn Lambert. "Seabed Mineral Discoveries within National Jurisdiction and the Future of the Law of the Sea." University of San Francisco Law Review. vol. 18, no. 3, Spring 1984, pp. 433-487.

850 Broadus, James M. "Seabed Materials." Science. vol. 235, 20 February 1987, pp. 853-860.

The article provides a status report on seabed materials which are basically minerals, in addition to offshore oil and gas resources.

851. _____ and Robert E. Bowen. "Developing a U. S. Research Strategy for Marine Polymetallic Sulfides." Ocean Development and International Law. vol. 17, nos. 1-3, 1986, pp. 91-130.

852. _____ and Robert E. Bowen. "Polymetallic Sulfides and Policy Spheres." Oceanus. vol. 27, no. 3, Fall 1984, pp. 26-31.

853. Bruce, Maxwell. "Ocean Energy: Some Perspectives on Economic Viability." Elisabeth Mann Borgese and Norton Ginsburg, eds. Ocean Yearbook 5. Chicago and London: University of Chicago Press, 1985, pp. 58-78.

854. Champ, M. A., W. P. Dillon and D. G. Powell. "Non-Living EEZ Resources: Minerals, Oil and Gas." Oceanus. vol. 27, no. 4, Winter 1984-85, pp. 28-34.

855. Charlier, Roger H. "Water, Energy and Non-living Ocean Resources." Elisabeth Mann Borgese and Norton Ginsburg, eds. Ocean Yearbook 4. Chicago and London: University of Chicago Press, 1983, pp. 75-120.

856. _____. "Other Ocean Resources." Elisabeth Mann Borgese and Norton Ginsburg, eds. Ocean Yearbook 1. Chicago and London: University of Chicago Press, 1978, pp. 160-210.

857. Charney, Jonathan I. "The Offshore Jurisdiction of the States of the United States and the Provinces of Canada: A Comparison." Douglas M. Johnston and Norman G. Letalik, eds. The Law of the Sea and Ocean Industry: New Opportunities and Restraints. Honolulu: The Law of the Sea Institute, University of Hawaii, 1984, pp. 426-454.

858. Cheever, Daniel. "Problems of Antarctic Resources." Choon-ho Park and Jae Kyu Park, eds. The Law of the Sea: Problems from the East Asian Perspective. Honolulu: The Law of the Sea Institute, University of Hawaii, 1987, pp. 116-120.

859. Clark, John and Scott McCreary. "Prospects for Coastal Resource Conservation in the 1980s." Oceanus. vol. 23, no. 4, Winter 1980-81, pp. 22-31.

Evaluates the Coastal Zone Management Act enacted by the United States Congress in the early 1970s and application of the concept of unit resource management.

860. Clay, Gerald S. Ocean Leasing for Hawaii. Honolulu: State of Hawaii, January 1981.

Provides an analysis of ocean leasing which encompasses ocean thermal energy conversion and fishing aggregation buoys.

861. Conference Proceedings, Seventh Ocean Energy Conference. Sponsored by U. S. Department of Energy, 1980.

Two-volume proceedings on this ocean energy conference containing valuable information about ocean engineering, resource development, wave energy, bio-fouling and open cycle power systems.

862. Cohen, Robert. "Ocean Thermal Gradients." Oceanus. vol. 22, no. 4, Winter 1979-80, pp. 12-22.

Discussion of technical aspects of fuel-free ocean thermal energy conversion (OTEC) by a government expert. Warns that OTEC power plants must be as carefully built to withstand hurricanes and heavy seas as oil drilling platforms in the rugged North Sea.

863. Conant, Melvin A. "Strategic Aspects of Pacific Petroleum Trade." Edward L. Miles and Scott Allen, eds. The Law of the Sea and Ocean Development Issues in the Pacific Basin. Honolulu: The Law of the Sea Institute, University of Hawaii, 1983, pp. 413-427.

864. Constans, Jacques. Marine Sources of Energy. New York: Pergamon Press, 1979.

An excellent treatment of offshore coastal wind energy conversion, ocean thermal energy conversion, the solar pond concept, wave and tidal energy conversion.

865. Craven, John P. "Present and Future Uses of Floating Platforms." Oceanus. vol. 19, no. 1, Fall 1975, pp. 67-71.

866. Cruickshank, Michael J. and Harold D. Hess. "Marine Sand and Gravel Mining." Oceanus. vol. 19, no. 1, Fall 1975, pp. 32-44.

Most authoritative discourse on gravel mining and the major use of marine sand and gravel in the construction industry.

867. Doumani, George A. Ocean Wealth: Policy and Potential. Rochelle Park, NJ: Hayden Book Company, Inc., 1973.

The book gives a detailed analysis of ocean resources. Discusses the legal concepts of the continental shelf and deposits on the seabed surface and below.

868. Dubs, Marne A.. "Minerals of the Deep Sea: Politics and Economics in Conflict." Elisabeth Mann Borgese and Norton Ginsburg, eds. Ocean Yearbook 6. Chicago and London: University of Chicago Press, 1980, pp. 55-83.

Discusses the principal issues of deep sea minerals: manganese nodules, technology for exploitation, ocean mining ventures, the Law of the Sea Treaty, and mine site conflict.

869. _____. "Development of the Ocean Resource Industry: The Impact of UNCLOS III." Douglas M. Johnston and Norman G. Letalik, eds. The Law of the Sea and Ocean Industry: New Opportunities and Restraints. Honolulu: The Law of the Sea Institute, University of Hawaii, 1984, pp. 4-9.

The director of Kennecott Copper Corporation's Ocean Mining Project wants to rewrite the Law of the Sea Treaty and make the needed changes.

870. Dupuy, R. J., ed. The Management of Humanity's Resources and the Law of the Sea. The Hague, Netherlands: Martinus Nijhoff; and London: Graham & Trotman, Ltd., 1982.

871. Earney, Fillmore C. F. Marine Mineral Resources. Marquette, MI: Northern Michigan University, 1989.

872. Eckert, Ross D. The Enclosure of Ocean Resources: Economics and the Law of the Sea. Stanford, CA: Hoover Institution Press, 1979.

The book analyzes economic problems and ocean policy development in the light of the law of the sea treaty negotiations. Discusses the changing economics of ocean uses, the continental margin enclosures, and navigation regulation.

873. Edgar, N. Terence and Kenneth C. Bayer. "Assessing Oil and Gas Resources on the U. S. Continental Margin." Oceanus. vol. 22, no. 3, Fall 1979, pp. 12-22.

874. Elliot, David H. "Antarctica: Is There Any Oil and Natural Gas?" Oceanus. vol. 31, no. 2, Summer 1988, pp. 32-38.

875. Emery, K. O. "Tectonic Evolution of the Yellow and East China Seas." Oceanus, vol. 26, no. 4, Winter 1983-84, pp. 26-32.

Research into the geological makeup of the East China Sea may provide clues to petroleum exploration.

876. _____. "Latitudinal Aspects of the Law of the Sea and of Petroleum Production." Ocean Development and

International Law.   vol. 2, no. 2, Summer 1974, pp. 137-150.

877. _____ and Elazer Uchupi. "The Oil Potential of the Caribbean." Elisabeth Mann Borgese and David Krieger, eds. The Tides of Change: Peace, Pollution and Potential of the Oceans. New York: Mason/Charter, 1975, pp. 239-253.

878. Farrington, John W. "The Biochemistry of Oil in the Ocean." Oceanus. vol. 20, no. 4, Fall 1977, pp. 5-10.

879. Fernholm, B. and G. Rudback. "Marine Resource Management for the Arctica." Journal of the Human Environment. vol. xviii, no. 1, 1989.

880. Flory, John F. "Oil Ports on the Continental Shelf." Oceanus. vol. 19, no. 1, Fall 1975, pp. 45-55.

881. "Foreign Metals: An Achilles' Heel for the U.S." U.S. News and World Report. 18 March 1985, p. 74.

882. Friedman, James M. "Atlantic Offshore Oil: The Need for Planning and Regulation." Oceanus. vol. 19, no. 1, Fall 1975, pp. 22-32.

An important discussion by a prominent attorney in ocean affairs on federal-state relations over Atlantic offshore oil development.

883. Fye, Paul M., Arthur E. Maxwell, Kenneth O. Emery and Bostwick H. Ketchum. "Ocean Science and Marine Resources." Edmund A. Gullion, ed. Uses of the Seas. Englewood Cliffs, NJ: Prentice-Hall, Inc., 1968, pp. 17-68.

884. Garrett, John Norton. "Hydrocarbons on the Continental Margins: Some of the Issues Addressed in the UNCLOS III Negotiations." Douglas M. Johnston and Norman G. Letalik, eds. The Law of the Sea and Ocean Industry: New Opportunities and Restraints. Honolulu: The Law of the Sea Institute, University of Hawaii, 1984, pp. 420-425.

885. Gaskell, T. F. and S. J. R. Simpson. "Oil: Two Billion B.C. - A.D. Two Thousand." Elisabeth Mann Borgese and Norton Ginsburg, eds. Ocean Yearbook 2. Chicago and London: University of Chicago Press, 1980, pp. 69-88.

886. Gault, Ian Townsend. "Recent Developments in the Cooperative Development of Offshore Petroleum Resources." Thomas A. Clingan, Jr., ed. The Law of the Sea: What Lies Ahead? Honolulu: The Law of the Sea Institute, University of Hawaii, 1988, pp. 207-227.

887. _____. "The Impact of Offshore Petroleum Regimes on Other Sea Users: The North Sea and North America." Douglas M. Johnston and Norman G. Letalik, eds. The Law of the Sea and Ocean Industry: New Opportunities

and Restraints. Honolulu: The Law of the Sea Institute, University of Hawaii, 1984, pp. 411-419.

Provides vital information about development of the North Sea petroleum regimes and exploration for oil in offshore Canada.

888. Gerson, Allan. "Offshore Oil Exploration by a Belligerent Occupant: The Gulf of Suez Dispute." American Journal of International Law. vol. 71, no. 4, October 1977, pp. 725-732.

889. Gorman, Brian. "Energy from the Sea: OTEC, the Sleeping Giant." NOAA Magazine. Fall 1981, pp. 5-9.

Discusses the experimental ocean thermal energy conversion plant in Hawaii which produced usable power without fouling.

890. Hage, Robert E. "Development of the Ocean Resource Industry: The Impact of UNCLOS III. Douglas M. Johnston and Norman G. Letalik, eds. The Law of the Sea and Ocean Industry: New Opportunities and Restraints. Honolulu: The Law of the Sea Institute, University of Hawaii, 1984, pp. 10-14.

891. Hajost, Scott A. "Authority to Manage Fisheries and Mineral Resources of the Southern Ocean: The Perspective of Non-Claimant Parties to the Antarctic Treaty." Thomas A. Clingan, Jr., ed. The Law of the Sea: What Lies Ahead? Honolulu: The Law of the Sea Institute, University of Hawaii, 1988, pp. 369-379.

892. Hanson, Arthur J. "Coastal and Ocean Resource Management: The Vietnam Case." Elisabeth Mann Borgese, Norton Ginsburg and Joseph R. Morgan, eds. Ocean Yearbook 7. Chicago and London: University of Chicago Press, 1988, pp. 241-262.

893. Harrison, Peter. "Offshore Oil and Gas: Development, Transporation and Coastal Impacts." Elisabeth Mann Borgese and Norton Ginsburg. Ocean Yearbook 4. Chicago and London: University of Chicago Press, 1983, pp. 319-346.

894. Hecker, Gary Alan. "Ocean Thermal Energy Conversion on the High Seas: Toward an International Regulatory Regime." San Diego Law Review. vol. 18, no. 3, April 1981, pp. 473-508.

895. Hedberg, Hollis D. "Deep Water Petroleum Prospects of the Oceans and Seas." Oceanus. vol. 26, no. 3, Fall 1983, pp. 9-16.

Finds flaws in the Law of the Sea Convention which may pose obstacles to drilling in deep sea waters of potentially oil-rich areas on the continental margin.

896. Henderson, Hamish McN. Oil and Gas: The North Sea Exploitation. Dobbs Ferry, NY: Oceana Publications, 1981.

897. Hennessey, Timothy M. "Multiple Uses of International Marine Resources: Theoretical Considerations." Douglas M. Johnston and Norman G. Letalik, eds. <u>The Law of the Sea and Ocean Industry: New Opportunities and Restraints</u>. Honolulu: The Law of the Sea Institute, University of Hawaii, 1984, pp. 34-50.

898. Hoagland, Porter, III. "Performance Requirements in Ocean Mineral Developments." <u>Marine Policy Reports</u>. vol. 9, no. 3, 1988, pp. 5-10.

899. Hunt, John M. "Introduction: Offshore Oil and Gas: Past, Present and Future." <u>Oceanus</u>. vol. 26, no. 3, Fall 1983, p. 2.

Points out that the offshore potential for oil and gas is still enormous, since only a small percentage of prospective areas in the deep seabed have been drilled; and that serious obstacles to exploration in very deep waters of the world's oceans may emerge if the 1982 Law of the Sea Convention is not modified.

900. _____. "Offshore Oil and Gas: Past, Present and Future." <u>Oceanus</u>. vol. 26, no. 3, Fall 1983, pp. 3-8.

901. Hurwood, David L. "Ocean Thermal Energy: Potentials and Pitfalls." <u>Ocean Development and International Law</u>. vol. 10, nos. 1-2, 1981, pp. 13-40.

902. "Indonesia, Australia Set Borders for Joint Oil Exploration Zone in Timor Sea." <u>Asian Wall Street Journal</u>. 23 February 1989, p. 6.

903. Jacobson, Mark P. "Convention on the Regulation of Antarctic Mineral Resources Activities; Opened for Signature, 25 November 1988." <u>Harvard International Law Journal</u>. vol. 30, no. 1, Winter 1989, pp. 237-239.

904. Johannas, Anai. "Activities of the Committee for Coordination of Joint Prospecting for Mineral Resources in Asian Offshore Areas (CCOP) 1966-1971." Douglas M. Johnston, Edgar Gold, Phiphat Tangsubkul, eds. <u>International Symposium on the New Law of the Sea in Southeast Asia: Developmental Effects and Regional Approaches</u>. Halifax, NS: Dalhousie Ocean Studies Programme, 1981, pp. 90-104.

905. Johnson, Charles J. and Allen L. Clark. "Expanding Horizons of Pacific Minerals." Elisabeth Mann Borgese, Norton Ginsburg and Joseph R. Morgan, eds. <u>Ocean Yearbook 7</u>. Chicago and London: University of Chicago Press, 1988, pp. 145-158.

A useful inventory of deep ocean minerals such as nodules, crusts and marine sulphide deposits in the Pacific, with tables and charts for reference.

906. Johnston, Douglas M. "Conservation and Management of the Marine Environment: Responsibilities and Required

Initiatives in Accordance with the 1982 UN Convention on the Law of the Sea." Robert B. Krueger and Stefan Riesenfeld, eds. The Developing Order of the Oceans. Honolulu: The Law of the Sea Institute, University of Hawaii, 1985, pp. 133-180.

907. _____ and Norman G. Letalik. The Law of the Sea and Ocean Industry: New Opportunities and Restraints. Honolulu: The Law of the Sea Institute, University of Hawaii, 1984.

908. Joyner, Christopher C. "The Antarctic Mineral Negotiating Process." American Journal of International Law. vol. 81, no. 4, 1987, pp. 888-905.

909. Kash, Don E. "Domestic Options to Offshore Oil and Gas." Oceanus. vol. 26, no. 3, Fall 1983, pp. 46-51.

Points out the high risks involved in alternative liquid-fuel options, but also argues the justification for federal support of liquid-fuel alternatives.

910. Keith, Kent M. "International Regulation of Ocean Floating Energy Platforms." John King Gamble, Jr., ed. Law of the Sea: Neglected Issues. Honolulu: The Law of the Sea Institute, University of Hawaii, 1979, pp. 275-296.

911. _____. "Laws Affecting the Development of Ocean Resources in Hawaii." Honolulu: University of Hawaii Law Review. vol. 4, no. 1, 1982, pp. 227-329.

This is a definitive study of the development of laws and regulation of ocean resources exploitation for the mid-ocean state of Hawaii. It focuses on Hawaii's planning laws for ocean resources development and the legal question of the extent of Hawaii's ocean jurisdiction.

912. Knight, Gary. "The Impact of the Law of the Sea Conference on Ocean Industry: Or, There Is Such a Thing as a Free Lunch, and Capitalism Is Paying for It." Douglas M. Johnston and Norman G. Letalik, eds. The Law of the Sea and Ocean Industry: New Opportunities and Restraints. Honolulu: The Law of the Sea Institute, University of Hawaii, 1984, pp. 15-19.

913. Koroma, Abdul G. "Perspective of Non-Parties to the Antarctic Treaty." Thomas A. Clingan, Jr. ed. The Law of the Sea: What Lies Ahead? Honolulu: The Law of the Sea Institute, University of Hawaii, 1988, pp. 380-385.

914. Koski, Randolph A., William R. Normark, Janet L. Morton and John R. Delaney. "Metal Sulfide Deposits on the Juan de Fuca Ridge." Oceanus. vol. 25, no. 3, Fall 1982, pp. 42-47.

915. Krem, Alexander J. "Financing Ocean Minderal Developments: Feasible under What Terms?" Robert B. Krueger and Stefan A. Reisenfeld, eds. The Developing Order of

the Oceans.   Honolulu: The Law of the Sea Institute,
University of Hawaii, 1985, pp. 319-339.

A banker's review and assessment of the financing provisions
for the deep seabed mining industry in the 1982 Law of the
Sea Convention.

916. Lagoni, Rainer. "Oil and Gas Deposits across National
Frontiers." American Journal of International Law.
vol. 73, no. 2, April 1979, pp. 215-243.

917. "A Leadership Agenda: State Management of Ocean
Resources." Report and Recommendation of the Ocean
Resource Committee, Western Legislative Conference,
January 1988.

918. Leger, Georges. "Partnerships in Hydrocarbon Develop-
ment: The Role of Petro-Canada International Assistance
Corporation." Douglas M. Johnston and Norman G. Leta-
lik, eds. The Law of the Sea and Ocean Industry: New
Opportunities and Restraints. Honolulu: The Law of the
Sea Institute, University of Hawaii, 1984, pp. 565-568.

919. Le Mehaute, Bernard. "Extracting Energy from the
Ocean." Robert L. Friedham, ed. Managing Ocean
Resources: A Primer. Boulder, CO: Westview Press, 1979,
pp. 51-66.

920. Lonsdale, Peter. "Hot Vents and Hydrocarbon Seeps in
the Sea of Cortez." Oceanus. vol. 27, no. 3, Fall
1984, pp. 21-25.

921. Luard, Evan. The Control of the Seabed: A New International Issue. London: Heinemann, 1974.

922. Mahmud, Abdul Aziz. "The Development of Non-Living
Resources: Problems and Opportunities for Marine
Regionalism in Southeast Asia: The Malaysian Perspec-
tive." Douglas M. Johnston, Edgar Gold and Phiphat
Tangsubkul, eds. International Symposium on the New Law
of the Sea in Southeast Asia: Developmental Effects and
Regional Approaches. Halifax, NS: Dalhousie Ocean
Studies Programme, 1981, pp. 73-81.

923. Malahoff, Alexander. "Polymetallic Sulfides and Cobalt
Crusts: New Mineral Resources of the Ocean Floor?"
Robert B. Krueger and Stefan A. Riesenfeld, eds. The
Developing Order of the Oceans. Honolulu: The Law of
the Sea Institute, University of Hawaii, 1985, pp. 270-
309.

This is a field research report on polymetallic sulfide
deposits found on the ocean floor along ridge crest segments
of the Juan de Fuca Straits, the East Pacific Rise, the
Galapagos Ridge, and on the submarine volcanos of the ridge
crests around the Hawaiian Ridge.

924. Mangone, G. J. American Strategic Minerals. New York:
Crane Russak and Co., 1984.

94   OCEAN POLITICS AND LAW

925. Meese, Sally A. "The Legal Regime Governing Seafloor Polymetallic Sulfide Deposits." Ocean Development and International Law. vol. 17, nos. 1-3, 1986, pp. 131-162.

926. Menzie, Charles A. "About Offshore Drilling: Muddy Issues." Oceanus. vol. 26, no. 3, Fall 1983, pp. 32-38.

927. Mero, John L. "Alternatives for Mineral Exploitation." Lewis M. Alexander, ed. The Law of the Sea: The Future of the Sea's Resources. Kingston, RI: University of Rhode Island, February 1968, pp. 94-97.

928. _____. The Mineral Resources of the Sea. New York: Elsevier Scientific Publishing Company, 1965.

929. Meyers, Herbert E. "How We're Fixed for Strategic Minerals." Fortune. 9 February 1981, pp. 68-70.

Discusses the United States industrial dependence on the supply from abroad of five strategic minerals: titanium, cobalt, manganese, platinum and chromium. A summary of the United Sstates stockpile of these strategic minerals is given.

930. Mottl, Michael J. "Submarine Hydrothermal Ore Deposits." Oceanus. vol. 23, no. 2, Summer 1980, pp. 18-27.

931. Murphy, John D. "Offshore Supply and Service: Chartering and Operations." Douglas M. Johnston and Norman G. Letalik, eds. The Law of the Sea and Ocean Industry: New Opportunities and Restraints. Honolulu: The Law of the Sea Institute, University of Hawaii, 1984, pp. 347-375.

932. Newman, J. N. "Power from Ocean Waves." Oceanus. vol. 22, no. 4, Winter 1979-80, pp. 38-45.

933. Nordquist, Myron H. "Jurisdictional Issues Affecting the Development of New Ocean Mineral Resources: Necessary Regimes." Robert B. Krueger and Stefan A. Riesenfeld, eds. The Developing Order of the Oceans. Honolulu: The Law of the Sea Institute, University of Hawaii, 1985, pp. 315-318.

934. _____ and Kent M. Keith. "Ocean Energy and Industrialization: Development Strategies." Edward L. Miles and Scott Allen, eds. The Law of the Sea and Ocean Development Issues in the Pacific Basin. Honolulu: The Law of the Sea Institute, University of Hawaii, 1983, pp. 382-394.

Discusses development strategies for the Pacific Islands-- the possibility of ocean thermal energy conversion for industrialization.

935. "Ocean Minerals: Dark Prospects." The Economist. 14 February 1981, pp. 87-88.

936. Oda, Shigera. _International Law of the Resources of the Sea_. Dordrecht, Netherlands: Martinus Nijhoff, and London: Graham & Trotman, Ltd., 1989.

This is a new edition of the book originally written in 1962 concerning ocean resources development in relation to the 1958 and 1960 Law of the Sea Conferences. The new edition contains the author's critical views with respect to the earlier two UN Law of the Sea Conferences on the high seas and resource development on the continental shelf.

937. Odell, Peter. "Offshore Resources: Oil and Gas." R. P. Barston and Patricie Birnie, eds. _The Maritime Dimension_. London: George Allen and Unwin, 1980, pp. 76-107

938. _____. "Oil and Gas Exploration and Exploitation in the North Sea." Elisabeth Mann Borgese and Norton Ginsburg, eds. _Ocean Yearbook 1_. Chicago and London: University of Chicago Press, 1978, pp. 139-159.

939. "Oil and Gas Technologies for the Arctic and Deep-water." Washington, DC: U. S. Congress Office of Technology Assessment, OTA-O-270, May 1985.

940. Packer, Tim. _Survey of Foreign Development Activities for Offshore Non-Fuel Mineral Resources: Part II_. Waterloo, ONT: University of Waterloo, 1988.

941. Park, Choon-ho. _East Asia and the Law of the Sea_. 2nd ed. Seoul, Korea: Seoul National University Press, 1985.

942. _____. "Offshore Oil Development in the China Seas: Some Legal and Territorial Issues." Elisabeth Mann Borgese and Norton Ginsburg, eds. _Ocean Yearbook 2_ Chicago and London: University of Chicago Press, 1980, pp. 302-316.

943. Pearson, Charles S. "Extracting Rent from Ocean Resources: Discussion of a Neglected Source." _Ocean Development and International Law_. vol. 1, no. 3, Fall 1973, pp. 221-238.

944. Penick, F. V. W. "The Legal Character of the Right to Explore and Exploit the Natural Resources of the Continental Shelf." _San Diego Law Review_. vol. 22, no. 4, July-August 1985, pp. 765-778.

This article discusses the legal characterization of the coastal state's right to develop natural resources on the continental shelf.

945. Pinto, M. C. W. "Authority to Manage Fisheries and Mineral Resources of the Southern Ocean: Objectives of Management." Thomas A. Clingan, Jr., ed. _The Law of the Sea, What Lies Ahead?_ Honolulu: The Law of the Sea Institute, University of Hawaii, 1988, pp. 343-365.

946. Pitzer, Pat. "The Ocean Source." <u>Spirit of Aloha</u>. August 1989, pp. 15-53.

Describes the water from the OTEC plant in Hawaii which provides the nutrients needed for aquaculture projects: pioneer commercial project in salmon and lobster breeding, and edible seaweeds.

947. <u>Proposed Marine Mineral Lease Sale in the Hawaiian Archipelago and Johnston Island Exclusive Economic Zones</u>. Draft Environmental Impact Statement. A Joint effort by the U. S. Department of the Interior and the Department of Planning and Economic Development. January 1987.

A comprehensive environmental impact statement regarding the leasing proposal for the mineral lease sale in the Hawaiian archipelago and Johnston Island Exclusive Economic Zones.

948. Rabinowitz, Philip and Sylvia Herrig. "Ocean Drilling Program: Altering Our Perception of Earth." <u>Oceanus</u>. vol. 29, no. 3, Fall 1986, pp. 36-41.

949. "Raw Materials: Global Military Consumption of Aluminium, Copper, Nickel and Platinum Is Greater than Overall Demand for These Minerals in Africa, Asia and Latin America Combined." <u>The UNESCO Courier</u>. March 1982, pp. 16-17.

950. Richardson, Jacques G., ed. <u>Managing the Ocean: Resources, Research, Law</u>. Mt. Airy, MD: Lomond Publications, Inc., 1985.

This is a collection of 35 essays by experts and scholars from 17 countries and three international organizations, edited by the former editor of a UNESCO journal on science and society. These essays attempt to explain the latest advances in science and technology on the management of ocean resources, oceanography and marine science.

951. Roberts, Kenneth G. "Offshore Petroleum Exploitation and Environmental Protection: The International and Norwegian Response." <u>San Diego Law Review</u>. vol. 17, no. 3, April 1980, pp. 629-660.

952. Ross, David A. "Resources of the Deep Sea Other than Manganese Nodules." John King Gamble, Jr., ed. <u>Law of the Sea: Neglected Issues</u>. Honolulu: The Law of the Sea Institute, University of Hawaii, 1979, pp. 54-79.

953. _____. <u>Opportunities and Uses of the Ocean</u>. New York: Springer-Verlag, 1978.

954. Rothe, Peter. "Marine Geology: Mineral Resources of the Sea" Jacques G. Richardson, ed. <u>Managing the Ocean: Resources, Research, Law</u>. Mt. Airy, MD: Lomond Publications, Inc., 1985, pp. 17-28.

955. Ruangsuvan, Charu-Udom. "The Development of Offshore Mineral Resources in Thailand." Douglas M. Johnston, Edgar Gold and Phiphat Tangsubukul, eds. _International Symposium on the New Law of the Sea in Southeast Asia: Developmental Effects and Regional Approaches_. Halifax, NS: Dalhousie Ocean Studies Programme, 1981, pp. 82-89.

956. Ryan, Paul R. "Cobalt-Rich Aeas Reported within EEZ." _Oceanus_. vol. 26, no. 2, Summer 1983, pp. 72-73.

Refers to the report released in September 1982 which confirmed the presence of cobalt-rich deposits in the Central Pacific near Hawaii and the U. S. Trust Territories.

957. Ryther, John H. "Fuels from Marine Biomass." _Oceanus_. vol. 22, no. 4, Winter 1979-80, pp. 48-58.

Presents the simple technology of generating fuel from marine biomass such as seaweeds and kelp--by a senior scientist at Woods Hole.

958. Santa Cruz, Fernando Zegers. "Authority to Manage Fisheries and Mineral Resources of the Southern Ocean." Thomas A. Clingan, Jr., ed. _The Law of the Sea: What Lies Ahead?_ Honolulu: The Law of the Sea Institute, University of Hawaii, 1988, pp. 366-368.

959. Scully, R. Tucker. "The Antarctic Mineral Resource Negotiations: A Report." Thomas A. Clingan, Jr., ed. _The Law of the Sea: What Lies Ahead?_ Honolulu: The Law of the Sea Institute, University of Hawaii, 1988, pp. 386-403.

960. Silverstein, Harvey B. "Ocean Energy and the Hydrogen Denominator." Elisabeth Mann Borgese and Norton Ginsburg, eds. _Ocean Yearbook 3_. Chicago and London: University of Chicago Press, 1982, pp. 105-117.

961. Skinner, Brian J. and Karl K. Turekian. _Man and the Ocean_. Englewood Cliffs, NJ: Prentice-Hall, Inc., 1973.

962. Sollie, Finn. "Trends and Prospects for Regimes for Living and Mineral Resources in the Antarctic." John King Gamble, Jr., ed. _The Law of the Sea: Neglected Issues_. Honolulu: The Law of the Sea Institute, University of Hawaii, 1979, pp. 193-208.

963. Spicer, W. Wylie. "Financing Offshore Regs." Douglas M. Johnston and Norman G. Letalik, eds. _The Law of the Sea and Ocean Industry: New Opportunities and Restraints_. The Law of the Sea Institute, University of Hawaii, 1984, pp. 380-401.

964. Spies, Robert B. "Natural Submarine Petroleum Seeps." _Oceanus_. vol. 26, no. 3, Fall 1983, pp. 24-29.

Discusses the natural seepage of oil from earth into the sea and its distribution and detection. Argues for future research to examine the marine life and and around the seep.

965. Steinhart, John and Mark Bultman. "How Undiscovered Oil Is Estimated." Oceanus. vol. 26, no. 3, Fall 1983, pp. 40-45.

A scientific study of the bleak future for U.S. oil discovery, except the offshore frontiers in Alaska and California offshore areas which represent the most significant possibilities.

966. Sullivan, Jeremiah J. Pacific Basin Enterprise and the Changing Law of the Sea. Lexington, MA: D. C. Heath and Company, 1977, pp. 85-107.

967. Summary of Ocean Minerals Activities and Related Research. Washington, DC: National Oceanic and Atmospheric Administration, U. S. Department of Commerce, 5 July 1988.

968. Symonds, Edward. "Offshore Oil and Gas." Elisabeth Mann Borgese and Norton Ginsburg, eds. Ocean Yearbook 1 Chicago and London: University of Chicago Press, 1978, pp. 114-138.

969. Talwani, Manik. "New Geophysical Techniques for Offshore Exploration." Oceanus. vol. 26, no. 3, Fall 1983, pp. 17-23.

Discusses new scientific and innovative techniques--seismic common-depth-point and echo-sounding method, for example-- for exploring the continental margins.

970. Tanner, James. "Du Pont's Conoco Discovers Oil, Gas off of Indonesia." Wall Street Journal. 16 January 1990, p. A-5.

971. Treves, Tullio. "Accommodation of Multiple Uses of the Seas in International Law, with Special Reference to the Mediterranean." Douglas M. Johnston and Norman G. Letalik, eds. The Law of the Sea and Ocean Industry: New Opportunities and Restraints. Honolulu: The Law of the Sea Institute, University of Hawaii, 1984, pp. 51-62.

972. Ulfstein, Geir. "The Conflict between Petroleum Production, Navigation and Fisheries in International Law." Ocean Development and International Law. vol. 19, no. 3, 1988, pp. 229-262.

973. Valencia, Mark J. "Northeast Asia: Petroleum Potential, Jurisdictional Claims and International Relations." Ocean Development and International Law. vol. 20, no. 3, 1989, pp. 297-298.

974. _____. "Taming Troubled Waters: Joint Development of Oil and Mineral Resources in Overlapping Claim

Areas." <u>San Diego Law Review</u>. vol. 23, no. 3, May-June 1986, pp. 661-684.

This article advocates joint exploration and development of oil and mineral resources in overlapping claim areas by examining six joint agreements: for Thailand and Malaysia, South Korea and Japan, Saudi Arabia and Kuwait, Iceland and Norway, Sudan and Saudi Arabia, and Tunisia and Libya.

975. _____ and Masahiro Miyoshi.   "Southeast Asian Seas: Joint Development of Hydrocarbons in Overlapping Areas?" <u>Ocean Development and International Law</u>. vol. 16, 3 November 1986, pp. 211-254.

976. Velocci, Tony. "Minerals: The Resource Gap." <u>Nation's Business</u>. vol. 68, no. 10, October 1980, pp. 33-38.

Discusses American dependence on importation of strategic minerals for industrial use.

977. Yuan, Paul C. "China's Offshore Oil Development: Prob- lems and Prospects." Douglas M. Johnston and Norman G. Letalik, eds. <u>The Law of the Sea and Ocean Industry: New Opportunities and Restraints</u>. Honolulu: The Law of the Sea Institute, University of Hawaii, 1984, pp. 455- 464.

Deep Seabed Mining

978. Adede, A. O. <u>The System for Settlement of Disputes under the United Nations Convention on the Law of the Sea: A Drafting History and A Commentary</u>. Dordrecht, Boston, Lancaster: Martinus Nijhoff, 1987.

This is a comprehensive drafting history of the dispute settlement system under the 1982 Law of the Sea Convention. Traces the evolution and development of the dispute settlement system from the 1974 Caracas session to the 1979-80 sessions of the Third UN Conference on the Law of the Sea.

979. _____. "The Basic Structure of the Dispute Settlement Part of the Law of the Sea Convention." <u>Ocean Development and International Law</u>. vol. 11, nos. 1-2, 1982, pp. 125-148.

980. _____. "Law of the Sea: The Scope of the Third-Party, Compulsory Procedures for Settlement of Disputes." <u>American Journal of International Law</u>. vol. 71, no. 2, April 1977, pp. 305-310.

981. "Agreement on the Resolution of Practical Problems with Respect to Deep Seabed Mining Areas, Belgium-Canada-Italy-Netherlands-USSR, 14 August 1987." <u>Harvard International Law Journal</u>. vol. 30, no. 1, Winter 1990, pp. 216-219.

982. Allen, Scott and John P. Craven, eds. <u>Alternative in Deepsea Mining</u>. Honolulu: Law of the Sea Institute, University of Hawaii, 1979.

A workshop, sponsored in 1978 by the Law of the Sea Institute, focused on the proposal for alternatives to deep seabed mining, then the center theme of international debate and importance.

983. Amsbaugh, J. K. and Jan L. Vander Voort. "The Ocean Mining Industry: A Benefit for Every Risk?" <u>Oceanus</u>. vol. 25, no. 3, Fall 1982, pp. 22-27.

984. Anand, R. P. "The Settlement of Disputes and the Law of the Sea Convention." Jon M. Van Dyke, ed. <u>Consensus and Confrontation: The United States and the Law of the Sea Convention</u>. Honolulu: The Law of the Sea Institute, University of Hawaii, 1985, pp. 483-487.

985. Andrassy, Juraj. <u>International Law and the Resources of the Sea</u>. New York: Columbia University Press, 1970.

986. Antrim, Lance N. and James K. Sebenius. "Incentives for Ocean Mining under the Convention." Bernard Oxman, David D. Caron, and Charles L. O. Buderi, eds. <u>Law of the Sea, U. S. Policy Dilemma</u>. San Francisco, CA: Institute for Contemporary Studies, 1983, pp. 79-99.

This article evaluates the commercial prospects for seabed mining. Begins with a discussion on the origins and alternatives for mining manganese nodules; then follows with discussions of the economics of seabed mining, and the political and legal environment in the light of United States law and the 1982 Law of the Sea Convention.

987. Arnold, Frederick. "Toward a Principled Approach to the Distribution of Global Wealth: An Impartial Solution to the Dispute over Seabed Manganese Nodules." <u>San Diego Law Review</u>. vol. 17, no. 3, April 1980, pp. 557-587.

988. Arrow, Dennis W. "The Customary Norm Process and the Deep Seabed." <u>Ocean Development and International Law</u>. vol. 9, nos. 1-2, 1981, pp. 1-60.

989. Auburn, F. M. "Some Legal Problems of the Commercial Exploitation of Manganese Nodules in the Pacific." <u>Ocean Development and International Law</u>. vol. 1, no. 2, Summer 1973, pp. 185-200.

990. Baram, Michael S., David Rice and William Lee. <u>Marine Mining of the Continental Shelf: Legal, Technical and Environmental Considerations</u>. Cambridge, MA: Ballinger Publishing Company, 1978.

This is an important study of marine mining and management of hard mineral resources on the continental shelf, a project sponsored by the National Science Foundation. The book discusses a wide range of technical, economic, legal, environmental and policy issues about mining of continental shelf hard minerals.

991. Barkenbus, Jack N. <u>Deep Seabed Resources: Politics and Technology</u>. New York and London: The Free Press, 1981.

Provides a legal background study on the evolution of U.S. policy for deep seabed mining, international negotiations vis-a-vis U.S. strategy, and the meaning of the New International Economic Order.

992. Barrett, Christopher. "Towards a Minerals Regime for Antarctica: The Problems Associated therewith and

Possible Solutions Offered by the Common Heritage of Mankind Principle." <u>Sea Changes</u>. no. 5, 1987, pp. 110-144.

993. "Belgium-France-Federal Republic of Germany-Italy-Japan-Netherlands-United Kingdom-United States: Provisional Understanding Regarding Deep Seabed Mining." <u>International Legal Materials</u>, vol. xxiii, no. 6, November 1984, pp. 1354-1365.

994. Biggs, Gonzalo. "Deep Seabed Mining and Unilateral Legislation." <u>Ocean Development and International Law</u>. vol. 8, no. 3, 1980, pp. 223-257.

995. Blissenbach, Erich and Zohair Nawab. "Metalliferous Sediments of the Seabed: The Atlantis II: Deep Deposits of the Red Sea." Elisabeth Mann Borgese and Norton Ginsburg, eds. <u>Ocean Yearbook 3</u>. Chicago and London: University of Chicago Press, 1982, pp. 77-104.

996. Borgese, Elisabeth Mann. "Implementing the Convention: Developments in the Preparatory Commission." Elisabeth Mann Borgese, Norton Ginsburg and Joseph R. Morgan, eds. <u>Ocean Yearbook 7</u>. Chicago and London: University of Chicago Press, 1988, pp. 1-7.

997. _____. "The Preparatory Commission for the International Seabed Authority and for the International Tribunal for the Law of the Sea: Third Session." Elisabeth Mann Borgese and Norton Ginsburg, eds. <u>Ocean Yearbook 6</u>. Chicago and London: University of Chicago Press, 1986, pp. 1-14.

A more detailed, but candid, study on the work of the Preparatory Commission and its operational tasks, the operating paralysis, and the future outlook for mining in the international area beyond national jurisdiction.

998. _____. "Making Part XI of the Convention Work." Jon M. Van Dyke, ed. <u>Consensus and Confrontation: The United States and the Law of the Sea Convention</u>. Honolulu: The Law of the Sea Institute, University of Hawaii, 1985, pp. 236-240.

999. _____. "Notes on the Work of the Preparatory Commission." Elisabeth Mann Borgese and Norton Ginsburg, eds. <u>Ocean Yearbook 5</u>. Chicago and London: University of Chicago Press, 1985, pp. 1-9.

1000. _____. "The Law of the Sea: Its Potential for Generating International Revenue." Elisabeth Mann Borgese and Norton Ginsburg, eds. <u>Ocean Yearbook 4</u>. Chicago and London: University of Chicago Press, 1983, pp. 22-33.

The article provides some answers to the question of how revenue can be generated by the operation of an international deep seabed mining license system.

1001. _____. "The Role of the International Seabed Authority in the 1980s." San Diego Law Review. vol. 18, no. 3, April 1981, pp. 395-407.

1002. Branco, Raul. "The Tax Revenue Potential of Manganese Nodules." Ocean Development and International Law. vol. 1, no. 2, Summer 1973, pp. 201-208.

1003. Breen, James H. "The 1982 Dispute Resolving Agreement: The First Step toward Unilateral Mining outside the Law of the Sea Convention." Ocean Development and International Law, vol. 14, no. 2, 1984, pp. 201-234.

1004. Brennan, Thomas S. and Ken H. Takayama. Compendium of State Ocean and Marine Related Policies. Honolulu: Legislative Reference Bureau, State of Hawaii, 1987.

1005. Brewer, William C., Jr. "The Prospect for Deep Seabed Mining in a Divided World." Ocean Development and International Law. vol. 14, no. 4, 1985, pp. 363-382.

This article points out that one cannot assess the prospects for deep seabed mining simply as another commercial mining venture, for there are many unknowns in deep seabed mining.

1006. _____. "Deep Seabed Mining: Can an Acceptable Regime Ever Be Found?" Ocean Development and International Law. vol. 11, nos. 1-2, 1982, pp. 25-68.

1007. Broadus, J. M. and Porter Hoaglund III. "Conflict Resolution in the Assignment of Area Entitlements for Seabed Mining." San Diego Law Review. vol. 21, no. 3, June 1984, pp. 541-576.

Describes conditions which created a need for procedures in achieving conflict resolution over deep seabed mining areas. Seabed mining most likely would proceed along two competing and conflicting tracks: provisions under the 1982 Law of the Sea Convention and domestic legislation or multilateral arrangements.

1008. Brown, E. D.. Seabed Energy and Mineral Resources and the Law of the Sea. 3 vols. London: Graham & Trotman, Ltd., 1986.

This is one of the best works dealing with the current state of international law relating to the exploration and exploitation of seabed resources--three volumes that are useful for lawyers, scholars and mining consortia.

1009. _____. "Freedom of High Seas Versus the Common Heritage of Mankind: Fundamental Principles in Conflict." San Diego Law Review. vol. 20, no. 3, April 1983, pp. 521-560.

1010. Brown, Heidi. "Recent Developments in the Law of the Sea 1986." San Diego Law Review. vol. 24, no. 3, May-June 1987, pp. 703-707.

1011. Buzan, Barry. Seabed Politics.   New York: Praeger
Publishers, 1976.

1012. Caflisch, Lucius C.   "The Settlement of Disputes
Relating to Activities in the International Seabed
Area." Christos L. Rozakis and Constantine Stephanow,
eds. The New Law of the Sea. North Holland, Amster-
dam, New York, Oxford: Elsevier Science Publishers
B.V., in collaboration with the Pantos School of
Political Science, Athens, 1983, pp. 303-344.

1013. Caron, David D. "Municipal Legislation for Exploitation of the Deep Seabed." Ocean Development and
International Law. vol. 8, no. 4, 1980, pp. 259-298.

1014. Charney, Jonathan I. "The International Regime for
the Deep Seabed: Past Conflicts and Proposals for
Progress." Harvard International Law Journal. vol. 17,
no. 1, 1976, pp. 1-50.

For a most comprehensive analysis about the proposals for
deep seabed mining as presented in the Informal Single
Negotiating Text in 1975-76, this has to be the article to
read.

1015. Clark, Joel P.   "The Rebuttal: The Nodules Are Not
Essential." Oceanus. vol. 25, no. 3, Fall 1982, pp.
18-21.

1016. Cohen, Lewis I. "International Cooperation on Seabed
Mining." Bernard H. Oxman, David D. Caron and Charles
L.O. Buderi, eds. Law of the Sea: U.S. Policy
Dilemma. San Francisco: I. C. S. Press, 1983, pp. 101-
109.

This short but concise article discusses the United States
mining law and its relationship to the Reciprocating State
Agreement (RSA) as its alternative to the deep seabed regime
established by the 1982 Law of the Sea convention.

1017. Craven, John P. "Mineral Futures of the Oceans." The
Management of Pacific Marine Resources: Present Problems and Future Trends. Boulder, CO: Westview Press,
1982.

Presents six seabed mining scenarios and predictions for the
future "global commons."

1018. Davin, E. M. and M. C. Gross. "Assessing the Seabed."
Oceanus. vol. 23, no. 1, Spring 1980, pp. 20-32.

1019. "Deep Seabed Hard Minerals Resources Act." Hearings
and Workup before the Subcommittee on International
Economic Policy and Trade and on International Organi-
zations of the Committee on Foreign Affairs, House of
Representatives, Ninety-sixth Congress, H. R. 2729, 11
July, 1 November and 19 December 1979, 30 April 1980.
Theodore G. Kronmiller and G. Wayne Smith, eds. The

Lawfulness of Deep Seabed Mining. Dobbs Ferry, NY: Oceana Publications, Inc., 1981.

1020. "Deep Seabed Hard Minerals Resources Act (DSHMRA) Reauthorization." Oceans Policy News. July 1989, pp. 3-4

1021. "Deep Seabed Mining: An Updated Environmental Assessment of NOAA Deep Seabed Mining Licensees' Exploration Plans," Washington, DC: Office of Ocean and Coastal Resources Management, Ocean Minerals and Energy Division, 1982.

1022. "Deep Sea Mining Dialogue: Law of the Sea Debate in the United Nations General Assembly." Oceans Policy News. December 1989, p. 2.

1023. Deese, David A. "Seabed Emplacement and Political Reality." Oceanus. vol. 20, no. 1, Winter 1977, pp. 47-63.

1024. Dubs, Marne A. "Minerals of the Deep Sea: Politics and Economics in Conflict." Elisabeth Mann Borgese and Norton Ginsburg, eds. Ocean Yearbook 6. Chicago and London: University of Chicago Press, 1986, pp. 55-83.

Discussion by a management consultant about many important aspects of deep seabed mining: mining sites for manganese nodules, technology associated, ocean mining ventures, and conflicts under the law of the sea.

1025. Dupuy, R. J., ed. The Settlement of Disputes on the New Natural Resources. The Hague, Netherlands: Martinus Nijhoff, and London: Graham & Trotman Ltd., 1983.

1026. Eckert, Ross D. "Deep Sea Mineral Resources." The Enclosure of Ocean Resources: Economics and the Law of the Sea. Stanford, CA: Hoover Institution Press, 1979, pp. 216-258.

A most comprehensive treatment of characteristics of manganese nodules, the ocean mining system, economic rents and rationale for regulating ocean mining.

1027. Evrivades, Euripides L. "The Third World's Approach to the Deep Seabed." Ocean Development and International Law. vol. 11, nos. 3-4, 1982, pp. 201-264.

1028. Filardi, Linda. "Canadian Perspectives on Seabed Mining: The Case of the Production Limitation Formula." Ocean Development and International Law. vol. 13, no. 4, 1983, pp. 457-480.

This study analyzes Canada's position on deep seabed mining at the Third UN Conference on the Law of the Sea. As a major land-based supplier of nickel and as an industrialized nation and ally of the United States with ties to most Third World developing nations, Canada played a leading role in advocating production controls on deep seabed mining.

1029. "Final Regulations Issued by U. S. Government for Commercial Recovery of Manganese Nodules." <u>Oceans Policy News</u>. April 1989, pp. 2-3.

1030. Fischer, David W. "Hard Mineral Resource Development Policy in the U. S. Exclusive Economic Zone: A Review of the Role of the Coastal States." <u>Ocean Development and International Law</u>. vol. 19, no. 2, 1988, pp. 101-112.

1031. _____. "Two Alternatives in National Governance of Marine Hard Minerals in the U. S. EEZ." <u>Ocean Development and International Law</u>. vol. 19, no. 4, 1988, pp. 287-298.

1032. Flipse, John E. "The Economic Viability of Deep Ocean Mining." Edward L. Miles and Scott Allen, eds. <u>The Law of the Sea and Ocean Development Issues in the Pacific Basin</u>. Honolulu: The Law of the Sea Institute, University of Hawaii, 1983, pp. 322-378.

1033. Foders, Federico. "International Organizations and Ocean Use: The Case of Deep-Sea Mining." <u>Ocean Development and International Law</u>, vol. 20, no. 5, 1989, pp. 519-530.

This is a view from Germany which analyzes the mining provisions of the Law of the Sea Convention as insufficient; offers alternative institutional arrangements for seabed mining.

1034. "France-Federal Republic of Germany-United Kingdom-United States: Agreement Concerning Interim Arrangements Relating to Polymetallic Nodules of the Deep Seabed." <u>International Legal Materials</u>. vol. xxi, no. 5, September 1982, pp. 950-962.

1035. Frank, Richard A. "Environmental Aspects of Deepsea Mining." <u>Virginia Journal of International Law</u>. vol. 15, no. 4, Summer 1975, pp. 815-826.

1036. Friedman, Alan G. and Cynthia A. Williams. "The Group of 77 at the United Nations: An Emergent Force in the Law of the Sea." <u>San Diego Law Review</u>. vol. 16, no. 3, April 1979, pp. 555-574.

1037. Gaertner, Marianne P. "The Dispute Settlement Provisions of the Convention on the Law of the Sea: Critique and Alternatives to the International Tribunal for the Law of the Sea." <u>San Diego Law Review</u>. vol. 19, no. 3, April 1982, pp. 577-597.

This article examines the complex provisions of dispute settlement in the 1982 Law of the Sea Convention; discusses the procedures for dispute settlement in Part XV of the Convention.

1038. Galey, Margaret E. "From Caracas to Geneva to New York: The International Seabed Authority as a Creator of Grants." _Ocean Development and International Law._ vol. 4, no. 2, 1977, pp. 171-194.

1039. Gamble, John King, Jr. "Assessing the Reality of the Deep Seabed Regime." _San Diego Law Review._ vol. 22, no. 4, July-August 1985, pp. 779-792.

A most penetrating analysis of the significant gap between legal prescription and state practice relative to the deep seabed mining provisions of the Law of the Sea Convention.

1040. Geddes, Roger A. "The Future of the United States Deep Seabed Mining: Still in the Hands of Congress." _San Diego Law Review._ vol. 19, no. 3, April 1982, pp. 613-630.

An important interesting commentary about the dilemma the U.S. ocean mining industry faced in view of the inadequate protection offered by Congress against the detrimental effects of the Law of the Sea Treaty.

1041. Gerstle, M. S. _The Politics of UN Voting: A View of the Seabed from the Glass Palace._ Honolulu: The Law of the Sea Institute, University of Hawaii, 1977.

This is a study about the politics and voting in the 24th UN General Assembly (December 1969) on the resolution for a moratorium on deep seabed mining.

1042. Goldblat, Jozef. "Review of the Seabed Treaty." Elisabeth Mann Borgese and Norton Ginsburg, eds. _Ocean Yearbook 2._ Chicago and London: University of Chicago Press, 1980, pp. 270-281.

1043. _____. "The Seabed Treaty." Elisabeth Mann Borgese and Norton Ginsburg, eds. _Ocean Yearbook 1._ Chicago and London: University of Chicago Press, 1978, pp. 386-411.

1044. Hardy, Michael. "Law of the Sea and the Prospects for Deep Seabed Mining: The Position of the European Community." _Ocean Development and International Law._ vol. 17, no. 4, 1986, pp. 309-324.

Outlines the relationship between the Law of the Sea Conference and internal development within the European community.

1045. Hayashi, Moritaka. "Registration of the First Group of Pioneer Investors by the Preparatory Commission for the International Seabed Authority and for the International Tribunal for the Law of the Sea." _Ocean Development and International Law._ vol. 20, no. 1, 1989, pp. 1-34.

India, France, Japan and the Soviet Union were registered in December 1987 as the first group of pioneer investors for the exclusive right to explore and exploit deep seabed mineral resources. This article traces the years of difficult negotiations in and outside of the Preparatory

Commission on the major issues, positions, and resolutions for the pioneer investors to mine in the international Area.

1046. _____. "Japan and Deep Seabed Mining." Ocean Development and International Law. vol. 17, no. 4, 1986, pp. 351-366.

1047. Heath, G. Ross. "Manganese Nodules: Unanswered Questions." Oceanus. vol. 25, no. 3, Fall 1982, pp. 37-42.

1048. Heirtzler, J. R. and A. E. Maxwell. "The Future of Deep Ocean Drilling." Oceanus. vol. 21, no. 3, Summer 1978, pp. 2-12.

1049. Hildreth, Richard G. "Legal Regimes for Seabed Hard Mineral Mining: Evolution at the Federal and State Levels." Ocean Development and International Law. vol. 20, no. 2, 1989, pp.141-156.

1050. Humphrey, Peter B., ed. Marine Mining: A New Beginning. (Proceedings of a Conference sponsored by the Department of Planning and Economic Development, County of Hawaii, and University of Hawaii Sea Grant College Project). Honolulu: Department of Planning and Economic Development, State of Hawaii, 1985.

An excellent volume which provides information and studies about marine minerals as world resources, marine mining technology, processing, and impact statements.

1051. Iguchi, Takeo. "Japan and the New Law of the Sea: Facing the Challenges of Deep Seabed Mining." Virginia Journal of International Law. vol. 27, no. 3, Spring 1987, pp. 527-550.

A most comprehensive analysis of Japan's position with respect to deep seabed mining.

1052. "Indian Ocean Marine Affairs Cooperation: Report of the First Meeting IOMAC Technical Group on Offshore Prospecting for Mineral Resources in the Indian Ocean." Government of Pakistan, 11-14 July 1988.

1053. Jaenicke, Gunther. "Conflicts between Mine Sites of Signatories and Non-Signatories of the Law of the Sea Convention." Thomas A. Clingan, Jr., ed. The Law of the Sea: What Lies Ahead? Honolulu: The Law of the Sea Institute, University of Hawaii, 1988, pp. 506-515.

1054. Jenisch, Uwe. "Bridging the Gap for Seabed Mining: Preparatory Instruments for the New Law of the Sea Convention." San Diego Law Review. vol. 18, no. 3, April 1981, pp. 409-413.

1055. Jenkins, Raymond W., M. Karl Jugel, Kent M. Keith and Maurice A. Meylan. The Feasibility and Potential Impact of Manganese Nodule Processing in the Puna and

<u>Kohala Districts of Hawaii</u>.   Honolulu: State of
Hawaii, Department of Planning and Economic Development, in cooperation with U.S. Department of Commerce
and National Oceanic and Atmospheric Administration,
November 1981.

Provides a study of the feasibility of a manganese nodule
processing industry in the State of Hawaii.   One of the
first such studies to be undertaken.

1056. Jesus, José Luis.   "Statement on the Issue of the
      Universality of the Convention."   Special Report,
      <u>Council on Ocean Law</u>, July 1990, pp. 1-5.

This is the latest statement from the Chairman of the
Preparatory Commission about questions to be considered--
including the agreed-upon system of amendments to the seabed
regime, decision-making and representation--to meet some of
the U.S. objections to the 1982 Law of the Sea Convention.

1057. Johnston, Douglas M. and Norman G. Letalik, ed. <u>The
      Law of the Sea and Ocean Industry: New Opportunities
      and Restraints</u>. Honolulu: The Law of the Sea Insti-
      tute, University of Hawaii, 1984.

1058. Jones, William B.   "Risk Assessment: Corporate
      Ventures in Deep Seabed Mining outside the Framework
      of the UN Convention on the Law of the Sea." <u>Ocean
      Development and International Law</u>. vol. 16, no. 4,
      1986, pp. 341-352.

One of the few articles which discusses and assesses various
categories of risk for U.S. deepsea mining industries
engaged in such activities outside of the UN Law of the Sea
framework.

1059. _____. "The International Seabed Authority with-
      out the U.S. Participation."   <u>Ocean Development and
      International Law</u>. vol. 12, nos. 3-4, 1982, pp. 151-
      172.

This paper focuses on what happens if and when the 1982 Law
of the Sea Convention comes into effect without United
States participation. The author then analyzes the dynamics
of international organizations, the operation of the
International Seabed Authority, and the dispute settlement
mechanisms.

1060. Kalinkin, G. F. "Problems of Legal Regulation of Sea-
      bed Uses beyond the Limits of the Continental Shelf."
      (Translated by Terese Sulikowski) <u>Ocean Development
      and International Law</u>. vol. 3, no. 2, 1975, pp. 127-
      154.

1061. Kanenas. "Wide Limits and 'Equitable' Distribution of
      Seabed Resources."   <u>Ocean Development and Inter-
      national Law</u>. vol. 1, no. 2, Summer 1973, pp. 137-158.

1062. Kimball, Lee A. "Conference Reports: Anticipation and Positioning; The 6th Session of the Preparatory Commission." Council on Ocean Law: Kingston, Jamaica, 14 March-8 April 1988; and New York, 15 August-2 September 1988.

1063. _____. "Conference Reports: Historic Steps at the Fifth Session of the Preparatory Commission," Council on Ocean Law: Kingston, Jamaica, 30 March-6 April 1987; and New York, 27 July-21 August 1987.

1064. _____. "Agreement on the Resolution of Practical Problems with Respect to Deep Seabed Mining Areas, and Exchange of Notes between the U.S. and the Parties to the Agreement." International Legal Materials. vol. xxvi, no. 6, November 1987, pp. 1725-1726.

1065. _____. "Statement of Understanding for Proceeding with Deep Seabed Mining Applications." International Legal Materials. vol. xxvi, no. 6, November 1987, pp. 1726-1727.

1066. _____. "Turning Points in the Future of Deep Seabed Mining." Ocean Development and International Law. vol. 17, no. 4, 1986, pp. 367-369.

An excellent paper which analyzes the prospects for deep seabed mining from legal and political perspectives. It points out the players and indicates the turning points in the development of future deep seabed mining.

1067. Knecht, Robert W. "Introduction: Deep Ocean Mining." Oceanus. vol. 25, no. 3, Fall 1982, pp. 3-11.

1068. Koh, Tommy T. B. "Deep Seabed Resources Are the Common Heritage of Mankind." Jon M. Van Dyke, ed. Consensus and Confrontation: The United States and the Law of the Sea Convention. Honolulu: The Law of the Sea Institute, University of Hawaii, 1985, pp. 228-232

1069. Kolodkin, Anatoly. "The Common Heritage of Mankind of the Seabed: The Notion and Substance." Jon M. Van Dyke, ed. Consensus and Confrontation: The United States and the Law of the Sea Convention. Honolulu: The Law of the Sea Institute, University of Hawaii, 1985, pp. 241-248.

1070. Kronmiller, Theodore G. and G. Wayne Smith, eds. The Unlawfulness of Deep Seabed Mining. 3 vols. Dobbs Ferry, NY: Oceana Publications, Inc., 1981.

This is a massive compilation of legal principles on deep seabed mining. It is detailed, comprehensive and well-documented, considering the voluminous material involved.

1071. Langevad, E. J. "Economists Leap into the Law of the Sea." LOS Lieder. vol. 3, no. 2. Honolulu: The Law of the Sea Institute, University of Hawaii, October 1989, pp. 1-4.

1072. Larschan, Bradley. "The International Status of the Contractual Rights of Contractors under the Deep Seabed Mining Provisions (Part XI) of the Third United Nations Convention on the Law of the Sea." _Denver Journal of International Law and Policy_. vol. 14, nos. 2-3, 1986, pp. 218-229.

This article discusses the contractual rights of contractors other than the Enterprise under the International Seabed Authority.

1073. Larson, David L. "Deep Seabed Mining: A Definition of the Problem." _Ocean Development and International Law_. vol. 17, no. 4, 1986, pp. 271-308.

A good summary analysis of the 1982 Reciprocating States Agreement and the international consortia on deep seabed mining.

1074. _____. "Deep Seabed Mining: American and Indian Perspectives." _Ocean Development and International Law_. vol. 14, no. 2, 1984, pp. 193-200.

1075. Lazarev, M. I. "Scientific-Technological Progress and the Search for Legal Regulations of Possible Seabed Uses." (Translated by Terese Sulikowski) _Ocean Development and International Law_. vol. 3, no. 1, 1975, pp. 75-86.

1076. Lee, Roy. Introductory Note: "United Nations Convention on the Law of the Sea: Understanding of the Preparatory Commission for the International Seabed Authority and for the International Tribunal for the Law of the Sea for Proceeding with Deep Seabed Mining Applications and for Resolving Disputes of Overlapping Claims of Mine Sites." _International Legal Materials_. vol. xxv, no. 5, September 1986, p. 1326.

1077. Luard, Evan. _The Control of the Seabed: A New International Issue_. London: Heinemann, 1974.

1078. Mahmoudi, Said. _The Law of Deep Seabed Mining: A Study of the Progressive Development of International Law Concerning the Management of Polymetallic Nodules of the Deep Seabed_. Stockholm: Almquist and Wiksell International, 1987.

1079. Malone, James L. "Freedom and Opportunity: Foundation for a Dynamic Oceans Policy." _Department of State Bulletin_. vol. 84, no. 2093, December 1984, pp. 76-79.

Outlines the U.S. official position on the Law of the Sea Convention--by the then Assistant Secretary of State for Oceans.

1080. Manansala, Mario C. "Deep Seabed Mining." Choon-ho Park and Jae Kyu Park, eds. _The Law of the Sea: Problems from the East Asian Perspective_. The Law of the Sea Institute, University of Hawaii, 1987, pp. 546-554

1081. <u>Marine Mining: A New Beginning</u>. Honolulu: State of Hawaii, Department of Planning and Economic Development, 1985.

1082. Markussen, Jan Magne. "The Asian Deepsea Projects: Different Motives, but a Common Objective?" <u>International Challenges</u>. vol. 8, no. 2, 1988.

1083. _____. "India and Deep Seabed Minerals: What Now?" <u>International Challenges</u>, vol. 8, no. 1, 1988, pp. 12-16.

1084. _____. "The Ocean Mining Project of the Fridljof Nansen Institute." Oslo, Norway: The Fridljof Nansen Institute, July 1988.

1085. Martin, Jochen. "Deep Sea Mining between Convention and National Legislation." <u>Ocean Development and International Law</u>. vol. 10, nos. 1-2, 1981, pp. 175-185.

1086. Marvosti, A. "Conceptual Model for the Management of International Resources: The Case of Seabed Minerals." <u>Ocean Development and International Law</u>. vol. 20, no. 3, 1989, pp. 273-284.

1087. Mero, John L. <u>The Mineral Resources of the Sea</u>. (Reprint) Amsterdam-Oxford-New York: Elsevier Scientific Publishing Co., 1973, pp. 127-241.

1088. Miller, Ken. "Deep Sea Mining Hits Opposition." <u>The Honolulu Star-Bulletin</u>. 15 January 1988, pp. A-1 and A-6.

1089. <u>Mining Development Scenario for Cobalt-Rich Manganese Crusts in the Exclusive Economic Zones of the Hawaii Archipelago and Johnston Island</u>. Honolulu: State of Hawaii, Department of Planning and Economic Development, and U. S. Department of the Interior Minerals Management Service, January 1987.

Another feasibility study on exploitation of the mineral resources of seamounts in the Exclusive Economic Zones surrounding the Hawaiian archipelago and Johnston Island.

1090. Molitor, Michael R. "The U. S. Deep Seabed Mining Regulations: The Legal Basis for an Alternative Regime." <u>San Diego Law Review</u>. vol. 19, no. 3, April 1982, pp. 599-612.

Points out the jurisdictional limitations in the United States domestic seabed mining legislation. Proposes continued development of deep seabed mining technology in the Exclusive Economic Zone.

1091. Molitor, Steven J. "The Provisional Understanding Regarding Deep Seabed Matters: An Ill-Conceived Regime for U. S. Deep Seabed Mining." <u>Cornell International Law Journal</u>. vol. 20, Winter 1987, pp. 223-252.

This article provides a full discussion regarding the Provisional Understanding Regarding Deep Seabed Mining.

1092. Moss, Ronald Scott. "Insuring Unilaterally Licensed Deep Seabed Mining Operations against Adverse Rulings by the International Court of Justice: An Assessment of the Risk." Ocean Development and International Law. vol. 14, no. 2, 1984, pp. 161-200.

Discusses the possibility of territorial disputes over the deep seabed if and when the 1982 Law of the Sea Convention comes into effect, and if the U.S. continues its refusal to sign the treaty.

1093. Murphy, John M. "The Politics of Manganese Nodules: International Considerations and Domestic Legislation." San Diego Law Review. vol. 16, no. 3, April 1979, pp. 531-554.

Congressman Murphy discusses unilateral legislation for deep seabed mining as being fully consonant with prevailing international law; feels that such enactment would spur Law of the Sea Conference negotiation.

1094. Nelson, Robert H. "Guiding the Ocean Search Process: Applying Public Land Experience to the Design of Leasing and Permitting Systems for Ocean Mining and Ocean Shipwrecks." Ocean Development and International Law. vol. 20, no. 6, 1989, pp. 577-600.

An interesting and novel concept in applying past U.S. government attempts in managing public lands and leasing systems for offshore oil and gas in contrast to designs for future systems of managing ocean resources.

1095. Nigrelli, Vincent. "Ocean Mineral Revenue Sharing." Ocean Development and International Law. vol. 5, nos. 2-3, 1978, pp. 153-180.

1096. "Notes: United States Activity outside of the Law of the Sea Convention: Deep Seabed Mining and Transit Passage." Columbia Law Review. vol. 84, no. 4, May 1984, pp. 1032-1058.

1097. "Ocean Mining: Economic, Technical, Political, Legal and Environmental Aspects." List of publications by International Challenges. vol. 8, no. 1, July 1988.

1098. Oda, Shigeru. The International Law of Ocean Development. 4 vols., 1975-1982. The Hague, Netherlands: Martinus Nijhoff, and London: Graham & Trotman, Ltd., 1989.

One of the most comprehensive studies on the subject--a must reference on the Law of the Sea.

1099. _____. The Law of the Sea in Our Time II: The United Nations Seabed Committee, 1968-1973. The

Hague, Netherlands: Martinus Nijhoff, and London: Graham & Trotman Ltd., 1977.

1100. Ogley, Roderick C. Internationalizing the Seabed. Brookfield, VT: Gower Publishing Company Limited, 1984.

1101. Oxman, Bernard H. "Summary of the Law of the Sea Convention."   Bernard H. Oxman, David D. Caron and Charles O. Buderi, eds. Law of the Sea: U. S. Policy Dilemma. San Francisco, CA: I. C. S. Press, Institute for Contemporary Studies, 1983, p. 159.

1102. Panel on the Law of the Ocean Uses. "Statement by Expert Panel: Deep Seabed Mining and the 1982 Convention on the Law of the Sea."   American Journal of International Law. vol. 82, no. 2, April 1988, pp. 363-369.

1103. Pendley, William Perry. "Commentary: It Ain't Broke; Don't Fix It: Mining in America's Exclusive Economic Zone Requires No New Legislation."   Marine Technology Society Journal. vol. 23, no. 1, March 1989, pp. 48-50

1104. _____. "The Argument: The U. S. Will Need Seabed Minerals." Oceanus. vol. 25, no. 3, Fall 1982, pp. 12-17.

1105. Penick, F. V. W. "The Legal Character of the Right to Explore and Exploit the Natural Resources of the Continental Shelf." San Diego Law Review. vol. 22, no. 4, July-August 1985, pp. 765-778.

Argues that coastal states enjoy real property rights over the minerals in situ on the continental shelf.

1106. Pirtle, Charles E. "Alternative Regimes for Harvesting the Seabed." Ocean Development and International Law. vol. 9, nos. 1-2, 1981, pp. 77-100.

1107. Plant, G. "The Third United Nations Conference on the Law of the Sea and the Preparatory Commission: Models for United Nations Law-making?" International Comparative Law Quarterly. vol. 36, part 3, July 1987, pp. 525-558.

1108. Platzoeder, Renate.   The Law of the Sea: Documents 1983-1989. Volumes 1-10.   Dobbs Ferry, NY: Oceana Publications, Inc., 1990.

This is a massive collection of documentary material on the work of the Preparatory Commission for the International Seabed Authority and the International Tribunal for the Law of the Sea.

1109. Pontecorvo, Giulio. "Musing about Seabed Mining, or Why What We Don't Know Can Hurt Us." Ocean Development and International Law. vol. 21, no. 1, 1990, pp. 117-118.

1110. Post, Alexander M. Deepsea Mining and the Law of the Sea. Dordrecht, Netherlands: Martinus Nijhoff, and London: Graham & Trotman, Ltd., 1983.

This book provides an analytical review of the development of deep seabed mining politics and calls for new inter-national law regulating the exploitation of ocean mining resources.

1111. _____.   "United Nations Involvement in Ocean Mining,"   Ocean Development and International Law, vol. 10, nos. 3-4, 1982, pp. 275-314.

1112. "The Preparatory Commission, Eighth Session." Oceans Policy News. April 1990, pp. 1-6.

Summarizes the latest work of the Preparatory Commission in the establishment of the international deep seabed mining regime.

1113. "The Preparatory Commission: The Resumed Seventh Session, 14 August - 1 September 1989." Oceans Policy News. September-October 1989.

1114. Proposed Marine Mineral Lease Sale: Exclusive Economic Zone Adjacent to Hawaii and Johnston Island. 2 vols. Honolulu: State of Hawaii Department of Business and Economic Development and U.S. Department of Interior. August 1990.

Latest study concerning the leasing proposal of 26,910 square kilometers of Exclusive Economic Zone in exploitation of potential metal resources in this zone.

1115. "Registration of Pioneer Investors in the Inter-national Seabed Area in Accordance with Resolution II of the Third United Nations Conference on the Law of the Sea." Special Issue II. Law of the Sea Bulletin. United Nations: Office for Ocean Affairs and the Law of the Sea, April 1988.

Contains the specifics with reference to registration of pioneer investors in the International Seabed Area by France, India, Japan and the Soviet Union.

1116. "Report on United States Deep Seabed Mining Program." Oceans Policy News. April 1990, p. 6.

1117. Richardson, Elliot L.   "The United States Posture toward the Law of the Sea Convention: Awkward but not Irreparable." San Diego Law Review. vol. 20, no. 3, April 1983, pp. 505-519.

1118. Scott, David Clark.   "Cobalt Rush?   U. S. Firm Explores Deepsea Mining." The Christian Science Monitor. 6 June 1989, p. 9.

1119. Scully, R. Tucker. "The Antarctic Mineral Resources

Negotiations." Oceanus. vol. 31, no. 2, Summer 1988, pp. 20-21.

1120. "Seabed Mineral Resource Development: Recent Activities of the International Consortia (ST/ESA/107)." United Nations: Department of Economic and Social Affairs, 1982.

1121. "Seabed Mineral Resource Development (ST/ESA/Add.1)." United Nations: Department of Economic and Social Affairs, 1982.

The above two key UN Secretariat studies provide summaries of international commercially oriented deep sea mining consortia and their activities.

1122. "Seabed Mining Technology Explored at UN Seminar." IMS Newsletter. no. 51, 1989.

1123. "Selected Documents and Proceedings; Documents of the Third Session of the Preparatory Commission for the International Seabed Authority and for the International Tribunal for the Law of the Sea." Elisabeth Mann Borgese and Norton Ginsburg, eds. Ocean Yearbook 6 Chicago and London: University of Chicago Press, 1986, pp. 527-571.

1124. "Selected Documents and Proceedings; The Preparatory Commission for the International Seabed Authority and for the International Tribunal for the Law of the Sea." Elisabeth Mann Borgese and Norton Ginsburg, eds. Ocean Yearbook 5. Chicago and London: University of Chicago Press, 1985, pp. 450-461.

This article contains information about submission of applications for registration as Pioneer Investor and resolution of conflicts with respect to overlapping areas.

1125. Shingleton, Brad. "UNCLOS III and the Struggle for Law: The Elusive Customary Law of Seabed Mining." Ocean Development and International Law. vol. 13, no. 1, 1983, pp. 33-64.

1126. Shusterich, Kurt Michael. Resource Management and the Oceans: The Political Economy of Deep Seabed Mining. Boulder, CO: Westview Press, 1982.

Focuses its concern on management of deep seabed mining in the International Area which was established by the 1982 Law of the Sea Convention. The author discusses and analyzes most succinctly the legal issues of both international and U.S. marine policy and resource management.

1127. Shyam, Manjula R. "Deep Seabed Mining: An Indian Perspective." Ocean Development and International Law. vol. 17, no. 4, 1986, pp. 325-350.

1128. Snyder, Joseph J. "Its' Time to Start Mining the Ocean." The Washington (DC) Post. 8 May 1988, p. 1.

1129. "Soviet Expedition Studied Central Atlantic Ocean Floor." _IMS Newsletter_, no. 51, 1989.

1130. "Special Report: The Preparatory Commission: Seventh Session, First Meeting, 27 February - 23 March 1989." Council on Ocean Law, September 1989.

1131. Starkey, J. C. "Australia's Offshore Petroleum Legal and Administrative Regime." _Maritime Studies_, vol. 37, November-December 1987.

1132. "Statement by Panel on the Law of Ocean Uses: Deep Seabed Mining and the 1982 Convention on the Law of the Sea." _American Journal of International Law_, vol. 82, no. 2, April 1988, pp. 363-369.

A most authoritative statement on deep seabed mining by the Panel on the Law of the Ocean Uses of the American Society for International Law. It urges reevaluation of nations' positions and taking the necessary steps to reconcile the differences.

1133. "Status of the 1982 LOS Treaty and Deep Seabed Mining: The Law of the Sea Institute's 23rd Annual Meeting." _Oceans Policy News_, June 1989, p. 5.

1134. Taniguchi, Chad. "Jurisdiction, Enforcement and Dispute Settlement in the Law of the Sea Convention." Jon M. Van Dyke, ed. _Consensus and Confrontation: The United States and the Law of the Sea Convention_. Honolulu: The Law of the Sea Institute, University of Hawaii, 1985, pp. 463-482.

1135. Touret, Denis G. "The French Deep Sea Mining Legislation of 1981." _Ocean Development and International Law_, vol. 13, no. 1, 1983, pp. 115-120.

1136. "U. S. Ocean Policy and Seabed Mining." _LOS Lieder_, vol. 3, no. 3. Honolulu: The Law of the Sea Institute, University of Hawaii, December 1989, p. 2.

1137. Van Dyke, Jon M. and David L. Teichmann. "Transfer of Seabed Mining Technology: A Stumbling Block to U. S. Ratification of the Convention on the Law of the Sea." Douglas M. Johnston and Norman G. Letalik, eds. _The Law of the Sea and Ocean Industry: New Opportunities and Restraints_. Honolulu: The Law of the Sea Institute, University of Hawaii, 1984, pp. 518-550.

1138. _____ and David L. Teichmann. "Transfer of Seabed Mining Technology: A Stumbling Block to U. S. Ratification of the Convention on the Law of the Sea." _Ocean Development and International Law_, vol. 13, no. 4, 1984, pp. 427-455.

Authors here argue that even though technology transfer provisions in the Law of the Sea Convention are ambiguous, the Preparatory Commission should be able to clarify the conflicts and that the issue should not be used as a stumbling block to prevent U. S. ratification of the treaty.

1139. Vicuna, Francisco Orrego. "The Deep Seabed Mining Regime: Terms and Conditions for Its Renegotiation." Ocean Development and International Law. vol. 20, no. 5, 1989, pp. 531-540.

An update on changing market conditions and the exploitation of deep seabed mining conditions since 1982. Vicuna argues for renegotiation of the deep seabed mining provisions in the 1982 treaty.

1140. Walkate, J. A. "Drafting the Deep Seabed Mining Code." Netherlands International Law Review. vol. xxxvi, no. 2, 1989, pp. 153-178.

1141. Welling, Conrad. "Conflict between Mining Sites of Non-Parties." Thomas A. Clingan, Jr., ed. The Law of the Sea: What Lies Ahead? Honolulu: The Law of the Sea Institute, University of Hawaii, 1988, pp. 501-505

1142. _____. "A View from the Industry." Jon M. Van Dyke, ed. Consensus and Confrontation: The United States and the Law of the Sea Convention. Honolulu: The Law of the Sea Institute, University of Hawaii, 1985, pp. 233-235.

1143. Whitney, Scott C. "Environmental Regulation of United States Deep Seabed Mining." William and Mary Law Review. vol. 19, Fall 1977, pp. 77-97.

1144. Williamson, Hugh R. "International Maritime Arbitration: Dispute Settlement without Recourse to the Courts." Elisabeth Mann Borgese, Norton Ginsburg and Joseph R. Morgan, eds. Ocean Yearbook 7. Chicago and London: University of Chicago Press, 1988, pp. 94-114.

1145. Willsey, F. Patterson. "The Deep Seabed Hard Mineral Resources Act and the Third United Nations Conference on the Law of the Sea: Can the Conference Meet the Mandate Embodied in the Act?" San Diego Law Review. vol. 18, no. 3, April 1981, pp. 509-532.

A most valuable discussion about the various legal aspects of the Law of the Sea provisions over deep seabed mining and on the acceptability to the U.S. 1980 domestic Deep Seabed Hard Mineral Resource Act.

1146. Yost, Kathryn E. "The International Seabed Authority Decision-Making Process: Does It Give a Proportionate Voice to the Participants' Interests in Deep Sea Mining?" San Diego Law Review. vol. 20, no. 3, April 1983, pp. 659-678.

This article focuses on the U.S. contention that the decision-making process for the International Seabed Authority under the 1982 Convention does not protect the interests of those participants engaged in deep seabed mining.

1147. Zacher, Mark W. and James G. McDonnell.   "Down to the Sea with Stakes: The Evolving Law of the Sea and the Future of the Deep Seabed Regime."   <u>Ocean Development and International Law</u>. vol. 21, no. 1, 1990, pp. 71-104.

Discusses a complex balancing of three principles in the 1982 Law of the Sea Convention: freedom of navigation, national enclosure of ocean space, and the common heritage of mankind.

Marine Pollution and Environmental Protection

1148. <u>An Act to Study, Control and Reduce the Pollution of Aquatic Environments from Plastic Materials and for other Purposes.</u> U. S. House of Representatives, 100th Congress, 2nd Session, 17 May 1988.

1149. Advisory Committee on Oil Pollution of the Sea. "Oil Pollution of the Sea: Excerpts from the ACOPS Annual Report 1980." Elisabeth Mann Borgese and Norton Ginsburg, eds. <u>Ocean Yearbook 3.</u> Chicago and London: University of Chicago Press, 1982, pp. 198-222.

1150. Advisory Committee on Pollution of the Sea. "Pollution of the Sea: Excerpts from the ACOPS Annual Report 1981." Elisabeth Mann Borgese and Norton Ginsburg, eds. <u>Ocean Yearbook 4.</u> Chicago and London: University of Chicago Press, 1983, pp. 295-307.

1151. Advisory Committee on Pollution of the Sea (ACOPS). <u>Yearbook: 1987-1988.</u> United Kingdom.

1152. "Alaska Oil Spill Hearing: U. S. Congress and Legislation." <u>Oceans Policy News.</u> April 1989, pp. 6-8.

1153. Alexander, Vera. "Arctic Ocean Pollution." <u>Oceanus.</u> vol. 29, no. 1, September 1986, pp. 31-35.

1154. Anderson, Susan H. "The Role of Recreation in the Marine Environment." Elisabeth Mann Borgese and Norton Ginsburg, eds. <u>Ocean Yearbook 2.</u> Chicago and London: University of Chicago Press, 1980, pp. 183-198.

1155. Andrianov, V. I. "The 1982 UN Convention on the Law of the Sea and the International Maritime Organization." Thomas A. Clingan, Jr., ed. <u>The Law of the Sea: What Lies Ahead?</u> Honolulu: The Law of the Sea Institute, University of Hawaii, 1988, pp. 539-542.

1156. "Announcement on Acid Rain, 17 March 1985." Prime Minister Mulroney and President Reagan. <u>U.S. Department of State Bulletin.</u> May 1985, pp. 3-4.

1157. Archer, Jack H.   "The Proposed Flower Garden Banks Marine Sanctuary: Protecting Marine Resources under International Law." Oceanus. vol. 31, no. 1, Spring 1988, pp. 54-58.

1158. Atema, Jelle.   "The Effects of Oil on Lobsters." Oceanus. vol. 20, no. 4, Fall 1977, pp. 67-73.

1159. Baba, N., Masashi Kiyota and Kazumoto Yoshida. "Distribution of Marine Debris and Northern Fur Seals in the Eastern Bering Sea."   Paper presented at the Second International Conference on Marine Debris, Honolulu, Hawaii, 2-7 April 1989.

1160. Barston, R. P. "Conference Reports: Implementing IMO Agreements, International Maritime Organization, 27th Session, Marine Environment Protection Committee, 13-17 March 1989." Marine Policy. vol. 13, no. 3, July 1989, pp. 267-268.

1161. _____ and P. W. Birnie. "The Marine Environment." R. P. Barston and Patricia Birnie, eds. The Maritime Dimension. London: George Allen and Unwin, 1980, pp. 108-127.

1162. Bascom, Willard. "The Disposal of Waste in the Ocean." American. vol. 231, no. 2, August 1974, pp. 16-25.

1163. Bavereis, Elizabeth I. and John N. Kraeuter. "Power Plants and Striped Bass: A Partnership." Oceanus. vol. 27, no. 1, Spring 1984, pp. 40-46.

1164. Beau, Michael J. "Redressing the Problem of Persistent Marine Debris through Law and Public Policy: Opportunities and Pitfalls." Paper presented at the Second International Conference on Marine Debris, Honolulu, Hawaii, 2-7 April 1989.

1165. Belsky, Martin H.   "Management of Large Marine Ecosystems: Developing a New Rule of Customary International Law." San Diego Law Review. vol. 22, no. 4, July-August 1985, pp. 733-763.

This paper examines the evolution of international law in establishing requirements for protection and management of the ocean ecosystem.

1166. Bernhardt, J. Peter A.   "Marine Pollution in the Law of the Sea." San Diego Law Review. vol. 24, no. 3, May-June 1987, pp. 689-700.

1167. Bertram, Kenneth M. and Danilo J. Santini. "United States Emergency Response Capabilities for Hazardous Materials Incidents in U.S. and Nearby Coastal Zones." Elisabeth Mann Borgese, Norton Ginsburg and Joseph R. Morgan, eds.   Ocean Yearbook 7. Chicago and London: University of Chicago Press, 1988, pp. 159-176.

1168. Boczek, Boleslaw A. "The Concept of Regime and the Protection and Preservation of the Marine Environment." Elisabeth Mann Borgese and Norton Ginsburg, eds. Ocean Yearbook 6. Chicago and London: University of Chicago Press, 1986, pp. 271-297.

1169. _____. "The Protection of the Antarctic Ecosystem: A Study in International Environmental Law." Ocean Development and International Law. vol. 13, no. 3, 1983, pp. 347-426.

1170. Booth, William. "Unravelling the Dolphin Soap Opera." Oceanus. vol. 32, no. 1, Spring 1989, pp. 76-79.

1171. Borgese, Elisabeth Mann. "The IMO and the UN Convention on the Law of the Sea." Elisabeth Mann Borgese, Norton Ginsburg and Joseph R. Morgan, eds. Ocean Yearbook 7. Chicago and London: University of Chicago Press, 1988, pp. 8-13.

1172. Boxer, Baruch. "Marine Environmental Protection in the Sea of Japan and Okhotsk." Ocean Development and International Law. vol. 21, no.2, 1990, pp. 193-212.

While marine environment protection is not a major issue of concern in the Japan/Okhotsk Sea area in contrast to issues of navigation, territorial claims, security and fisheries, four regional states in the region--Japan, South and North Korea, and the Soviet Union--have become more aware of the need and benefit for pollution control and conservation of fisheries.

1173. _____. "Marine Pollution Research Needs in the EEZ." Oceanus. vol. 27, no. 4, Winter 1984-85, pp. 23-27.

1174. Boyle, Alan E. "Marine Pollution under the Law of the Sea Convention." American Journal of International Law. vol. 79, no. 2, April 1985, pp. 347-372.

Provides a comprehensive analysis of the general responsibility for coastal states to regulate all sources of marine pollution, the need for international rules to control both the content and standard for the regulations, and the need to impose a duty on states in order to enforce regulations over sources of marine pollution.

1175. Braham, Howard W. "Eskimos, Yankees and Bowheads." Oceanus. vol. 32, no. 1, Spring 1989, pp. 54-62.

1176. Breem, Paul A. "Ghost Fishing in Trap Fisheries: A Review." Paper presented at the Second International Conference on Marine Debris, Honolulu, Hawaii, 2-7 April 1989.

1177. Brigham, Lawson W. "The Soviet Antarctic Program." Oceanus. vol. 31, no. 2, Summer 1988, pp. 87-92.

1178. Brown, E. D. "Pollution from Sea-Bed Mining." Seabed Energy and Mineral Resources and the Law of the Sea. vol. II, pt. 4. London: Graham & Trotman, Ltd., 1986, pp. II.9.4-35.

Provides one of the most comprehensive assessments of the environmental implications of seabed mining, in addition to a brief view of national legislation, particularly U.S. laws.

1179. Bruce, Maxwell. "The London Dumping Convention, 1972: First Decade and Future." Elisabeth Mann Borgese and Norton Ginsburg, eds. Ocean Yearbook 6. Chicago and London: University of Chicago Press, 1986, pp. 298-318.

Presents a brief history of the London 1972 Dumping Convention, an outline of the problems in a decade's experience, and prospects for the future.

1180. Bruner, Ronald G. "Plastic Industry and Marine Debris: Solutions through Education." Paper presented at the Second International Conference on Marine Debris, Honolulu, Hawaii, 2-7 April 1989.

1181. Burns, John F. "Canada Losing Patience with U. S. on Acid Rain." The New York Times. 25 April 1988, p. A-10:5.

1182. Burrough, R. H. "Ocean Dumping: Information and Policy in the U.S.A." Marine Policy. vol. 12, no. 2, April 1988.

1183. Busby, Richard H. "The Convention for the Prevention of Marine Pollution from Land-based Sources: An Effective Method for Arbitrating International Effluent Pollution Disputes." California Western International Law Journal. vol. 5, no. 350, 1974-75, pp. 350-375.

Presents the thesis that the international arbitration process can help remove major impediments to solutions for the problem of waste material flow into rivers and coastal seas.

1184. Busha, Thomas S. "The Response of the International Maritime Organization to References in the 1982 Convention to the 'Competent International Organization.'" Jon M. Van Dyke, Lewis M. Alexander and Joseph R. Morgan, eds. International Navigation: Rocks and Shoals Ahead? Honolulu: The Law of the Sea Institute, University of Hawaii, 1988, pp. 237-259.

1185. _____. "The IMO Conventions." Elisabeth Mann Borgese and Norton Ginsburg, eds. Ocean Yearbook 6. Chicago and London: University of Chicago Press, 1986, pp. 160-170.

1186. Campbell, Douglas, II. "Marine Pollution." David L. Larson, ed. Major Issues of the Law of the Sea. Durham, NH: University of New Hampshire, 1976, pp. 107-124.

1187. Capuzzo, Judith M. "Predicting Pollution Effects in the Marine Environment." Oceanus. vol. 24, no. 1, Spring 1981, pp. 25-33.

1188. Cates, Melissa B. "Offshore Oil Platforms which Pollute the Marine Environment: A Proposal for an International Treaty Imposing Strict Liability." San Diego Law Review. vol. 21, no. 3, June 1984, pp. 691-708.

Suggests that there is a need for a new international treaty imposing liability on a nation when an offshore structure causes transnational oil pollution.

1189. Champ, Michael A. "A Global Overview of Ocean Dumping, with Discussion of the Assimilative Capacity Concept for Sewage Sludge." Douglas M. Johnston and Norman G. Letalik, eds. The Law of the Sea and Ocean Industry: New Opportunities and Restraints. Honolulu: The Law of the Sea Institute, University of Hawaii, 1984, pp. 282-311.

Provides an overview of the world's critical problem of waste treatment and disposal, particularly dumping in coastal and oceanic areas by developed coastal states. Argues that ocean disposal will increase "until the assimilative capacity of the world ocean is ultimately exceeded."

1190. "Claims: Damages Resulting from Operation of Smelter at Trail, British Columbia." Charles I. Vevans, ed. Treaties and Other International Agreements. U.S. Department of State Publication 8549, vol. 6, pp. 60-64.

1191. Clark, R. B. Marine Pollution. Oxford: Clarendon Press, 1986.

1192. Clingan, Thomas A., Jr. "Vessel-Source Pollution, Problems of Hazardous Cargo, and Port State Jurisdiction." Jon M. Van Dyke, Lewis Alexander and Joseph R. Morgan, eds. International Navigation: Rocks and Shoals Ahead? Honolulu: The Law of the Sea Institute, University of Hawaii, 1988, pp. 273-279.

1193. Coe, James M. "Marine Debris in the North Pacific." Paper presented at the Second International Conference on Marine Debris, Honolulu, Hawaii, 2-7 April 1989.

Reviews research and management activities and results since 1984 on the marine debris problem focusing on North Pacific species such as seabirds and marine mammals.

1194. Commission of the European Communities. Law and Practice Relating to Pollution Control in the Member States of the European Communities. New ed. London: Graham & Trotman, Limited, 1983.

1195. "Conservation and Management of Marine Environment Responsibilities and Required Initiatives in Accordance with the 1982 UN Convention on the Law of the Sea." Chart presented by Douglas M. Johnston and prepared by Dalhousie Ocean Studies Programme in cooperation with the Commission for Environmental Policy, Law and Administration of the International Union for the Conservation of Nature and Natural Resources. Robert B. Kreuger and Stefan A. Riesenfeld, eds. The Developing Order of the Oceans. Honolulu: The Law of the Sea Institute, University of Hawaii, 1985, pp. 133-179.

1196. "Consideration and Adoption of the Final Report of the Intergovernmental Panel of Experts on Radioactive Waste Disposal at Sea." First meeting, 19-23 October 1987, International Maritime Organization, LDC/IGPRAD 1/6. 10 November 1987, p. 59.

1197. "Convention on Movements of Hazardous Wastes." Oceans Policy News. April 1989, p. 1.

1198. "Convention on Transboundary Movement of Hazardous Wastes." Oceans Policy News. February 1989, p. 1.

1199. Cordle, Frank. "The FDA Responds: Mercury Levels in Fish." Oceanus. vol. 24, no. 1, Spring 1981, pp. 42-43

1200. Corredor, J.E. and J. M. Morell. "Cooperative Research on Petroleum Pollution in the Caribbean: The Caripol Program." Paper presented at the Second International Conference on Marine Debris, Honolulu, Hawaii, 2-7 April 1989.

1201. Corwin, Edward. "Prospects for Increased State and Public Control over OCS Leasing: The Timing of the Environmental Impact Statement." San Diego Law Review. vol. 21, no. 3, June 1984, pp. 709-731.

This important comment suggests that environmental impact statements be made available to the public in the federal decision-making process, as more local governments in the U.S. and the public provide input regarding oil and gas leases on the outer continental shelf.

1202. Craven, John P. "A Legal Regime for Arms Control and Pollution Control of the Oceans." Elisabeth Mann Borgese and David Krieger. The Tides of Change: Peace, Pollution and Potential of the Oceans. New York: Mason/Charter, 1975, pp. 100-109.

1203. Curtis, Clifton E. "Legality of Seabed Disposal of High-Level Radioactive Wastes under the London Dumping Convention." Ocean Development and International Law. vol. 14, no. 4, 1985, pp. 383-416.

An important discussion about the definition of "disposal at sea" to support his thesis that seabed disposal of certain wastes, including high-level radioactive, is prohibited by the London   Dumping Convention and   other international agreements.

1204. _____. "Recent Developments under Special Environmental Conventions." Robert B. Krueger and Stefan A. Riesenfeld, eds. The Developing Order of the Oceans. Honolulu: The Law of the Sea Institute, University of Hawaii, 1985, pp. 117-132.

1205. _____. "Radwaste Disposal Risks Assessed at LDC Meeting." Oceanus. vol. 27, no. 2, Summer 1984, pp. 68-71.

1206. _____. "The Environmental Aspects of Deep Ocean Mining." Oceanus. vol. 25, no. 3, 1982, pp. 31-36.

1207. Davis, W. Jackson.   "Global Aspects of Marine Pollution Policy: The Need for a New International Convention." Marine Policy. vol. 14, no. 3, May 1990, pp. 191-197.

1208. Davison, Art. On the Wake of the Exxon Valdez: The Devastating Impact of the Alaska Oil Spill. San Francisco: Sierra Club Books, 1990.

1209. Debenham, Patty.   "Education and Awareness: Keys to Solving the Marine Debris Problem." Paper presented at the Second International Conference on Marine Debris, Honolulu, Hawaii, 2-7 April 1989.

1210. "Deteriorating Environment Highlight of Conference." National Research Council. News Report.   vol. xxxiv, no. 6, 1989.

1211. "Disasters: Close Shave off Morocco." TIME. 15 January 1990, p. 38.

1212. "Discussion: Implementing the Environmental Provisions of the 1982 Law of the Sea Convention." Jon M. Van Dyke, Lewis M. Alexander and Joseph R. Morgan, eds. International Navigation: Rocks and Shoals Ahead? Honolulu: The Law of the Sea Institute, University of Hawaii, 1988, pp. 299-304.

1213. Ditz, Daryl.   "Interpretation of Need in U. S. Ocean Incineration Policy." Marine Policy. vol. 13, no. 1, January 1989, pp. 43-55.

1214. Dixon, Trevor R.   "Marpol 73/78: Training Education and Information: Meeting the Challenge." Paper presented at the Second International Conference on Marine Debris, Honolulu, Hawaii, 2-7 April 1989.

1215. "Draft Guidelines on Removal of Offshore Structures." IMO News. no. 2, 1988.

1216. "Draft Salvage Convention." Oceans Policy News. March 1989, p. 1.

1217. Dubois, Bernard A. "The 1976 London Convention on Civil Liability for Oil Pollution Damage from Offshore Operations." Journal of Maritime Law and Commerce. vol. 9, no. 61, 1977, pp. 61-77.

1218. Du Bois, Random. "Catchment Land Use and Its Implications for Coastal Resources Conservation in East Africa and the Indian Ocean." Elisabeth Mann Borgese and Norton Ginsburg, eds. Ocean Yearbook 5. Chicago and London: University of Chicago Press, 1982, pp. 192-222.

1219. "Dumping Liability to Be Considered by Task Team." IMO News. no. 1, 1989.

1220. Dunbar, Maxwell J. "Arctic Marine Ecosystems." Oceanus. vol. 29, no. 1, September 1986, pp. 36-40.

1221. Dunham, Bob. "Japan's Collision Course with Ocean Pollution." Oceans. vol. 9, no. 6, November-December 1976, pp. 58-61.

1222. Edwards, David T. and Edward Rymarz. "International and Regional Regulations for the Prevention and Control of Pollution by Debris from Ships." Paper presented at the Second International Conference on Marine Debris, Honolulu, Hawaii, 2-7 April 1989.

1223. Farrington, John W. "Oil Pollution: A Decade of Research and Monitoring." Oceanus. vol. 28, no. 3, Fall 1985, pp. 2-12.

1224. _____. "Sources and Distribution Processes of Chemical Contaminants in the Coastal Zone." Douglas M. Johnston and Norman G. Letalik, eds. The Law of the Sea and Ocean Industry: New Opportunities and Restraints. Honolulu: The Law of the Sea Institute, University of Hawaii, 1984, pp. 246-269.

1225. _____. "Bivalves as Sentinels of Coastal Chemical Pollution: The Mussel (and Oyster) Watch." Oceanus. vol. 26, no. 2, Summer 1983, pp. 18-29.

1226. _____, Judith M. Capuzzo, Thomas M. Leschine and Michael A. Champ. "Ocean Dumping." Oceanus. vol. 25, no. 4, Winter 1982-83, pp. 39-50.

1227. Finn, Daniel P. "Nuclear Waste Management Activities in the Pacific Basin and Regional Cooperation on the Nuclear Fuel Cycle." Ocean Development and International Law. vol. 13, no. 2, 1983, pp. 213-246.

1228. Fleischer, Carl August. "Oil Spills: Convention to Limit Liability." Environmental Policy and Law. no. 3, 1977, pp. 76-78.

Discusses the key provisions of the 1977 civil liability convention on oil spills.

1229. Flinterman, Cees, Barbara Kwiatkowska and Johan G. Lammers, ed. _Transboundary Air Pollution: International Legal Aspects of the Cooperation of States_. Dordrecht, Boston, Lancaster: Martinus Nijhoff, 1986.

This book is a collection of essays on control of transboundary air pollution or acid rain. These essays discuss international agreements, bilateral and multilateral regimes, as well as remedies in private international law on acid rain control.

1230. Foster, Nancy and Michael L. Lemay. "Managing Marine Protected Areas: An Action Plan." Washington, DC: U.S. Department of Commerce, NTIS Service, March 1989.

1231. Fowler, Alfred N. "Antarctic Logistics." _Oceanus_. vol. 31, no. 2, Summer 1988, pp. 80-86.

1232. Fowler, Charles W. "Studies of the Population Level Effects of Entanglement on Northern Fur Seals." Paper presented at the Second International Conference on Marine Debris, Honolulu, Hawaii, 2-7 April 1989.

1233. Fraker, Mark A. "A Rescue that Moved the World." _Oceanus_. vols. 32, no. 1, Spring 1989, pp. 96-102.

1234. Frank, Richard A. "Environmental Aspects of Deep Sea Mining." _Virginia Journal of International Law_, vol. 15, no. 4, 1975, pp. 815-826.

Describes the potential environmental effects of deep sea mining and suggests ways to deal with them through domestic and international regulation.

1235. French, Deborah P. and Mark Reed. "Potential Impact of Entanglement in Marine Debris on the Population Dynamics of the Northern Fur Seal, Callorhinus Ursinus." Paper presented at the Second International Conference on Marine Debris, Honolulu, Hawaii, 2-7 April 1989.

1236. Frosch, Robert A. "Disposing of High-Level Radioactive Waste." _Oceanus_. vol. 20, no. 1, Winter 1977, pp. 4-17

Reveals scientific study of land and seabed locations as possible long-term sites for isolating high-level radioactive reactor wastes.

1237. _____, Charles D. Hollister and David A. Deese. "Radioactive Waste Disposal in the Oceans." Elisabeth Mann Borgese and Norton Ginsburg, eds. _Ocean Yearbook 1_ Chicago and London: University of Chicago Press, 1978, pp. 340-349.

1238. Fulghum, Clay. "What to Do with Those Old Oil Rigs." _EPA Journal_. vol. 4, no. 5, June 1988.

1239. Galey, M. _Marine Environmental Affairs Bibliography_.

Honolulu: Law of the Sea Institute, University of Hawaii, 1977.

An annotated bibliography covering the literature about marine environmental protection up to 1977.

1240. Glasby, G. P. "Pacific Is Favored for Sub-Seabed Radioactive Waste Disposal." _Pacific Islands Monthly_. vol. 54, no. 4, April 1983, pp. 15-17.

1241. Glass, Kathy and Kirsten Englund. "Why the Japanese Are So Stubborn about Whaling." _Oceanus_. vol. 32, no. 1, Spring 1989, pp. 45-51.

1242. Gold, Edgar. "The Control of Pollution from Ships: Responsibilities and Rights." Thomas A. Clingan, Jr., ed. _The Law of the Sea: What Lies Ahead?_ Honolulu: The Law of the Sea Institute, University of Hawaii, 1988, pp. 276-291.

While the paper argues for a balance between rights and resonsibilities in ship-generated marine pollution, it has an excellent review of the development of marine pollution responsibilities.

1243. _____. "New Directions in Ship-generated Marine Pollution Control: The New Law of the Sea and Developing Countries." Elisabeth Mann Borgese, Norton Ginsburg and Joseph R. Morgan, eds. _Ocean Yearbook 7_. Chicago and London: University of Chicago Press, 1988, pp. 191-204.

1244. _____ and Douglas M. Johnston. "Pollution Control in the Semi-Enclosed Seas of East Asia." Choon-ho Park and Jae Kyu Park, eds. _The Law of the Sea: Problems from the East Asian Perspective_. Honolulu: The Law of the Sea Institute, University of Hawaii, 1987, pp. 96-105.

Presents the hypothesis that marine pollution control is developed through successful efforts to form coalitions at the right time.

1245. _____ and Douglas M. Johnston. "Ship-generated Pollution: The Creator of Regulated Navigation." Thomas A. Clingan, Jr., ed. _Law of the Sea: State Practice in Zones of Special Jurisdiction_. Honolulu: The Law of the Sea Institute, University of Hawaii, 1982, pp. 156-197.

1246. Goldberg, Edward D. "The Oceans as Waste Space." Elisabeth Mann Borgese and Norton Ginsburg, eds. _Ocean Yearbook 5_. Chicago and London: University of Chicago Press, 1985, pp. 150-161.

1247. _____. "The Oceans as Waste Space: The Argument." _Oceanus_. vol. 24, no. 1, Spring 1981, pp. 2-9.

1248. _____. "Pollution History of Estuarine Sediments." Oceanus. vol. 19, no. 3, Spring 1976, pp. 18-26.

1249. Goodall, R. Natalie. "The Lost Whales of Tierra del Fuego." Oceanus. vol. 32, no. 1, Spring 1989, pp. 89-95.

1250. Goodrich, Laurence J. "Long Road to a Superfund Clean-up." The Christian Science Monitor. 3 October 1989, p. 7.

1251. Gould, J. R. "Problems of Pollution of the Sea." Thomas A. Clingan, Jr. and Lewis M. Alexander, eds. Hazards of Maritime Transit. Cambridge, MA: Ballinger Publishing Company, 1973, pp. 67-75.

Discusses fabricated plastic items seen on the shores of all isolated and unpopulated islands so far visited around the region and the environmental problem of entanglement and ingestion.

1252. Gregory, Murray R. "Plastics: Accumulation, Distribution and Environmental Effects of Meso-, Macro- and Mega-Litter in Surface Waters across the Southwest Pacific to Sub-Antarctic New Zealand, and on Adjacent Shores." Paper presented at the Second International Conference on Marine Debris, Honolulu, Hawaii, 2-7 April 1989.

1253. Guthrie, Dan. "Castoff Plastic Debris." Oceanus. vol. 31, no. 3, Fall 1988, pp. 29-36.

1254. Hagelin, L. "A Call for a World Park Antarctica." Journal of Human Environment. vol. xviii, no. 1, 1989.

1255. Hain, James H. W. "Low-Level Radioactivity in the Irish Sea." Oceanus. vol. 29, no. 3, Fall 1986, pp. 16-27.

1256. _____. "URI Symposium Report: The Future of the World's Oceans." Oceanus. vol. 29, no. 3, Fall 1986, pp. 68-69.

1257. Hardy, Michael. "Offshore Development and Marine Pollution." Ocean Development and International Law. vol. 1, no. 3, Fall 1973, pp. 239-274.

1258. Harrison, Craig S. "Costs to the United States in Environmental Protection and Marine Scientific Research by not Joining the Law of the Sea Convention." Jon M. Van Dyke, ed. Consensus and Confrontation: The United States and the Law of the Sea Convention. Honolulu: The Law of the Sea Institute, University of Hawaii, 1985, pp. 425-437.

1259. Hart, Paul Dudley. "The Growth of Antarctic Tourism." Oceanus. vol. 31, no. 2, Summer 1988, pp. 93-100.

1260. Hawley, T. M.   "The Whale, A Large Figure in the Collective Unconscious: Or, A Freudian Field Day." Oceanus. vol. 32, no. 1, Spring 1989, pp. 112-120.

1261. "Hazardous and Noxious Substances Liability and Compensation." Oceans Policy News. March 1989, p. 2.

1262. Heath, G. Ross. "Barriers to Radioactive Waste Migration." Oceanus. vol. 20, no. 1, Winter 1977, pp. 26-30

A study has been done to determine the speed at which radionuclides buried in the seabed can move up through sediments and whether it can be slowed by containment.

1263. Helmer, Richard and Nikki Meith. "Marine Environment and Coastal Resources in Southeast Asia: A Threatened Heritage."   Elisabeth Mann Borgese and Norton Ginsburg, eds. Ocean Yearbook 4.   Chicago and London: University of Chicago Press, 1983, pp. 260-294.

1264. Henderson, John R. "Recent Entanglement of Hawaiian Monk Seals in Marine Debris." Paper presented at the Second International Conference on Marine Debris, Honolulu, Hawaii, 2-7 April 1989.

1265. Heneman, Burr. Persistent Marine Debris in the North Sea, Northwest Atlantic Ocean, Wider Caribbean Area and the West Coast of Baja, California: A Report to the Marine Mammal Commission and the National Ocean Pollution Program Office. Washington, DC: U.S. Department of Commerce, National Oceanic and Atmospheric Administration, 1982.

1266. "Herald Aftermath: Further SOLAS Amendments Adopted." IMO News. no. 1, 1989.

1267. Hessler, Robert R. and Peter A. Jumars. "Abyssal Communities and Radioactive Waste Disposal." Oceanus. vol. 20, no. 1, Winter 1977, pp. 41-46.

Materials deposited under central gyre waters would be exposed to the most sparsely settled community which might accelerate the movement of accidentally leaked radioactive wastes.

1268. Heyerdahl, Thor. "How Vulnerable Is the Ocean?" Maurice F. Strong, ed. Who Speaks for Earth? New York: W. W. Norton & Company, Inc., 1973, pp. 45-63.

1269. Hofman, Robert J. "A First of Its Kind Anywhere." Oceanus. vol. 32, no. 1, Spring 1989, pp. 21-36.

1270 Hollister, Charles D. "The Seabed Option." Oceanus. vol. 20, no. 1, Winter 1977, pp. 18-25.

Presents the results of a 3-year research project--that the highly sorptive clay sediments of the mid-plate, mid-gyre on the Pacific Ocean floor have the potential to isolate wastes from the ocean and from man.

1271. _____, D. Richard Anderson and G. Ross Heath. "Sub-seabed Disposal of Nuclear Wastes." Science, vol. 213, no. 4514, 18 September 1981, pp. 1321-1326.

Brief, but authoritative, analysis of the management of disposal of radioactive wastes in the submarine areas of the ocean.

1272. Hoss, Donald E. and Lawrence R. Settle. "Ingestion of Plastics by Fishes." Paper presented at the Second International Conference on Marine Debris, Honolulu, Hawaii, 2-7 April 1989.

1273. Hull, E. W. Seabrook. Introduction to a Convention of the International Environment Protection Agency. Honolulu: The Law of the Sea Institute, University of Hawaii, 1971.

1274. _____ and Albert W. Koers. "A Regime for World Ocean Pollution Control." Robert G. Wirsing, ed. International Relations and the Future of Ocean Space. Columbia, SC: University of South Carolina Press, 1974, pp. 83-116.

1275. Hume, Howard. "Commentary." Robert B. Krueger and Stefan A. Riesenfeld, ed. The Developing Order of the Oceans. Honolulu: The Law of the Sea Institute, University of Hawaii, 1985, pp. 187-188.

1276. "IMO Projects Help Combat Pollution." IMO News. no. 1, 1989.

1277. "Incineration at Sea May End by 1995." IMO News. no. 1, 1989.

1278. "International Maritime Organization (IMO)." Oceans Policy News. July 1989, p. 3.

1279. "International Oil Pollution Compensation Fund." Oceans Policy News. March 1989, pp. 1-2.

1280. Ishihara, Takehiko. "Radioactive Waste Disposal." Oceanus. vol. 30, no. 1, Spring 1987, pp. 61-70.

1281. Jackson, C. I. "The Dimensions of International Pollution." Oregon Law Review. vol. 50, no. 3, Spring 1971, pp. 223-243.

Examines three dimensions to international pollution: atmospheric pollution, pollution of water bodies, and pollution that arises through trade.

1282. Jarman, M. Casey. "Marine Pollution: Injury without a Remedy?" San Diego Law Review. vol. 24, no. 3, May-June 1987, pp. 603-626.

This article analyzes the use of U.S. federal courts as forums for redress of damages resulting from pollution of coastal and ocean waters. It points to the conflicting federal common law and state statutory remedies in marine pollution.

1283. Johnston, Douglas M. "Conservation and Management of the Marine Environment Responsibilities and Required Initiatives in Accordance with the 1982 UN Convention on the Law of the Sea." Robert B. Krueger and Stefan A. Riesenfeld, eds. The Developing Order of the Oceans. Honolulu: The Law of the Sea Institute, University of Hawaii, 1985, pp. 133-179.

Surveys the various tasks which must be discharged in ful-filment of the general environmental purposes of the 1982 Law of the Sea Convention.

1284. Kadej, Blanka. "International Environmental Law: Selective Bibliography." New York University Journal of International Law and Politics. vol. 20, no. 3, Spring 1988, pp. 825-860.

An excellent bibliography on international environmental law--this is a most useful reference on the subject.

1285. Kamlet, Kenneth S. "The Oceans as Waste Space: The Rebuttal." Oceanus. vol. 24, no. 1, Spring 1981, pp. 10-17.

1286. Kaplan, David E. "When Incidents Are Accidents: The Silent Saga of the Nuclear Navy." Oceans. vol. 16, no. 4, July-August 1983, pp. 26-33.

Introduces controversial evidence that indicates the disposal of large quantities of high level radioactive wastes from the U.S. Navy nuclear propulsion center as well as dumping in the waters of wastes from the nuclear subs.

1287. Kasoulides, George C.. "State Responsibility and Assessment of Liability for Damage Resulting from Dumping Operations." San Diego Law Review. vol. 26, no. 3, August-September 1989, pp. 497-524.

The London Dumping Convention contains provisions for the establishment of a liability regime for ocean dumping opera-tions, including the dumping of radioactive waste. This article presents a discussion of the principles of state responsibility for environmental protection and obligation of states and individuals.

1288. _____. "Removal of Offshore Platforms and Development of International Standards." Marine Policy. vol. 13, no. 3, July 1989, pp. 249-265.

1289. Katona, Steven K. "Getting to Know You." Oceanus. vol. 32, no. 1, Spring 1989, pp. 37-44.

1290. Kelly, John E. and Cordelia E. Shea. "The Sub-seabed Disposal Program for High-Level Radioactive Waste: Public Response." Oceanus. vol. 25, no. 2, Summer 1982, pp. 42-53.

Describes the program for the placing of radioactive waste canisters in sediments beneath the deep ocean.

1291. Kidder, Rushworth M. "Ocean Cleanup Teaches Lessons." The Christian Science Monitor. 20 September 1989, p. 12.

1292. Kindt, John Warren. "International Environmental Law and Policy: An Overview of Transboundary Pollution." San Diego Law Review. vol. 23, no. 2, May-June 1986, pp. 583-609.

1293. _____. Marine Pollution and the Law of the Sea. 4 vols. Buffalo, NY: William S. Hein & Co., Inc., 1986

As the author claims, this massive 4-volume work is aimed at assisting both the United States and the international legal communities by providing in-depth analyses and overviews of international environmental law, U. S. environmental law, and the 1982 Law of the Sea Convention.

1294. _____. "The Claim for Limiting Marine Research: Compliance with International Environmental Standards." Ocean Development and International Law. vol. 15, no. 1, 1985, pp. 13-36.

1295. _____. "Marine Pollution and Hydrocarbons: The Goal of Minimizing Damage to the Marine Environment." California Western International Law Journal. vol. 14, 1984, pp. 233-288.

A most comprehensive analysis of problems of the effects of oil pollution, liquified natural gas, organicides, and plastics in marine pollution and their prevention for minimizing damage to the marine environment.

1296. _____. "Offshore Siting of Nuclear Power Plants." Ocean Development and International Law. vol. 8, no. 1, 1980, pp. 57-104.

1297. Knauss, John A. "Ocean Pollution: Status and Prognostication." John King Gamble, Jr. and Giulio Pontecorvo, eds. Law of the Sea: The Emerging Regime of the Oceans. Cambridge, MA: Ballinger Publishing Company, 1974, pp. 313-328.

1298. Koebas, Suleyman. "Assessment of Marine Pollution from Land-based Sources in the Eastern Mediterranean." Paper presented at the Second International Conference on Marine Debris, Honolulu, Hawaii, 2-7 April 1989.

1299. Koval, Arlene. "Extension of Ocean Dumping Legislation under the Marine Protection, Research and Sanctuaries Act to a United States Exclusive Economic Zone." San Diego Law Review. vol. 21, no. 3, June 1984, pp. 733-749.

Examines the issue of application of national laws in the United States Exclusive Economic Zone, such as the Marine

Protection, Research, and Sanctuaries Act, which is designed to control ocean dumping.

1300. Kuribayashi, Tado. "Commentary." Robert B. Krueger and Stefan A. Riesenfeld, eds. The Developing Order of the Oceans. Honolulu: The Law of the Sea Institute, University of Hawaii, 1985, pp. 180-182.

1301. Kuzin, A. E. "The Estimation of Mortality Rates for Callorhinus Ursinus from Commercial Fishing Waste Pollution." Paper presented at the Second International Conference on Marine Debris, Honolulu, Hawaii, 2-7 April 1989.

1302. Kwiatkowska, Barbara. "Marine Pollution from Land-based Sources: Current Problems and Prospects." Ocean Development and International Law. vol. 14, no. 3, 1984, pp. 315-335.

1303. Lampse, Wilhelm G. "The New International Maritime Organization and Its Place in Development of International Maritime Law." Journal of Maritime Law and Commerce. vol. 14, no. 3, July 1983, pp. 305-329.

One of the most detailed analyses of the IMO's development, the primary responsibilities of its Maritime Safety Committee, and the future.

1304. Laska, Shirley. "Designing Effective Educational Programs: The Attitudinal Basis of Marine Littering." Paper presented at the Second International Conference on Marine Debris, Honolulu, Hawaii, 2-7 April 1989.

1305. Law and Practice Relating to Pollution Control in the Member States of the European Community. New ed. London: Graham & Trotman, Ltd., 1983.

A major work on law and practice in pollution control by the European Economic Community.

1306. The Law of the Sea: Pollution by Dumping. A legislative history on the establishment and enforcement of rules and standards. United Nations, 1981.

1307. Leary, Warren E. "Reagan, in Switch, Agrees to a Plan on Acid Rain." The New York Times. 7 August 1988, p. I-1:2.

Discusses switch by President Reagan's agreement over freeze emission levels of nitrogen oxide, the most important transboundary pollutant between Canada and the U.S.

1308. Lester, James P. "Domestic Structure and International Technology Collaboration: Ocean Pollution Regulation." Ocean Development and International Law. vol. 8, no. 4, 1980, pp. 299-336.

1309. Levandowski, Richard. "Civil Liability for Oil Pollution Damage on the Norwegian Continental Shelf." Ocean

Development and International Law. vol. 5, no. 4, 1978, pp. 397-420.

1310. Livingston, D. Marine Pollution Articles in the Law of the Sea Single Informal Negotiating Text. Honolulu: The Law of the Sea Institute, University of Hawaii, 1976.

1311. "London Dumping Convention (LDC)."   Oceans Policy News. December 1989, pp. 1-3.

1312. "London Dumping Convention Meeting."   Oceans Policy News. March 1989, p. 2.

1313. Long, William L. "Economic Aspects of Transport and Disposal of Hazardous Wastes."   Marine Policy. vol. 14, no. 3, May 1990, pp. 198-204.

1314. McCaffrey, Stephen C. "The Work of the International Law Commission Relating to Transfrontier Environmental Harm."   Journal of International Law and Politics. vol. 20, no. 3, Spring 1988, pp. 715-732.

1315. McDade, Paul V. "The Removal of Offshore Installations and Conflicting Treaty Obligations as a Result of Emergence of the New Law of the Sea: A Case Study." San Diego Law Review. vol. 24, no. 3, May-June 1987, pp. 645-687.

This article takes up the problem of binding obligations on the part of states for the removal of offshore installations.

1316. McDougal, Myres S. and Jan Schneider. "The Protection of Environment and World Public Order: Some Recent Developments." Mississippi Law Journal. vol. 45, November 1974, pp. 1085-1124.

A leading scholar on public policy of the oceans discusses the confused and conflicting perspectives of state-centered elites in responding to marine environmental protection and the need for collective fundamental education worldwide to change these perspectives.

1317. McManus, Robert J "The New Treaty on Vessel Pollution." Oceans. vol. 7, no. 4, July-August 1974, pp. 59-65.

1318. _____. "The New Law on Ocean Dumping: Statute Treaty." Oceans. vol. 6, no. 5, September-October 1973, pp. 25-32.

A most succinct analysis of the 1972 London Convention on Ocean Dumping.

1319. "Major Change Ahead for SOLAS and Load Lines Convention." IMO News. no. 2, 1988.

1320. Manville, Albert M., II. "Aleutian Island Plastic, Wildlife Entanglement and Use of These Data in Influencing Legislation." Paper presented at the Second International Conference on Marine Debris, Honolulu, Hawaii, 2-7 April 1989.

1321. Mapes, Glynn and Philip Revzin. "British Spat with EC over Pollution Shows What 1992 May Bring." The Wall Street Journal. 14 December 1989, p. A-1.

1322. "Marine Environmental Protection Committee (MEPC) Meeting." Oceans Policy News. May 1989, pp. 1-2.

1323. "MARPOL Annex V Regulations." Oceans Policy News. May 1989, pp. 2-3.

1324. "MARPOL 73/78: The International Convention for the Prevention of Marine Pollution from Ships 1973, as Modified by Its Protocol of 1978." Selected Documents and Proceedings. Elisabeth Mann Borgese and Norton Ginsburg, eds. Ocean Yearbook 6. Chicago and London: University of Chicago Press, 1986, pp. 574-581.

1325. Martinez, Lissa A. "Shipboard Waste Disposal: Taking Out the Trash under the New Rules." Paper presented at the Second International Conference on Marine Debris, Honolulu, Hawaii, 2-7 April 1989.

1326. Mate, Bruce R. "Watching Habits and Habitats from Earth Satellites." Oceanus. vol. 24, no. 1, Spring 1981, pp. 14-18.

1327. Matsumura, Satsaki and Yoshinobu Wakata. "Movements of Floating Debris in the North Pacific." Paper presented at the Second International Conference on Marine Debris, Honolulu, Hawaii, 2-7 April 1989.

1328. Meade, Norman F. and Kathleen M. Drazek. "An Economic Perspective on the Problem of Persistent Marine Debris." Paper presented at the Second International Conference on Marine Debris, Honolulu, Hawaii, 2-7 April 1989.

1329. Mearns, Alan J. "Ecological Effects of Ocean Sewage Outfalls: Observations and Lessons." Oceanus. vol. 24, no. 1, Spring 1981, pp. 44-54.

1330. Meese, Sally A. "When Jurisdictional Interests Collide: International Domestic and State Efforts to Prevent Vessel Source Oil Pollution." Ocean Development and International Law. vol. 12, nos. 1-2, 1982, pp. 71-140.

1331. Meng, Qing-Nan. Land-Based Marine Pollution: International Law Development. London, Dordrecht, Boston: Graham & Trotman Ltd., 1987.

This is a book which pays some attention to international law on land-based pollution, the source of some 80% of all marine pollution.   The book attempts to provide a comprehensive examination of the issues concerning land-based marine pollution and control through international efforts.

1332. Menzie, Charles A. "Environmental Concerns about Offshore Drilling: Muddy Issues." Oceanus. vol. 26, no. 3, Fall 1983, pp. 32-39.

Argues the need to maintain environmental safeguards to ensure that offshore drilling operations continue to be done in a responsible manner.

1333. M'Gonigle, R. Michael and Mark W. Zacher. Pollution, Politics and International Law: Tankers at Sea. Berkeley, CA: University of California Press, 1979.

Another view by two scholars of marine pollution, particularly on the role of the International Maritime Consultative Organization.

1334. Miles, Edward L., Robert B. Krueger and Stefan A. Riesenfeld, eds. The Developing Order of the Oceans. Honolulu: The Law of the Sea Institute, University of Hawaii, 1985, pp. 183-186.

1335. Milgram, Jerome. "The Cleanup of Oil Spills from Unprotected Waters: Technology and Policy." Oceanus. vol. 20, no. 4, Fall 1977, pp. 86-93.

1336. Molina, Mario J. "The Antarctic Ozone Hole." Oceanus. vol. 31, no. 2, Summer 1988, pp. 47-52.

1337. Moore, Berrien, III and Bert Bolin. "The Oceans, Carbon Dioxide and Global Climate Change." Oceanus. vol. 29, no. 4, Winter 1986-87, pp. 9-15.

1338. Murakawa, Masamichi. "Marine Pollution and Countermeasures in Japan." Oceanus. vol. 30, no. 1, Spring 1987, pp. 55-60.

1339. Nakajima, Masayuki, Yasuda Hiroki and Kazumoto Yoshida. "Historical Observation on Damage to Dermal Tissue of Fur Seals Caused by Net Entanglement." Paper presented at the Second International Conference on Marine Debris, Honolulu, Hawaii, 2-7 April 1989.

1340. Nanda, Ved P. "Protection of the Internationally Shared Environment and the United Nations Convention on the Law of the Sea." Jon M. Van Dyke, ed. Consensus and Confrontation: The United States and the Law of the Sea Convention. Honolulu: The Law of the Sea Institute, University of Hawaii, 1985, pp. 403-420.

The view of a participant at the Law of the Sea negotiations on the contribution of the 1982 Convention to international environmental law.

1341. _____ and Bruce C. Bailey. "Export of Hazardous Waste and Hazardous Technology: Challenges for International Environmental Law." <u>Denver Journal of International Law and Policy</u>. vol. 17, no. 1, Fall 1988, pp. 155-206.

1342. "The Navy Defends the Nuclear Navy." <u>Oceans</u>. vol. 16, no. 5, September-October 1983, pp. 62-63.

1343. Negroponte, John D. "State Department Perspectives on Environmental Issues." Address before the International Environmental Forum, 18 September 1987. <u>U. S. State Department Bulletin</u>, December 1987, pp. 63-65.

Presents the U.S. official view on the State Department's role in environmental issues, including acid rain and other transboundary environmental concerns, such as the United States-Mexico border.

1344. Neidler, G.T. and W. L. Templeton. "Radioactive Waste: The Need to Calculate an Ocean Capacity." <u>Oceanus</u>. vol. 24, no. 1, Spring 1981, pp. 60-65.

1345. "A New Programme for Assessment and Control of Marine Pollution." <u>CEP News</u>. vol. 12, no. 2, December 1988.

1346. Nweihed, Kaldone G. "The International Maritime Organization: A Venezuelan Perspective." Elisabeth Mann Borgese and Norton Ginsburg, eds. <u>Ocean Yearbook 6</u>. Chicago and London: University of Chicago Press, 1986, pp. 171-196.

1347. Officer, Charles B. and John H. Ryther. "Swordfish and Mercury: A Case History." <u>Oceanus</u>. vol. 24, no. 1, Spring 1981, pp. 34-41.

1348. O'Hara, Kathryn J. "National Marine Debris Data Base." Paper presented at the Second International Conference on Marine Debris, Honolulu, Hawaii, 2-7 April 1989.

1349. "Oil Spill Legislation." <u>Oceans Policy News</u>. July 1989, p. 4.

1350. "Oil Spill Legislation: U.S. Legislation and Congress." <u>Oceans Policy News</u>. December 1989, p. 4.

1351. "Oil Spill Liability and Compensation." <u>Oceans Policy News</u>. September-October 1989, pp. 2-3.

1352. "Oil Spill Liability and Compensation: U. S. Congress and Cooperation." <u>Oceans Policy News</u>. March 1989, p. 3

1353. "Oil Spill Protocol: U. S. Congress and Legislation." <u>Oceans Policy News</u>. April 1989, p. 8.

1354. "Oil Spills and Compensation." <u>Oceans Policy News</u>. August 1989, p. 3.

1355. "Oil Spills Legislation: U. S. Congress and Legislation." <u>Oceans Policy News</u>. May 1989, pp. 3-4.

1356. O'Keefe, Constance. "Transboundary Pollution and the Strict Liability Issue: The Work of the International Law Commission on the Topic of International Liability for Injurious Consequences Arising out of Acts Not Prohibited by International Law." Denver Journal of International Law and Policy. vol. 18, no. 2, 1990, pp. 146-208.

The article examines the risk vs. harm distinction introduced in the 1989 report of the International Law Commission in its attempt to draft a model treaty dealing with the ramifications of transboundary pollution.

1357. Ostronskii, Ia A. "International Legal Protection of the Seas from Pollution." Ocean Development and International Law. vol. 3, no. 3, 1976, pp. 287-302.

1358. Paul, Linda M. "Using the Protective Principle to Unilaterally Enforce Transnational Marine Pollution Standards." Paper presented at the Second International Conference on Marine Debris, Honolulu, Hawaii, 2-7 April 1989.

1359. Pearson, Charles S. International Marine Environment Policy: The Economic Dimension. Baltimore and London: Johns Hopkins University Press, 1975.

1360. "Plastics Dumping to Be Annexed with Annex V's Entry into Force." IMO News. no. 1, 1988.

1361. Polacheck, Tom. "Harbor Porpoises and the Gillnet Fishery." Oceanus. vol. 32, no. 1, Spring 1989, pp. 63-70.

1362. "Pollution by Dumping: Legislative History of Articles 1, Paragraph 1(5), 210 and 216 of the United Nations Convention on the Law of the Sea." United Nations: Office of the Special Representative of the Secretary-General for the Law of the Sea, 1985.

1363. "President Signs Protocol on Ozone-Depleting Substances: President's Statement of 5 April 1988." Washington, DC: U. S. Department of State Bulletin. June 1988, p. 30.

1364. "Promises, Promises on Acid Rain." The New York Times. 30 April 1988, p. I-30.

1365. "Proposal by the Delegation of the United States of America: Annex on Hazardous Substances other than Oil." UNEP (OCA)/CAR IG.2/CRP.1. 26 October 1987, p. 2

1366. Proposed Marine Mineral Lease Sale: Exclusive Economic Zone Adjacent to Hawaii and Johnston Island. Final Environmental Impact Statement. 2 vols. Washington, DC and Honolulu: A Joint Effort of Minerals Management Service, U. S. Department of the Interior and Department of Business and Economic Development, State of Hawaii, August 1990.

This document is concerned with the environmental impact of the proposed lease sale of about 26,910 square kilometers, or 6.65 million acres, of Exclusive Economic Zone lands for exploitation of non-oil and gas minerals.   The potential metal resources in the proposed lease sale area are esti- mated to be 2.6 million metric tons of cobalt, 1.6 million metric tons of nickel, and 81 million metric tons of manganese.

1367. "Protection of Marine Environment: The Law of the Sea Institute's 23rd Annual Meeting." Oceans Policy News. June 1989, pp. 4-5.

1368. "Protocol Amending the Paris Convention for the Pre- vention of Marine Pollution from Land-based Sources." International Legal Materials. vol. xxvii, no. 3, May 1988. p. 1112.

1369. Redford, David P.   "Status of the U.S. Environmental Protection Agency Marine Debris Activities and Pro- grams."   Paper presented at the Second International Conference on Marine Debris, Honolulu, Hawaii, 2-7 April 1989.

1370. "Report on the Status of Conventions and other Multi- lateral Instruments in Respect of which the Organi- zation Performs Functions."   Note by the Secretary General. IMO No. C60/5, 12 April 1988.

1371. Report to the Congress on Ocean Pollution, Monitoring and Research, October 1986 through September 1987. Washington, DC: U. S. Department of Commerce, National Oceanic and Atmospheric Administration, June 1988.

1372. Revelle, Roger.   "The Oceans and the Carbon Dioxide Problem." Oceanus. vol. 26, Summer 1983, pp. 3-9.

1373. Ribic, Christine A. " An Index of Fur Seal Entangle- ment in Floating Net Fragments." Paper presented at the Second International Conference on Marine Debris, Honolulu, Hawaii, 2-7 April 1989.

1374. Richardson, Elliot L.   "Prevention of Vessel-Source Pollution: An Attainable Goal." Oceans. vol. 13, no. 2, March-April 1980, pp. 2-5.

The one-time chief U. S. negotiator at the Law of the Sea Conference discusses   the   prevention   of   vessel-source pollution as an attainable goal and the issues of compensa- tion, monitoring and enforcement.

1375. _____. "Prevention of Vessel-Source Pollution, Part II: Compensation, Monitoring and Enforcement." Oceans. vol. 13, no. 3, May-June 1980, pp. 58-61.

1376. "Ro-Ro Safety: Draft SOLAS Amendments Discussed." IMO News. no. 2, 1988.

1377. Rose, Bob. "The Marine Plastic Debris Action Plan for Washington: The First in the Nation." Paper presented at the Second International Conference on Marine Debris, Honolulu, Hawaii, 2-7 April 1989.

1378. Rosen, Yereth. "Oil Spill Update: Cleanup Too Confined, Critics Say." The Christian Science Monitor, 24 August 1989, p.8.

1379. Ruben, Alfred P. "Pollution by Analogy: The Trail Smelter Arbitration." Oregon Law Review. vol. 50, 1971, pp. 259-282.

A case study of the famous Trail Smelter Arbitration Case which established state liability and may serve as a basis for asserting rights in international law over pollution damage.

1380. Ryan, Peter G. "The Effects of Ingesting Plastic and Other Marine Debris on Seabirds." Paper presented at the Second International Conference on Marine Debris, Honolulu, Hawaii, 2-7 April 1989.

1381. _____. "The Marine Plastic Debris Problem off Southern Africa: Types of Debris, Their Environmental Effects and Control Measures." Paper presented at the Second International Conference on Marine Debris, Honolulu, Hawaii, 2-7 April 1989.

Discusses plastic debris as marine pollutant that endangers marine life in the seas off southern Africa and the adjacent southern ocean.

1382. Sadove, Samuel S. and Stephen Morreale. "Marine Mammal and Sea Turtle Encounters with Marine Debris in the New York Bight and the Northeast Atlantic." Paper presented at the Second International Conference on Marine Debris, Honolulu, Hawaii, 2-7 April 1989.

1383. Schatz, Gerald S. "Protecting the Antarctic Environment." Oceanus. vol. 31, no. 2, Summer 1988, pp. 101-107.

1384. Schmandt, Jurgen and Hilliard Roderick, eds. Acid Rain and Friendly Neighbors: The Policy Dispute between Canada and the United States. Durham, NC: Duke University Press, 1985.

This is a collaborative work by a policy specialist and a physicist over the policy problems derived from acid rain in the United States and Canada. It analyzes the acid rain issue between the two neighboring nations and the interplay of science and policy.

1385. Scott, George. "The Philosophy and Practice of Degradable Plastics." Paper presented at the Second International Conference on Marine Debris, Honolulu, Hawaii, 2-7 April 1989.

1386. Sebek, Viktor. "Pollution of the Marine Environment." ACOPS International Conference on Pollution of the Marine Environment, 27-30 October 1987.

1387. Seebald, Ray E. "Implementation and Enforcement of Annex V of MARPOL 73/78 in the United States." Paper presented at the Second International Conference on Marine Debris, Honolulu, Hawaii, 2-7 April 1989.

1388. Shabecoff. "U. S. Bars Proposal to Limit Acid Rain." The New York Times. 27 April 1988, p. A-5:1.

1389. Shah, M. J. "Model Maritime Legislation for Developing Countries: The UNCTAD Experience." Elisabeth Mann Borgese and Norton Ginsburg, eds. Ocean Yearbook 4. Chicago and London: University of Chicago Press, 1983, pp. 140-149.

1390. Sheffer, Victor B. "How Much Is a Whale's Life Worth, Anyway?" Oceanus. vol. 32, no. 1, Spring 1989, pp. 109-111.

1391. Sigurjonsson, Johann. "To Icelanders, Whaling Is a Godsend." Oceanus. vol. 32, no. 1, Spring 1989, pp. 29-36.

1392. Simon, Ann W. Neptune's Revenge: The Ocean of To-morrow. New York and Toronto: Franklin Watts, 1984.

A popular and compelling book which examines the environ-mental degeneration of an island and of the entire world's marine life.

1393. Skinner, Brian J. and Karl K. Turekian. Man and the Ocean. Englewood Cliffs, NJ: Prentice-Hall, Inc., 1973.

1394. Smith, Brian D. State Responsibility and the Marine Environment: The Rules of Decision. Oxford: Clarendon Press, and New York: Oxford University Press, 1988.

This book provides a description of the primitive state of the law of environmental responsibility as applied to marine pollution. Focuses its discussion on state obligation to prevent injury to other states under bilateral arrangements.

1395. Sohn, Louis B. "Implications of the Law of the Sea Convention Regarding the Protection and Preservation of the Marine Environment." Robert B. Krueger and Stefan A. Riesenfeld, eds. The Developing Order of the Seas. Honolulu: The Law of the Sea Institute, University of Hawaii, 1985, pp. 103-116.

1396. "SOLAS Amended to Improve Ro-Ro Safety." IMO News. no. 2, 1988.

1397. "South Pacific Driftnet Convention." Oceans Policy News. December 1989, p. 6.

144   OCEAN POLITICS AND LAW

1398. Speranskaya, L. V. "Marine Environmental Protection and Freedom of Navigation in International Law." Elisabeth Mann Borgese and Norton Ginsburg, eds. Ocean Yearbook 6. Chicago and London: University of Chicago Press, 1986, pp. 197-202.

1399. Springer, Allen L. The International Law of Pollution: Protecting the Global Environment in a World of Sovereign States. Westport, CT: Quorum Books, 1983.

1400. Srivastava, C. P. "IMO and the Law of the Sea." E. D. Brown and R. R. Churchill, eds. The UN Convention on the Law of the Sea: Impact and Implementation. Honolulu: The Law of the Sea Institute, University of Hawaii, 1987, pp. 419-425.

1401. "The State of the Marine Environment 1988." The Siren. no. 36, April 1988, pp. 13-32.

1402. Stegeman, John J. "Fate and Effects of Oil in Marine Mammals." Oceanus. vol. 20, no. 4, Fall 1977, pp. 59-66.

1403. Sterba, James P. "Save the Oil Rigs? Yes, They Are an Ecologists' Pet." Asian Wall Street Journal. 5 May 1989, pp. 1 and 9.

1404. Stewart, Brent S. and Pamela K. Yochem. ""Pinniped Entanglement in Synthetic Materials in the Southern California Bight." Paper presented at the Second International Conference on Marine Debris, Honolulu, Hawaii, 2-7 April 1989.

1405. "Sting of a Dead Scorpion: Where Should Old Nuclear Submarines Go?" Oceans. vol. 16, no. 1, January-February 1983, pp. 66-67.

1406. Swartzman, Gordon L., Christine A. Ribie and Chisheng P. Huang. "Marine Debris Entanglement Mortality and Fur Seal Population: A Modeling Perspective." Paper presented at the Second International Conference on Marine Debris, Honolulu, Hawaii, 2-7 April 1989.

1407. Thacher, Peter S. and Nikki Meith-Avcin. "The Oceans: Health and Prognosis." Elisabeth Mann Borgese and Norton Ginsburg, eds. Ocean Yearbook 1. Chicago and London: University of Chicago Press, 1978, pp. 293-339.

1408. Tillman, Michael F. "Marine Debris in the Antarctic." Paper presented at the Second International Conference on Marine Debris, Honolulu, Hawaii, 2-7 April 1989.

Reports the results of monitoring the problem of marine debris in the relatively pristine Antarctic.

1409. Timagenes, Gregorios J. International Control of Marine Pollution. 2 vols. Dobbs Ferry, NY: Ocean Publications, Inc., 1980.

Until the publication of John Warren Kindt's work in 1986, this was the comprehensive and up-to-date study of marine pollution. Still a most useful reference book on the subject.

1410. Tolba, Mostafa K. "The Global Agenda and the Hazardous Wastes Challenge." Marine Policy. vol. 14, no. 3, May 1990, pp. 205-209.

1411. Triggs, Gillian D., ed. The Antarctica Treaty Regime: Law, Environment and Resources. Cambridge (UK): Cambridge University Press, 1987.

1412. Tyack, Peter L. "Let's Have Less Public Relations and More Ecology." Oceanus. vol. 32, no. 1, Spring 1989, pp. 103-108.

1413. _____ and Laela S. Sayigh. "Those Dolphins Aren't Just Whistling in the Dark." Oceanus. vol. 32, no. 1, Spring 1989, pp. 80-83.

1414. "UNEP Calls for Tough Controls on Hazardous Waste Movements." The Siren. no. 37, July 1988.

1415. "The United Nations Environment Programme Conference on Plenipotentiaries on the Global Convention on the Control of Transboundary Movements of Hazardous Wastes: Final Act and Text of Basel Convention." International Legal Materials. vol. xxviii, no. 3, May 1989, pp. 649-686.

1416. "The United Nations General Assembly Report on the Marine Environment." Oceans Policy News. December 1989, pp. 5-6.

1417. United Nations, Office of the Special Representative of the Secretary-General for the Law of the Sea. Pollution by Dumping. New York: 1985.

This is a volume devoted to the legislative history of Articles 1, 210 and 216 of the 1982 Law of the Sea Convention on pollution by dumping. The bulk of the volume is concerned with negotiations at the Third Law of the Sea Conference relating to the ocean dumping issue.

1418. "U. S. A.: Problem of Ship-Generated Garbage/Marine Debris in the Marine Environment." UNEP (OCA) CAR IG.2.CRP.10, 28 October 1987, (1).

1419. "U. S. Is Denounced on Acid Rain Study." The New York Times. 9 January 1988, p. I-7.

1420. "Using the Protective Principle to Unilaterally Enforce Transnational Marine Pollution Standards." LOS Lieder. vol. 3, no. 3. Honolulu: The Law of the Sea Institute, University of Hawaii, December 1989, pp. 2-4.

1421. Vacarro, Ralph, Judith M. Capuzzo and Nancy H. Marcus. "The Oceans and U.S. Sewage Sludge Disposal Strategy." Oceanus. vol. 24, no. 1, Spring 1981, pp. 55-59.

1422. "Vacuum Method of Reducing Oil Pollution Proposed." IMO News. no. 1, 1989.

1423. Valenzuela, Mario. "IMO: Public International Law and Regulation." Douglas M. Johnston and Norman G. Letalik, eds. The Law of the Sea and Ocean Industry: New Opportunities and Restraints. Honolulu: The Law of the Sea Institute, University of Hawaii, 1984, pp. 141-151.

1424. Valiela, Ivan and Susan Vince. "Green Borders of the Sea." Oceanus. vol. 19, no. 3, Spring 1976, pp. 10-17.

1425. Vandermeulen, John H. "Effects of Chemical Contaminants in the Coastal Zone." Douglas M. Johnston and Norman G. Letalik, eds. The Law of the Sea and Ocean Industry: New Opportunities and Restraints. Honolulu: The Law of the Sea Institute, University of Hawaii, 1984, pp. 270-295.

1426. Van Dyke, Jon M. "Ocean Disposal of Nuclear Wastes." Marine Policy. vol. 12, no. 2, April 1988, pp. 82-95.

1427. Waldichuk, Michael. "Control of Marine Pollution: An Essay Review." Ocean Development and International Law. vol. 4, no. 3, 1977, pp. 269-296.

1428. Wallace, Barbara. "Shipping Industry Marine Debris Education Plan." Paper presented at the Second International Conference on Marine Debris, Honolulu, Hawaii, 2-7 April 1989.

1429. Walsh, James P. "U. S. Policy on Marine Pollution: Changes Ahead." Oceanus. vol. 24, no. 1, Spring 1981, pp. 18-24.

1430. Wang, Cheng-Pang. "A Review of the Enforcement Regime for Vessel-Source Oil Pollution Control." Ocean Development and International Law. vol. 16, no. 4, 1986, pp. 305-340.

Identifies the currently applicable international law intended to regulate vessel-source pollution and the enforcement regime in IMCO conventions and the 1982 Law of the Sea Convention.

1431. Wells, P. G. and R. P. Cate. "Protecting Marine Environment Quality from Land-based Pollutants: The Strategic Role of Ecotoxicology." Marine Policy. vol. 12, no. 1, January 1988.

1432. Wilber, R. Jude. "Plastic in the North Atlantic." Oceanus. vol. 30, no. 3, Fall 1987, pp. 61-68.

1433. Wiswall, F. L., Jr.   "The IMO: Private International Law and Regulation." Douglas M. Johnston and Norman G. Letalik, eds. The Law of the Sea and Ocean Industry: New Opportunities and Restraints. Honolulu: The Law of the Sea Institute, University of Hawaii, 1984, pp. 183-189.

1434. Wolfe, D. A., M. A. Champ, F. A. Cross, D. R. Kester, P. K. Park and R. L. Swanson. "Marine Pollution in China." Oceanus. vol. 26, no. 4, Winter 1983-84, pp. 40-47.

1435. Wolman, Abel.   "Pollution as an International Issue." Foreign Affairs. vol. 47, no. 1, October 1968, pp. 164-175.

1436. Woodiffe, J. C.   "Port Visits by Nuclear Armed Naval Vessels: Recent Practice." International and Comparative Law Quarterly.   vol. 35, part 3, July 1986, pp. 730-736.

1437. Woodward, Jennifer. "International Pollution Control: The United States and Canada: The International Joint Commission." New York Law School Journal of International and Comparative Law. vol. 9, nos. 2-3, 1988, pp. 325-344.

The article discusses the joint effort by the United States and Canada in enacting and enforcing legislation for water pollution control in the Great Lakes; it is another study on transboundary pollution control.

1438. Yagi, Nobuyuki and Yoshie Otsuka. "Clean-Up Program in Japan." Paper presented at the Second International Conference on Marine Debris, Honolulu, Hawaii, 2-7 April 1989.

1439. Yoshida, Kazumoto, N. Baba and Masashi Kiyota. "Studies of the Effects of Net Fragment Entanglement on Northern Fur Seals. Part 1: Daily Activity Pattern of Entangled and Non-Entangled Fur Seals." Paper presented at the Second International Conference on Marine Debris, Honolulu, Hawaii, 2-7 April 1989.

1440. _____, N. Baba and Masashi Kiyota. "Studies of the Effects of Net Fragment Entanglement on Northern Fur Seals. Part 2: Swimming Behavior of Entangled and Non-Entangled Fur Seals." Paper presented at the Second International Conference on Marine Debris, Honolulu, Hawaii, 2-7 April 1989.

Regional Arrangements for Marine Environmental Protection and Pollution Control

1441. "Agreement on the Implementation of a European Project on Pollution, on the Topic 'Sewage Sludge Processing.'" International Legal Materials. vol. xii, no. 1, January 1973, pp. 863-878.

1442. Alexander, Lewis M. "Regionalism and the Law of the Sea: The Case of Semi-enclosed Seas." Ocean Development and International Law. vol. 2, no. 2, Summer 1974, pp. 151-186.

1443. _____. "Regionalism at Sea: Concept and Reality." Douglas M. Johnston, ed. Regionalization of the Law of the Sea. Cambridge, MA: Ballinger Publishing Company, 1978, pp. 3-16.

1444. Andreev, Anatoly. "Activities of the Intergovernmental Maritime Consultative Organization in the Field of Prevention and Control of Operational and Accidental Pollution Emanating from Ships." Thomas A. Clingan, Jr. and Lewis M. Alexander, eds. Hazards of Maritime Transit. Cambridge, MA: Ballinger Publishing Company, 1973, pp. 29-47.

1445. Andresen, Steinar. "The Environmental North Sea Regime: A Successful Regional Approach?" Elisabeth Mann Borgese, Norton Ginsburg and Joseph R. Morgan, eds. Ocean Yearbook 8. Chicago and London: University of Chicago Press, 1989, pp. 378-401.

The author, from Norway's Fridtjof Nansen Institute, discusses the extensive regulation of contaminants by various regional ad hoc agreements for the North Sea environmental regime.

1446. Atwood, Donald K., Fred J. Burton, Jorge E. Corredor, George R. Harvey, Alfonso J. Mata-Jiminez, Alfonso Vasquez-Botello and Barry A. Wade. "Petroleum Pollution in the Caribbean." Oceanus. vol. 30, no. 4, Winter 1987-88, pp. 25-32.

Discusses the effects of oil pollution in the Caribbean by investigating the existence of tar on beaches, floating tar and sources of oil contamination.

1447. Bender, Klaus. "Marine Environmental Protection in the Scandinavian Countries." Comparative Marine Policy. Brooklyn, NY: J. F. Bergin Publishers, Inc., 1981, pp. 179-185.

1448. Bilder, Richard B. "The Canadian Arctic Waters Pollution Prevention Act." Lewis M. Alexander, ed. The Law of the Sea: The United Nations and Ocean Management. Kingston, RI: University of Rhode Island, 1971, pp. 204-223.

1449. Boczek, Boleslaw A. "International Protection of the Baltic Sea Environment against Pollution: A Study in Marine Regionalism." American Journal of International Law. vol. 72, no. 4, October 1978, pp. 782-814

This is a detailed study which shows how the seven Baltic states approached the problem of combating and controlling the pollution of their common marine heritage. Focuses on the international regional approach embodied in the 1974 Baltic Convention and other agreements attempting to solve the environmental problems of the Baltic Sea.

1450. Boxer, Baruch. "Mediterranean Pollution: Problem and Response." Ocean Development and International Law. vol. 10, nos. 3-4, 1982, pp. 315-356.

Discusses the unique regional effort to control pollution of the Mediterranean Sea, but expresses some doubts whether the many dimensions of Mediterranean environmental problems will ever be dealt with adequately.

1451. Busha, Thomas S. "The Role of IMCO in Environmental Monitoring." Lewis M. Alexander, ed. The Law of the Sea: The United Nations and Ocean Management. Kingston, RI: University of Rhode Island, 1971, pp. 198-203

1452. "Caribbean Environment Program." Oceans Policy News. February 1990, p. 1-5.

1453. "Caribbean Environment Program." Oceans Policy News. July 1989, pp. 1-3.

1454. "CEP Strategy for Regional Cooperation." CEP News. vol. 3, no. 1, March 1989.

1455. Chasis, Sarah. "Marine Environmental Protection in the United States." Comparative Marine Policy. Brooklyn, NY: J. F. Bergin Publishers, Inc., 1981, pp. 187-194.

1456. Chircop, Aldo. "Participation in Marine Regionalism: An Appraisal in a Mediterranean Context." Elisabeth Mann Borgese, Norton Ginsburg and Joseph R. Morgan, eds. Ocean Yearbook 8. Chicago and London: University of Chicago Press, 1989, pp. 402-420.

This article discusses regionalism as a concept in the 1982 Law of the Sea Convention and a definition of Mediterranean regionalism. The article also provides a discussion of the guidelines for participation in regionalism by users and non-users.

1457. "Conference of Plenipotentiaries of the Coastal States of the Mediterranean Region for the Protection of the Mediterranean Sea, Barcelona, 2-16 February, 1976." Elisabeth Mann Borgese and Norton Ginsburg, eds. Ocean Yearbook 1. Chicago and London: University of Chicago Press, 1978, pp. 702-733.

1458. "Conference of Plenipotentiaries on Cooperation in the Protection and Development of the Marine and Coastal Environment of West and Central African Region, Abidjan, 16-23 March 1981." International Legal Materials. vol. xx, no. 3, May 1981, pp. 67-75.

1459. "Conference of Plenipotentiaries on the Protection and Development of the Marine Environment of the Wider Caribbean Region, 21-24 March 1983." International Legal Materials. vol. xxii, no. 2, March 1983, pp. 221-234.

1460. "Convention on the Protection of the Environment between Denmark, Finland, Norway and Sweden, 19 February 1974." International Legal Materials. vol. xii, no. 3, May 1974, pp. 591-597.

1461. Couper, A. D. and H. D. Smith. "The North Sea: Bases for Management and Planning in a Multi-State Sea Region." Douglas M. Johnson and Norman G. Letalik, eds. The Law of the Sea and Ocean Industry: New Opportunities and Restraints. Honolulu: The Law of the Sea Institute, University of Hawaii, 1984, pp. 63-88.

1462. Danusaputro, Munadjat. "Elements of an Environmental Policy and Navigational Scheme for Southeast Asia, with Special Reference to the Straits of Malacca." Douglas M. Johnston, ed. Regionalization of the Law of the Sea. Cambridge, MA: Ballinger Publishing Company, 1978, pp. 171-198.

1463. Davidson, Lynn. An Evaluation of International Protection Offered to Caribbean Coral Reefs and Associated Ecosystems. Woods Hole, MA: Woods Hole Oceanographic Institution, 1989.

1464. Dubais, Bernard A. "The 1976 London Convention on Civil Liability for Oil Pollution Damage from Offshore Operations." Journal of Maritime Law and Commerce. vol. 9, no. 61, 1977, pp. 61-77.

1465. Eriksson, Gudmundar. "Some Thoughts on Regional Marine Arrangements in the Developing World." Douglas M. Johnston, ed. Regionalization of the Law of the Sea. Cambridge, MA: Ballinger Publishing Company, 1978, pp. 95-102.

1466. "Environmental Priorities." Douglas M. Johnston, ed. Arctic Ocean Issues in the 1980s. Honolulu: The Law of the Sea Institute, University of Hawaii, 1982.

1467. "Goals Set for Programmes in Central Indian Ocean." IMS Newsletter. no. 51, 1989.

1468. Gold, Edgar. A New Law of the Sea for the Caribbean: An Examination of Marine Law and Policy Issues in the Lesser Antilles. NY: Springer-Verlag, 1989.

1469. _____. "The Protection of the Marine Environment: Compatability through Cooperation." Douglas M. Johnston, Edgar Gold and Phiphat Tangsubkul, eds. International Symposium on the New Law of the Sea in Southeast Asia: Developmental Effects and Regional Approaches. Halifax, NS: Dalhousie Ocean Studies Programme, 1983, pp. 121-125.

1470. Goldberg, Edward D. "The Oceans as Waste Space." Elisabeth Mann Borgese and Norton Ginsburg, eds. Ocean Yearbook 5. Chicago and London: University of Chicago Press, 1985, pp. 150-161.

1471. Haas, Peter M. Saving the Mediterranean: The Politics of International Environmental Cooperation. New York: Columbia University Press, 1990.

This is a significant contribution in the available literature for examining in detail the work of the Mediterranean Action Plan and its success with international environmental cooperation.

1472. "HELMEPA Protection Association: An Overview." Elisabeth Mann Borgese and Norton Ginsburg, eds. Ocean Yearbook 5 Chicago and London: University of Chicago Press, 1985, pp. 313-316.

Describes briefly the work of the Hellenic Marine Environment Protection Association for Greek-flag vessels and seafarers for the purpose of preserving the health of the oceans.

1473. "The International Convention Concerning Pollution and the Mediterranean." Elisabeth Mann Borgese and Norton Ginsburg, eds. Ocean Yearbook 6. Chicago and London: University of Chicago Press, 1986, pp. 572-573.

A brief view of the structures of the IMO relating to global marine pollution control and the progress made with respect to the three regional legal instruments of the Convention for Protection of the Mediterranean Sea against pollution.

1474. Jaenicke, Guenther. "Cooperation in the Baltic Area." Choon-ho Park, ed. The Law of the Sea in the 1980s. Honolulu: The Law of the Sea Institute, University of Hawaii, 1983, pp. 493-513.

1475. Janis, Mark W. "The Development of European Regional Law of the Sea." Ocean Development and International Law. vol. 1, no. 3, Fall 1973, pp. 275-290.

1476. _____. "The Roles of Regional Law of the Sea." San Diego Law Review. vol. 12, no. 3, 1975, pp. 553-568.

1477. Jenisch, Uwe. "Recent Law of the Sea Development in the Baltic Sea." German Foreign Affairs Review. no. 4, 1987.

1478. Douglas M. Johnston, ed. Regionalization of the Law of the Sea. Cambridge, MA: Ballinger Publishing Company, 1978.

1479. _____, Edgar Gold and Phiphat Tangsubkul, eds. International Symposium on the New Law of the Sea in Southeast Asia; Development Effects and Regional Approaches. Halifax, NS: Dalhousie Ocean Studies Programme, 1983.

1480. Kimball, Lee. "Regional Marine Resources Development: Growth by Necessity." Elisabeth Mann Borgese and Norton Ginsburg, eds. Ocean Yearbook 3. Chicago and London: University of Chicago Press, 1982, pp. 157-197

1481. Kingham, James. "Marine Environmental Protection: A Canadian Perspective." Comparative Marine Policy. Brooklyn, NY: J. F. Bergin Publisher, Inc., 1981, pp. 195-205.

1482. _____. "Marine Resources Management in the North Pacific Rim and Problems of Environmental Protection." Douglas M. Johnston, ed. Regionalization of the Law of the Sea. Cambridge, MA: Ballinger Publishing Company, 1978, pp. 161-163.

1483. Kirton, Allan. "Developing Country View of Environmental Issues." Edward Miles and John King Gamble, Jr., eds. Law of the Sea: Conference Outcomes and Problems of Implementation. Cambridge, MA: Ballinger Publishing Company, 1977, pp. 279-283.

1484. "Kuwait Regional Conference on the Protection and Development of the Marine Environment and the Coastal Areas of Bahrain, Iran, Iraq, Kuwait, Oman, Qatar, Saudi Arabia and the United Arab Emirates." International Legal Materials. vol. xvii, no. 3, May 1978, pp. 501-540.

1485. "Kuwait Regional Convention for Cooperation on the Protection of the Marine Environment from Pollution." Elisabeth Mann Borgese and Norton Ginsburg, eds. Ocean Yearbook 2. Chicago and London: University of Chicago Press, 1980, pp. 516-546.

1486. LeGault, L. "Canadian Arctic Waters Pollution Prevention Legislation." Lewis M. Alexander, ed. The Law of the Sea: The United Nations and Ocean Management. Kingston, RI: University of Rhode Island, 1971, pp. 294-300.

1487. Lundholm, Bengt. "The Oceans: Their Production and Pollution with the Baltic as a Case Study." Elisabeth Mann Borgese, ed. Pacem in Maribus. New York: Dodd Mead and Company, 1972, pp. 25-31.

1488. McManus, Robert. "Environmental Provisions in the Revised Single Negotiating Text." Edward Miles and John King Gamble, Jr., eds. Law of the Sea: Conference Outcomes and Problems of Implementation. Cambridge, MA: Ballinger Publishing Company, 1977, pp. 269-277.

1489. "Marine Pollution in the South-Eastern Caribbean Sea." CEP News. vol. 3, no. 1, March 1989.

1490. Meith, Nikki and Richard Helmer. "Marine Environment and Coastal Resources in Southeast Asia: A Threatened Heritage." Elisabeth Mann Borgese and Norton Ginsburg, eds. Ocean Yearbook 4. Chicago and London: University of Chicago Press, 1983, pp. 260-294.

This paper tells the story of the action plan adopted by the five members of the Association of Southeast Asian Nations (ASEAN)--Indonesia, Malaysia, Philippines,Singapore and Thailand--to control pollution from oil and from land-based sources. It was a regional sea action plan sponsored by the United Nations Environmental Programme.

1491. M'Gonigle, R. Michael and Mark W. Zacher. Pollution, Politics and International Law: Tankers at Sea. Berkeley, CA: University of California Press, 1979.

1492. Miles, Edward L. and Scott Allen, ed. The Law of the Sea and Ocean Development Issues in the Pacific Basin. Honolulu: The Law of the Sea Institute, University of Hawaii, 1983.

1493. Negroponte, John D. "Introduction, Caribbean Marine Science." Oceanus. vol. 30, no. 4, Winter 1987-88, pp. 2-8.

The article discusses the cooperative projects dealing with marine pollution in the Caribbean area.

1494. "OAS Marine Protected Areas Inventory." Oceans Policy News. April, 1989, pp. 1-2.

1495. "Oil Spill Incidents." CEP News. vol. 3, no. 1, March 1989.

1496. Okidi, C. O. Regional Control of Ocean Pollution: Legal and Institutional Problems and Prospects. The Hague, Netherlands: Martinus Nijhoff, and London: Graham & Trotman, LTD., 1978.

1497. _____ . "Toward Regional Arrangements to Regulation of Marine Pollution: An Appraisal of Options." Ocean Development and International Law. vol. 4, no. 1, 1977, pp. 1-26.

1498. Oxman, Bernard H. "Ocean Pollution: What Can the Law of the Sea Conference Do?" John King Gamble, Jr. and Giulio Pontecorvo, eds. Law of the Sea: The Emerging Regime of the Oceans. Cambridge, MA: Ballinger Publishing Company, 1974, pp. 343-346.

1499. Parry, John. "Regional Seas: United Nations Environmental Programme Expands beyond the Mediterranean." Oceans. vol. 14, no. 2, March-April, 1981, pp. 65-67.

Describes the work of the ten regional seas programs of the UN Environmental Programme for some 110 countries of the world.

1500. Pathmarajah, Meera and Nikki Meith. "A Regional Approach to Marine Environmental Problems in East Africa and the Indian Ocean." Elisabeth Mann Borgese and Norton Ginsburg, eds. Ocean Yearbook 5. Chicago and London: University of Chicago Press, 1985, pp. 162-191

1501. Piyakarnchana, Twesukdi. "Some Thailand Strategies on Marine Pollution." Douglas M. Johnston, Edgar Gold and Phiphat Tangsirbkul, ed. International Symposium on the New Law of the Sea in Southeast Asia: Developmental Effects and Regional Approaches. Halifax, NS: Dalhousie Ocean Studies Programme, 1983, pp. 113-114.

1502. Price, R. The Maritime Law of the Arabian Gulf Cooperation Council States. The Hague, Netherlands: Martinus Nijhoff, and London: Graham & Trotman, Ltd., 1986.

1503. "Protocol for the Protection of the Mediterranean Sea against Pollution from Land-based Sources." Elisabeth Mann Borgese and Norton Ginsburg, eds. Ocean Yearbook 3. Chicago and London: University of Chicago Press, 1982, pp. 489-496.

1504. "Recommendatons for the Prevention and Control of Marine Pollution in the Wider Caribbean Region." IMO-UNEP-IOC Government of Mexico Seminar on the Control of Dumping and Other Waste Disposal Methods in the Wider Caribbean Region, Mexico City, 28 September - 1 October 1987. CARISEM/6/Rev.1, 1 October 1987 (8).

1505. "Regional Organizations, Law of the Sea Debate in the United Nations General Assembly." Oceans Policy News. December 1989, p. 3.

1506. "Report of the Meeting of Experts for the Development of a Protocol Concerning Specially Protected Areas and Wildlife in the Wider Caribbean." United Nations Environmental Programme. Meeting of Experts, St. Croix, 24-26 October 1989.

1507. Ritcher-Calder, Lord. "The Pollution of the Mediterranean." Elisabeth Mann Borgese and David Krieger,
eds. The Tides of Change: Peace, Pollution and Potential of the Oceans. New York: Mason/Charter, 1975,
pp. 144-165.

1508. Ross, David A. "The Red Sea: A New Ocean." Oceanus.
vol. 22, no. 3, Fall 1979, pp. 33-39.

1509. Saetevik, Sunneva. Environmental Cooperation between
the North Sea States: Success or Failure? Washington,
DC: Belhaven Press, 1988.

Translated into English, the study provides a general background of environmental cooperation in the North Sea, as
well as analyses of the legal and institutional framework of
the 1974 Paris Convention on Land-Based Pollution.

1510. Saliba, L. J. "Regional Measures for Marine Pollution
Control in the Mediterranean." Marine Pollution
Bulletin. vol. 26, no. 1, January 1989, pp. 12-17.

This article provides a study of the Mediterranean Action
Plan sponsored by the United Nations Environmental Programme
which culminated in the signing of the 1976 Convention for
the Protection of the Mediterranean Sea against Pollution at
Barcelona.

1511. Sambrailo, B. "Preservation of Marine Environment with
Special Reference to the Mediterranean and Adriatic
Seas." John King Gamble, Jr. and Giulio Pontecorvo,
eds. Law of the Sea: The Emerging Regime of the
Oceans. Cambridge, MA: Ballinger Publishing Company,
1974, pp. 333-341.

1512. Sarna, A. H. V. "Environmental Protection in Southeast
Asia." Douglas M. Johnston, Edgar Gold and Phiphat
Tangsubkul, eds. International Symposium on the New
Law of the Sea in Southeast Asia: Developmental
Effects and Regional Approaches. Halifax, NS:
Dalhousie Ocean Studies Programme, 1983, pp. 115-120.

1513. "SEAPOL International Conference: Ocean Development
and Management in Southeast Asia: Prospects for Implementation of the UN Convention on the Law of the Sea."
Marine Policy. vol. 12, no. 1, January 1987, pp. 49-66

1514. "Second International Conference on the Protection of
the North Sea: Ministerial Declaration Calling for
Reduction of Pollution." International Legal Materials
vol. xxvii, no. 3, May 1988, pp. 835-848.

1515. Thacher, Peter S. "UNEP: An Update on the Regional Sea
Programme." Elisabeth Mann Borgese and Norton
Ginsburg, eds. Ocean Yearbook 4. Chicago and London:
University of Chicago Press, 1984, pp. 450-461.

This paper provides a brief history of the origin, purposes
and progress of the regional approach to solving ocean

pollution problems through the United Nations Environmental Programme (UNEP).

1516. _____, "The Caribbean Example." Elisabeth Mann Borgese and Norton Ginsburg, eds. Ocean Yearbook 3. Chicago and London: University of Chicago Press, 1982, pp. 223-257.

A fairly thorough analysis of the action plan for marine environmental protection in the wider Caribbean region in all aspects.

1517. _____ and Nikki Meith. "Approaches to Regional Marine Problems: A Progress Report on UNEP's Regional Seas Program." Elisabeth Mann Borgese and Norton Ginsburg, eds. Ocean Yearbook 2. Chicago and London: University of Chicago Press, 1980, pp. 153-182.

1518. "UNEP: An Update on the Regional Seas Programme." Elisabeth Mann Borgese and Norton Ginsburg, eds. Ocean Yearbook 4. Chicago and London: University of Chicago Press, 1984, pp. 450-462.

Provides update material on the work of the UN Regional Seas Programme.

1519. United Nations Office of Special Representative of the Secretary-General for the Law of the Sea. "Symposium on Marine Cooperation in the Mediterranean Sea; Third Tunis Declaration, 28 November 1986." Law of the Sea Bulletin. no. 9, April 1987, pp. 62-64.

1520. Valencia, Mark J. "Southeast Asia: National Marine Interests and Marine Regionalism." Ocean Development and International Law. vol. 5, no. 4, 1978, pp. 421-476.

Discusses the semi-enclosed South China Sea as a logical site for regional cooperation on marine resources protection and regional marine arrangements.

1521. Vallega, Adalberto. "A Human Geographical Approach to Semi-enclosed Seas: The Mediterranean Case." Elisabeth Mann Borgese and Norton Ginsburg, eds. Ocean Yearbook 7. Chicago and London: University of Chicago Press, 1987, pp. 372-393.

Analyzes the present situation, the Mediterranean community's relation to the sea, the semi-enclosed sea nature, and human geography of the sea.

1522. Voigt, Klaus. "The Baltic Sea: Pollution Problems and Natural Environmental Changes." Jacques G. Richardson, ed. Managing the Ocean: Resources, Research, Law. Mt. Airy, MD: Lomond Publications, Inc., 1985, pp. 159-167

1523. Vrancken, P. "Sub-Saharan African Regional Marine and Coastal Environment Conventions: Analysis and Possible

Implications for South Africa." <u>Sea Changes</u>. no. 7, 1988, pp. 62-78.

1524. Wilson, A. Meriwether. "Caribbean Marine Resources: A Report on Economic Opportunities." <u>Oceanus</u>. vol. 30, no. 4, Winter 1987-88, pp. 33-41.

1525. Woodley, Jeremy D. "Jamaica: Managing Marine Re- sources." <u>Oceanus</u>. vol. 30, no. 4, Winter 1987-88, pp. 85-86.

Military Uses of the Ocean
Space: Legality, Prohibitions
and Restrictions

1526. Abbadi, Abdelkader K. "Security and Cooperation in the Mediterranean Basin." Ocean Development and International Law. vol. 14, no. 1, 1984, pp. 55-78.

1527. Abir, Mordechai. Oil, Power and Politics: Conflict in Arabia, the Red Sea and the Gulf. London: Frank Case, 1974.

1528. Alexander, Lewis M. and Joseph R. Morgan. "Choke Points of the World Ocean: A Geographic and Military Assessment." Elisabeth Mann Borgese, Norton Ginsburg and Joseph R. Morgan, eds. Ocean Yearbook 7. Chicago and London: University of Chicago Press, 1988, pp. 340-355.

Discusses closure or restricting of flow of ocean traffic in localities around the world; three case studies for coastal states to control these "choke points."

1529. Allen, Scott. "The Elements of Seapower: Mahan Revisited." Elisabeth Mann Borgese, Norton Ginsburg and Joseph R. Morgan, eds. Ocean Yearbook 7. Chicago and London: University of Chicago Press, 1988, pp. 317-339.

Discusses the purposes of navies, conditions affecting sea power as Mahan envisioned.

1530. Allmendinger, Eugene. "Submersibles: Past-Present-Future." Oceanus. vol. 25, no. 1, Spring 1982, pp. 18-29.

1531. Arkin, William M. "Troubled Waters: The Navy's Aggressive War Strategy." Technology Review. vol. 92, no. 1, January 1989.

1532. Aune, Bjorn. "Piracy and Its Repression under the 1982 Law of the Sea Convention." Elisabeth Mann Borgese, Norton Ginsburg and Joseph R. Morgan, eds. Ocean Year-

book 8.   Chicago and London: University of Chicago
Press, 1989, pp. 18-43.

Provides background on types of piracy today and repression
of piracy in the multizonal regime.

1533. "The Australians and the Indian Ocean: The Strategic
Dimensions of Australia's Increasing Naval Involvement
in the Indian Ocean." Center for Indian Ocean Regional
Studies, Custin University of Technology, 28-30 March
1988.

1534. Badurina, Berislav.   "Military Force in the Mediterranean." Elisabeth Mann Borgese and David Krieger,
eds.   The Tides of Change: Peace, Pollution and
Potential of the Oceans. New York: Mason/Charter,
1975, pp. 197-209.

1535. Baradolia, P. D. "Limiting Naval Armaments and Controlling Conversion from Military Production." Marine
Policy. vol. 14, no. 2, March 1990, pp. 125-136.

1536. Barber, Jack E. "The Legality of the Right of a Non-
Belligerent to Shoot Down a Civilian Airline over
International Waters: Use of Force in International
Law." Towson State Journal of International Law. vol.
xxiii, no. 2, Spring 1989, pp. 43-58.

1537. Barnaby, C. F. "Superpower Military Activities in the
World's Oceans." Elisabeth Mann Borgese and Norton
Ginsburg, eds. Ocean Yearbook 5. Chicago and London:
University of Chicago Press, 1982, pp. 223-239.

1538. Barnaby, F. "Antarctica: The First of Five Nuclear
Weapon Free Zones."   Journal of Human Environment.
vol. xviii, no. 1, 1989.

1539. _____. "Military Uses of the Ocean." Jacques G.
Richardson, ed. Managing the Oceans: Resources,
Research, Law. Mt. Airy, MD: Lomond Publications,
Inc., 1985, pp. 357-370.

1540. _____. The ASW Problem: ASW Detection and Weapon
Systems." Elisabeth Mann Borgese and Norton Ginsburg,
eds. Ocean Yearbook 1. Chicago and London: University
of Chicago Press, 1978, pp. 380-385.

1541. _____. "Strategic Submarines and Anti-submarine
Warfare." Elisabeth Mann Borgese and Norton Ginsburg,
eds. Ocean Yearbook 1. Chicago and London: University
of Chicago Press, 1978, pp. 376-379.

1542. Barry, James A., Jr. "The Seabed Arms Control Issue,
1967-1971: A Superpower Symbiosis?" Richard B. Lillich
and John Norton Moore, eds. U. S. Naval War College
International Law Studies, Readings in International
Law from War College Review 1974-1977. vol. 61. Newport, RI: Naval War College Press, 1980, pp. 572-585.

1543. Boczek, Boleslaw A. "Law of Warfare at Sea and Neutrality: Lessons from the Gulf War." Ocean Development and International Law. vol. 20, no. 3, 1989, pp. 239-272.

1544. _____. "Peaceful Purposes Provisions of the United Nations Convention on the Law of the Sea." Ocean Development and International Law. vol. 20, no. 4, 1989, pp. 359-390.

Discusses those provisions in the 1982 Law of the Sea Convention that address peaceful purposes. It examines the term "peaceful purpose" through antecedents such as the 1959 Antarctic Treaty, 1967 Outer Space and Moon Treaties, and 1971 Seabed Arms Control Treaty. The focus of the paper is an analysis of the peaceful purposes clauses contained in the Law of the Sea Convention.

1545. _____. "The Peaceful Purposes Reservation of the United Nations Convention on the Law of the Sea." Elisabeth Mann Borgese, Norton Ginsburg and Joseph R. Morgan, eds. Ocean Yearbook 8. Chicago and London: University of Chicago Press, 1989, pp. 329-361.

The article, almost identical to the previous entry, is a more recent inquiry into the peaceful purpose provisions in the 1982 Law of the Sea Convention. Analyzes and interprets the meaning of those provisions dealing with peaceful uses of the seas.

1546. _____. "Peacetime Military Activities in the Exclusive Economic Zone of Third World Countries." Ocean Development and International Law. vol. 19, no. 6, 1988, pp. 445-468.

1547. Booth, Kenneth. "The Military Implications of the Changing Law of the Sea." John King Gamble, Jr., ed. Law of the Sea: Neglected Issues. Honolulu: The Law of the Sea Institute, University of Hawaii, 1979, pp. 328-397.

Takes the position that there has always been a connection between naval strategy and law of the sea. The key question is: "In what fundamental way do international legal ocean regimes affect the exercise of naval power?"

1548. Bosma, John T. "The Alternative Future of Naval Force." Ocean Development and International Law. vol. 5, nos. 2-3, 1978, pp. 181-248.

1549. Breckner, Norman V. "Some Dimensions of Defense Interest in the Legal Delimitations of the Continental Shelf." Lewis M. Alexander, ed. The Law of the Sea: National Policy Recommendations. Kingston, RI: University of Rhode Island, March 1970, pp. 188-192.

1550. Brill, Richard. "Disarmament Interests on the Shelf." Lewis M. Alexander, ed. The Law of the Sea: International Rules and Organization for the Sea. Kingston,

RI: University of Rhode Island, March 1969, pp. 234-238.

1551. Brittin, Burdick H. "The Two Faces of Piracy." Thomas A. Clingan, Jr., ed. The Law of the Sea: What Lies Ahead? Honolulu: The Law of the Sea Institute, University of Hawaii, 1988, pp. 424-431.

1552. Burbridge, P. R. "Coastal and Marine Resource Management in the Straits of Malacca." AMBIO. vol. xvii, no. 3, 1988, pp. 170-177.

1553. Burke, William T. "Threats to the Public Order of the Oceans." Jon M. Van Dyke, Lewis M. Alexander and Joseph R. Morgan, eds. International Navigation: Rocks and Shoals Ahead? Honolulu: The Law of the Sea Institute, University of Hawaii, 1988, pp. 384-391.

1554. Busha, Thomas S. "Monitoring and Surveillance: Navigation." Elisabeth Mann Borgese and Norton Ginsburg, eds. Ocean Yearbook 3. Chicago and London: University of Chicago Press, 1982, pp. 118-125.

1555. Buzan, Barry. "Naval Power, the Law of the Sea and the Indian Ocean as a Zone of Peace." Marine Policy. July 1981, pp. 194-204.

Discusses the rights of warships and the implementation of the declaration of the Indian Ocean as a Zone of Peace--by raising the issues of superpower rivalry, the geostrategic position and the incompatibilities between the zone and the law of the sea.

1556. Clingan, Thomas A., Jr. "The Implications of the New Law of the Sea for Foreign Policy, National Security Policy and Economic Development Issues in the Pacific Basin." Edward L. Miles and Scott Allen, eds. The Law of the Sea and Ocean Development Issues in the Pacific Basin. Honolulu: The Law of the Sea Institute, University of Hawaii, 1983, pp. 20-32.

1557. _____. "The Next Twenty Years of Naval Mobility." Proceedings; Naval Review. 1980, pp. 82-93.

In terms of naval mobility, examines legal constraints in shaping naval forces by the provisions of the Law of the Sea Treaty then under negotiation.

1558. Conant, Melvin A. "Polar Strategic Concerns." Oceanus. vol. 28, no. 2, Summer 1985, pp. 62-66.

Discusses the Arctic region as an area of major power conflict and the relative quiet in Antarctic waters.

1559. Cottrell, Alvin J. and Associates. Sea Power and Strategy in the Indian Ocean. Beverly Hills, CA and London: Sage Publications, Inc., 1981.

This is a three-part volume, with an introduction by Thomas
H. Moorer, on naval strategy in the Indian Ocean.

1560. _____ and R. M. Burrell. "Soviet-U. S. Naval
Competition in the Indian Ocean." ORBIS. vol. xviii,
no. 4, Winter 1975, pp. 1109-1128.

1561. Craven, John P. "International Security on the
Seabed." Lewis M. Alexander, ed. The Law of the Sea:
International Rules and Organization for the Sea.
Kingston, RI: University of Rhode Island, March 1969,
pp. 414-419

1562. Cunha, Derek da. Soviet Naval Power in the Pacific.
Boulder, CO: Lynne Rienner Publishers, 1990.

1563. Dalton, Harvey. "Comments on National Security Concerns." Jon M. Van Dyke, Lewis M. Alexander and
Joseph R. Morgan, eds. International Navigation: Rocks
and Shoals Ahead? Honolulu: The Law of the Sea Institute, University of Hawaii, 1988, pp. 373-375.

1564. Daniel, Donald C. "Antisubmarine Warfare in the
Nuclear Age." ORBIS. vol. 28, no. 3, Fall 1984, pp.
527-552.

1565. Darby, Joseph J. "The Soviet Doctrine of the Closed
Sea." San Diego Law Review. vol. 23, no.3, May-June
1986, pp. 685-699.

This article examines the Soviet doctrine of the closed sea:
warships of any non-littoral nation possess the right to
enter and navigate enclosed or semi-enclosed seas such as
the Black Sea. The application of the doctrine, which has
never been a part of customary international law, is analyzed in view of recent history and developments in law of
the sea.

1566. "Discussion: Security Concerns and Coastal State
Interests." Jon M. Van Dyke, Lewis M.Alexander and
Joseph R. Morgan, eds. International Navigation: Rocks
and Shoals Ahead? Honolulu: The Law of the Sea Institute, University of Hawaii, 1988, pp. 377-382.

1567. Duncan, Jeffrey S. "The Tomahawk Nuclear Cruise Missile: Arguments For and Against." Oceanus. vol. 28,
no. 2, Summer 1985, pp. 55-61.

Before the Desert Shield of 1991, discusses the sea-launched
cruise missile and how it affects both arms control and
military strategy.

1568. Egge, Bjorn. "An International Multipurpose Surveillance System." Elisabeth Mann Borgese and David
Krieger, eds. The Tides of Change: Peace, Pollution
and Potential of the Oceans. New York: Mason/Charter,
1975, pp. 121-139.

1569. Farid, Abdel Majid. The Red Sea: Prospects for Stabil-
      ity. New York: St. Martin Press, 1984.

1570. "Fighting the Mines of August." NEWSWEEK, 20 August
      1984, pp. 48-49.

Provides a good description of American ships, choppers and
men engaged in the mine sweep in the Persian Gulf during the
Iran-Iraqi war.

1571. "Final Declaration of the Review Conference of Parties
      to the Treaty on the Prohibition of the Emplacement of
      Nuclear Weapons and Other Weapons of Mass Destruction
      on the Seabed and the Ocean Floor and in the Subsoil
      Thereof." Elisabeth Mann Borgese and Norton Ginsburg,
      eds. Ocean Yearbook 2.   Chicago and London: Univer-
      sity of Chicago Press, 1980, pp. 555-558.

1572. Fong, Gracie.   "Comments on the South Pacific Nuclear
      Free Zone Treaty." Jon M. Van Dyke, Lewis M. Alexander
      and Joseph R. Morgan, eds. International Navigation:
      Rocks and Shoals Ahead? Honolulu: The Law of the Sea
      Institute, University of Hawaii, 1988, pp. 365-366.

1573. Friedham, Robert L., George O. Totten III, Haruhiro
      Fukui, Tsuneo Akaha, Masayuki Takeyama, Mamoru Koga
      and Hiroyuki Nakahara. Japan and the New Ocean Regime.
      Boulder, CO: Westview Press, 1984.

1574. Friedman, Norman. The U. S. Maritime Strategy. London:
      Janes Publishing, Inc., 1988.

Written by a respected naval authority, the book addresses
the United States doctrine known as "Maritime Strategy." It
opens discussion with a cogent exposition on national strategy and sea power.

1575. Friedmann, Wolfgang. The Future of the Oceans.   New
      York: George Braziller, 1971.

1576. Gardner, Paul F. "Tuna Poaching and Nuclear Testing in
      the South Pacific." ORBIS. vol. 32, no. 2, Spring
      1988, pp. 249-262.

1577. Garwin, Richard L. "Anti-submarine Warfare and
      National Security." Scientific American. vol. 227,
      no. 1, July 1972, pp. 14-25.

A useful technical discussion about missile-submarine deter-
rents of the superpowers; distinguishes anti-submarine
warfare techniques from techniques of submarines carrying
strategic offensive missiles.

1578. German, Robert K.   "Nuclear Free Zones: Norwegian
      Interest, Soviet Encouragement." ORBIS. vol. 26, no.
      2, Summer 1982, pp. 451-476.

1579. Ghebhardt, Alexander O. "Soviet and U. S. Interests in the Indian Ocean." <u>Asian Survey</u>. vol. xv, no. 8, August 1975, pp. 672-683.

1580. Goldblat, Jozef. "Law of the Sea and the Security of Coastal States." France T. Christy, Jr, Thomas A. Clingan, Jr., John King Gamble, Jr., H. Gary Knight and Edward Miles, eds. <u>Law of the Sea: Caracas and Beyond</u>. Cambridge, MA: Ballinger Publishing company, 1975, pp. 301-317.

1581. _____. "Review of the Seabed Treaty." Elisabeth Mann Borgese and Norton Ginsburg, eds. <u>Ocean Yearbook 2</u>. Chicago and London: University of Chicago Press, 1980, pp. 270-281.

1582. _____. "The Seabed Treaty." Elisabeth Mann Borgese and Norton Ginsburg, eds. <u>Ocean Yearbook 1</u>. Chicago and London: University of Chicago Press, 1978, pp. 386-411.

1583. Goldie, L. F. E. "Low Intensity Conflict at Sea." <u>Syracuse Journal of International Law and Commerce</u>. vol. 14, no. 4, 1988, pp. 597-656.

1584. Grunawalt, Captain Richard Jack, USN. "Belligerent and Neutral Rights in Straits and Archipelagoes." Thomas A. Clingan, Jr., ed. <u>The Law of the Sea: What Lies Ahead?</u> Honolulu: The Law of the Sea Institute, University of Hawaii, 1988, pp. 137-140.

1585. _____. "New Legal Issues Resulting from the U.S. Global Military Commitment: A Naval Perspective of the Persian Gulf Tanker War." <u>Proceedings</u>. The Law of the Sea Institute Annual Conference, University of Rhode Island, June 1988.

1586. Haerr, Roger Cooling. "The Gulf of Sidra." <u>San Diego Law Review</u>. vol. 24, no. 3, May-June 1987, pp. 751-767

1587. Halberstam, Malvina. "Terrorism on the High Seas: The Achille Lauro, Piracy and the IMO Convention on Maritime Safety." <u>American Journal of International Law</u>. vol. 82, no. 2, April 1988, pp. 269-310.

1588. Hanks, Robert J. and Alvin J. Cottrell. "The Strait of Hormuz: Strategic Chokepoint." Alvin J. Cottrell and Associates, eds. <u>Sea Power and Strategy in the Indian Ocean</u>. Beverly Hills, CA: Sage Publications, 1981, pp. 73-116.

An excellent discussion of the political changes in the Persian Gulf and the importance of the Strait of Hormuz with respect to the threat of piracy, terrorism, and military protection measures.

1589. Harlow, Bruce A. "UNCLOS III and Conflict Management in the Straits." Robert B. Krueger and Stefan A. Riesenfeld, eds. <u>The Developing Order of the Oceans</u>.

Honolulu: The Law of the Sea Institute, University of
Hawaii, 1985, pp. 678-686.

1590. Harrison, Selig S. and K. Subrahmangam. Superpower
Rivalry in the Indian Ocean. NY: Oxford University
Press, 1989.

Issues and problems in the Indian Ocean region as seen from
the views of three Americans and three Indians.

1591. Hill, Clarence A, Jr. "U. S. Law of the Sea Position
and Its Effect on the Operating Navy: A Naval
Officer's View." Ocean Development and International
Law. vol. 3, no. 4, 1976, pp. 341-360.

1592. Hirdman, Sven. "Prospects for Arms Control in the
Oceans." Elisabeth Mann Borgese and David Krieger,
eds. The Tides of Change: Peace, Pollution and Potential of the Oceans. New York: Mason/Charter, 1975, pp.
197-209.

1593. Hoagland, Porter, III. "The Roll of the U. S. Coast
Guard." Oceanus. vol. 28, no, 2, 1985, pp. 67-73.

1594. Holloway, James L., III. "The U. S. Navy: A Functional
Appraisal." Oceanus. vol. 28, no. 2, Summer 1985,
pp. 3-11.

1595. Hong, Moon-Shin. "Changing Direction of Power Balance
and the Sea Lanes Security in the Pacific Basin."
Edward L. Miles and Scott Allen, eds. The Law of the
Sea and Ocean Development Issues in the Pacific Basin.
Honolulu: The Law of the Sea Institute, University of
Hawaii, 1983, pp. 471-475.

Some important comments on the sea-lane security problem in
the Far East and Asia in the context of changing strategic
relationships of the major maritime powers.

1596. Hughes, Oscar. "The New Submarine Project." Maritime
Studies. vol. 37, November-December 1987.

1597. Huisken, Ronald. "Naval Forces." Elisabeth Mann
Borgese and Norton Ginsburg, eds. Ocean Yearbook 1.
Chicago and London: University of Chicago Press, 1978,
pp. 412-435.

1598. "Iraq-United States: Agreement on Compensation in
U.S.S. Stark Incident." International Legal Materials.
vol. xviii, no. 3, May 1989, pp. 644-648.

1599. Janis, Mark W. "Dispute Settlement in the Law of the
Sea Convention: The Military Activities Exception."
Ocean Development and International Law. vol. 4, no.
1, 1977, pp. 51-66.

1600. _____. Sea Power and the Law of the Sea. Lexington, MA: D. C. Heath and Company, 1976.

166 OCEAN POLITICS AND LAW

1601. _____. "The Soviet Navy and Ocean Law." Richard B. Lillich and John Norton Moore, eds. U. S. Naval War College International Law Studies, Readings in International Law from War College Review 1974-1977. vol. 61 Newport, RI: U. S. Naval War College Press, 1980, pp. 609-615.

1602. Jasani, Bhupendra M. "A Note on Ocean Surveillance from Space." Elisabeth Mann Borgese and Norton Ginsburg, eds. Ocean Yearbook 5. Chicago and London: University of Chicago Press, 1985, pp. 240-253.

1603. _____. "Ocean Surveillance by Earth Satelites." Elisabeth Mann Borgese and Norton Ginsburg, eds. Ocean Yearbook 2. Chicago and London: University of Chicago Press, 1980, pp. 250-269.

1604. Jones, Rodney W. "Ballistic Missile Submarine and Arms Control in the Indian Ocean." Asian Survey. vol. xx, no. 3, March 1980, pp. 269-279.

1605. Joyner, Christopher C. "Security Issues and the Law of the Sea: The Southern Ocean." Ocean Development and International Law. vol. 15, no. 2, 1985, pp. 171-196.

1606. Karkoszka, Andrzej. "Naval Forces." Elisabeth Mann Borgese and Norton Ginsburg, eds. Ocean Yearbook 2. Chicago and London: University of Chicago Press, 1980, pp. 199-225.

1607. Katchen, Martin H. "The Spratly Islands and the Law of the Sea: Dangerous Ground for Asian Peace." Asian Survey. vol. xvii, no. 12, December 1977, pp. 1167-1181.

1608. Keating, Colin. "The Nuclear Free Zone in the South Pacific." Thomas A. Clingan, Jr., ed. The Law of the Sea: What Lies Ahead? Honolulu: The Law of the Sea Institute, University of Hawaii, 1988, pp. 150-156.

1609. Kemp, Geoffrey. "Maritime Access and Maritime Power: The Past, the Persian Gulf and the Future." Alvin J. Cottrell and Associates, eds. Sea Power and Strategy in the Indian Ocean. Beverly Hills, CA: Sage Publications, 1981, pp. 15-71.

Discusses the various concepts of maritime power and the emerging maritime environment with focus on the growth of the Soviet Navy and its threat to Western oil sea lines of communication.

1610. Kime, Adm. J. W., U.S.C.G., and Daniel F. Sheehan. "Violence at Sea: Scope of the Problem." Thomas A. Clingan, Jr., ed. The Law of the Sea: What Lies Ahead? Honolulu: The Law of the Sea Institute, University of Hawaii, 1988, pp. 419-423.

1611. Kinley, Geoffrey. "The Law of Self-Defense, Contemporary Naval Operations and the United Nations Convention on the Law of the Sea." E.D. Brown and R.R. Churchill, eds. <u>The U. N. Convention on the Law of the Sea: Impact and Implementation</u>. Honolulu: The Law of the Sea Institute, University of Hawaii, 1987, pp. 10-40.

1612. Knauss, John A. "The Military Role in the Ocean and Its Relation to the Law of the Sea." Lewis M. Alexander, ed.<u>The Law of the Sea: A New Geneva Conference</u>. Kingston, RI: The Law of the Sea Institute, University of Rhode Island, 1972, pp. 77-86.

1613. Larkin, Bruce D. "East Asian Ocean Security Zones." Elisabeth Mann Borgese and Norton Ginsburg, eds. <u>Ocean Yearbook 2</u>. Chicago and London: University of Chicago Press, 1980, pp. 282-301.

1614. Larson, David L. "Naval Weaponry and the Law of the Sea." <u>Ocean Development and International Law</u>. vol. 18, no. 2, 1987, pp. 125-199.

This paper examines in considerable detail the major naval weapons systems as related to the law of the sea. It points out that the use of naval weapons systems is largely unrestricted by international law and the law of the sea. The author provides a summary of naval weaponry used, their legal status, and areas employed.

1615. _____. "Security Issues and the Law of the Sea: A General Framework." <u>Ocean Development and International Law</u>. vol. 15, no. 2, 1985, pp. 99-146.

1616. _____. and Michael W. Roth. "The Law of the Sea and Maritime Strategy." <u>Marine Policy</u>. vol. 13, no. 3, July 1989, pp. 193-217.

1617. Laursen, Finn. "Security Aspects of Danish and Norwegian Law of the Sea Policies." <u>Ocean Development and International Law</u>. vol. 18, no. 2, 1987, pp. 199-233.

The paper discusses the security issues that affect the law of the sea policies of Norway, Denmark and the Soviet Union, as the latter's Baltic Fleet must gain access to the North Atlantic Ocean by passing the Belts and the Danish or Norwegian strategic straits.

1618. _____. "Security versus Access to Resources: Explaining a Decade of U.S. Ocean Policy." <u>World Politics</u>. vol. xxxiv, no. 2, January 1982, pp. 197-229

1619. _____. <u>Superpower at Sea: U. S. Ocean Policy</u>. New York: Praeger, 1983.

1620. Lee, Roy S. "New Law of the Sea and the Pacific Basin." Edward L. Miles and Scott Allen, eds. <u>The Law of the Sea and Ocean Development Issues in the Pacific Basin</u>. Honolulu: The Law of the Sea Institute, University of Hawaii, 1983, pp. 5-19.

1621. Lissitzyn, Oliver J. "Electronic Reconnaissance from the High Seas and International Law." Richard B. Lillich and John Norton Moore, eds. U. S. Naval War College International Law Studies, Readings in International Law from War College Review 1974-1977. vol. 61. Newport, RI: Naval War College Press, 1980, pp. 563-571.

1622. Lowe, Vaughan. "The Impact of the Law of the Sea on Naval Warfare." Syracuse Journal of International Law and Commerce. vol. 14, no. 4, Special Issue, 1988, pp. 657-698.

While discussing some of the key provisions and problems contained in the Law of the Sea Treaty, raises questions about the traditional war and peace dichotomy as a satisfactory basis of modern law of armed conflict.

1623. Luard, Evan. The Control of the Seabed: A New International Issue. London: Heinemann, 1974.

1624. Luton, Gary. "Strategic Issues in the Arctic Region." Elisabeth Mann Borgese and Norton Ginsburg, eds. Ocean Yearbook 6. Chicago and London: University of Chicago Press, 1986, pp. 399-416.

1625. McCann, Kevin. "The Soviet Navy: Structure and Purposes." Elisabeth Mann Borgese and Norton Ginsburg, eds. Ocean Yearbook 6. Chicago and London: University of Chicago Press, 1986, pp. 346-361.

1626. McCormick, Gordon H. and Mark E. Miller. "American Seapower at Risk: Nuclear Weapons in Soviet Naval Planning." ORBIS. vol. 25, no. 2, Summer 1981, pp. 351-368.

1627. McDougal, Myres S. "Authority to Use Force on the High Sea." Richard B. Lillich and John Norton Moore, eds. U.S. Naval War College International Law Studies, Readings in International Law from War College Review 1974-1977. vol. 61. Newport, RI: Naval War College Press, 1980, pp. 551-562.

1628. MccGwire, Michael. "Changing Naval Operations and Military Intervention." Richard B. Lillich and John Norton Moore, eds. U. S. Naval War College International Law Studies, Readings in International Law from War College Review 1974-1977. vol. 61. Newport, RI: Naval War College Press, 1980, pp. 586-608.

Provides a historic perspective on the growth and objectives of the Soviet Navy.

1629. _____. "The Geopolitical Importance of Strategic Waterways in the Asian Pacific Region." ORBIS. vol. xviii, no. 4, Winter 1975, pp. 1037-1057.

1630. McIntosh, Malcolm. Arms across the Pacific: Security

and Trade Issues around the Pacific.   New York: St. Martin's, 1988.

1631. Maiava, Iosefa.   "The South Pacific   Nuclear Free Zone Treaty."   Jon M. Van Dyke, Lewis M. Alexander and Joseph R. Morgan, eds. International Navigation: Rocks and Shoals Ahead?   Honolulu: The Law of the Sea Institute, University of Hawaii, 1988, pp. 363-364.

1632. Martin, J. J. "Trident's Role in US Strategy: View I." Oceanus. vol. 28, no. 2, Summer 1985, pp. 38-44.

Discusses   the   role   of   the   Trident   submarine-launched missiles.

1633. Martin, L. W. and Hedley Bull. "The Strategic Consequences of Britain's Revised Naval Role." Edmund A. Gullion, ed. Uses of the Sea.   Englewood Cliffs, NJ: Prentice-Hall, 1968, pp. 113-137.

1634. Mauer, John Henry. "Sea Power and Crisis Diplomacy." ORBIS. vol. 26, no. 3, Fall 1982, pp. 569-572.

1635. Mehr, Farhaug. "Neutrality in the Gulf War." Ocean Development and International Law.   vol. 20, no. 1, 1989, pp. 105-107.

1636. Menefee, Samuel P. "Peaceful Uses of the Seas: Principles and Complexities." Marine Policy. vol. 12, no. 2, April 1988.

1637. Misra, K. P. "Developments in the Indian Ocean: The Littoral Response." International Studies. no. 16, July-December 1977, pp. 17-22.

1638. "Missile Test Aborted." Greenpeace. November-December 1989, p. 18.

1639. Mitchell, Peter A.   "The Navy's Mission in Space." Oceanus. vol. 28, no. 2, Summer 1985, pp. 22-30.

1640. Modelski, George and William R. Thompson. Seapower in Global Politics. New York: Oxford University Press, 1988.

This is a very informative book which compiles basic data on the strength of the world's navies between 1494 and 1993.

1641. Mooney, Rear Admiral J. B., Jr. "Naval Research and National Security." Oceanus. vol. 28, no. 2, Summer 1985, pp. 12-21.

1642. Moorer, Thomas and Alvin J. Cottrell.   "A Permanent U.S. Naval Presence in the Indian Ocean." Alvin J. Cottrell and Associates, eds. Sea Power and Strategy in the Indian Ocean. Beverly Hills, CA: Sage Publications, 1981, pp. 117-133.

Discusses the need for U.S. naval presence in the region.

1643. Morgan, Joseph R. "Naval Operations in the Antarctic Region: A Possibility?" Elisabeth Mann Borgese, Norton Ginsburg and Joseph R. Morgan, eds. Ocean Yearbook 8. Chicago and London: University of Chicago Press, 1989, pp. 362-377.

Discusses the military provisions of the Antarctic Treaty and the geostrategy in the region.

1644. _____. "Naval Bases, Base Rights and Port Access." Oceanus. vol. 32, no. 3, Fall 1989, pp. 85-88

1645. _____. "Small Navies." Elisabeth Mann Borgese and Norton Ginsburg, eds. Ocean Yearbook 6. Chicago and London: University of Chicago Press, 1986, pp. 362-389

1646. _____. "Structure and Prospects of Latin American Navies." Elisabeth Mann Borgese and Norton Ginsburg, eds. Ocean Yearbook 4. Chicago and London: University of Chicago Press, 1983, pp. 347-365.

1647. Morris, Michael A. "Southern Cone Maritime Security after the 1984 Argentine-Chilean Treaty of Peace and Friendship." Ocean Development and International Law. vol. 18, no. 2, 1987, pp. 235-254.

This paper is a study of the 1984 Argentine-Chilean Treaty of Peace and Friendship that removed the conflict between the two nations in the Southern Cone of South America adjacent to the South Atlantic and South Pacific Oceans.

1648. _____. "Military Aspects of the Exclusive Economic Zone." Elisabeth Mann Borgese and Norton Ginsburg, eds. Ocean Yearbook 3. Chicago and London: University of Chicago Press, 1982, pp. 320-348.

1649. _____. "Have U. S. Security Interests Really Been Sacrificed? A Reply to Admiral Hill." Ocean Development and International Law. vol. 4, no. 4, 1977, pp. 381-398.

1650. Morse, Robert W. "Acoustics and Submarine Warfare." Oceanus. vol. 20, no. 2, Spring 1977, pp. 67-72.

1651. "Navies in Foreign Policy." Orbis: A Journal of World Affairs. Fall, 1982, pp. 569-589.

Five experts contributed their views about the various questions relating to new maritime technologies and the impact of strategic deployment of navies.

1652. Narokobi, Camillus S. N. "Military Activities in the Exclusive Economic Zone." Jon M. Van Dyke, Lewis M. Alexander and Joseph R. Morgan, eds. International Navigation: Rocks and Shoals Ahead? Honolulu: The Law of the Sea Institute, University of Hawaii, 1988, pp. 342-343.

1653. Oda, Judge Shigeru. The Passage of Warships through Straits and Archipelagic Waters." Jon M. Van Dyke, Lewis M. Alexander and Joseph R. Morgan, eds. International Navigation: Rocks and Shoals Ahead? Honolulu: The Law of the Sea Institute, University of Hawaii, 1988, pp. 155-157.

1654. Osgood, Robert E. "U. S. Security Interests in Ocean Law." Ocean Development and International Law. vol. 2, no. 1, Spring 1974, pp. 1-36.

1655. Oxman, Bernard. "The Regime of Warships under the UNCLOS." Virginia Journal of International Law. vol. 24, 1948, pp. 809-863.

1656. Park, Choon-ho. "The 50-mile Military Boundary Zone of North Korea." American Journal of International Law. vol. 72, vol. 72, no. 4, October 1978, pp. 866-874.

1657. "The Persian/Arabian Gulf Tanker War: International Law of International Chaos." Ocean Development and International Law. vol. 19, no. 4, 198, pp. 381-399.

1658. Postal, Theodore A. "Trident and Strategic Stability: View II." Oceanus. vol. 28, no. 2, Summer 1985, pp. 45-54.

Another view on the complex design and capability of submarine launced missiles.

1659. Power, Paul F. "The South Pacific Nuclear-Weapon-Free Zone." Pacific Affairs. vol. 59, no. 3, Fall 1986, pp. 455-475.

Analyzes the main provisions of the Raratonga Treaty for a nuclear-free-zone in the South Pacific and the positions of China, France, Soviet Union and the United States.

1660. Purver, Ronald. "Arctic Security: The Murmansk Initiative and Its Impact." Current Research on Peace and Violence. vol. xi, no. 4, 1988, pp. 147-158.

1661. Queneudec, Jean-Pierre. "The Peaceful Use of International Maritime Areas." Christos Rozakis and Constantine A. Stephanou, eds. The New Law of the Sea. Amsterdam, North Holland: Elsevier Science Publishers B.V., 1983.

1662. Rais, Rasul B. The Indian Ocean and the Superpowers. Totowa, NJ: Rowman and Littlefield Publishers, Inc., 1987.

The central theme is that naval deployment by superpowers in the Indian Ocean should be seen in the context of economic and security interests rather than military rivalry.

1663. _____. "An Appraisal of U. S. Strategy in the Indian Ocean." Asian Survey. vol. xxiii, no. 9, September 1983, pp. 1043-1051.

Analyzes the diminishing U.S. influence in the Indian Ocean
as the result of many decades of "strategic neglect."

1664. Raphael, Perl. The Falkland Islands Dispute in Inter-
      national Law and Politics. Dobbs Ferry, NY: Oceana
      Publications, Inc., 1983.

1665. Richardson, Elliot L. "Power, Mobility and the Law of
      the Sea." Foreign Affairs. vol. 58, no. 4, Spring
      1980, pp. 902-919.

This paper analyzes the new importance of the classical uses
of seapower in the light of the oil crisis in the Middle
East and the need for keeping open the supply lines for
carrying oil from the Persian Gulf to the rest of the world.

1666. Rieman, Arthur M. "Creating a Nuclear Free Zone
      Treaty that is True to Its Name: The Nuclear Free Zone
      Concept and a Model Treaty." Denver Journal of Inter-
      national Law and Diplomacy. vol. 18, no. 2, Winter
      1990, pp. 209-278.

A most comprehensive analysis of the concept of the nuclear
free zone to remove the dangers of nuclear weapons, radioactive contamination and pollution, as well as a review of
some of the existing nuclear free zone treaties.

1667. Robertson, Cdr. J. W. "Security Interests and Regimes
      of the Sea." Lewis M. Alexander, ed. The Law of the
      Sea: The Future of the Sea's Resources. Kingston, RI:
      University of Rhode Island, February 1968, pp. 47-51.

1668. Ronzitti, N. The Law of Naval Warfare: A Collection of
      Agreements and Documents with Commentaries. Dordrecht,
      the Netherlands: Martinus Nijhoff, and London: Graham
      & Trotman Ltd., 1988.

This volume is a collection of materials dealing with the
law of naval warfare. The material consists of international conventions now in force, as well as agreements in
force and not in force, on naval warfare rules.

1669. Rose, Stephen. "Naval Activity in the Exclusive Eco-
      nomic Zone--Troubled Waters Ahead?" Ocean Development
      and International Law. vol. 21, no. 2, 1990, pp. 123-
      146.

The article surveys the types of exclusive economic zone
claims made since the Third UN Conference on the Law of the
Sea began in the 1970s.

1670. Russo, Francis V., Jr. "Neutrality at Sea in Transi-
      tion: State Practice in the Gulf War as Emerging
      International Customary Law." Ocean Development and
      International Law. vol. 19, no. 4, 1988, pp. 381-400.

By examining the belligerent and neutral conducts in the
"Tanker War," discusses naval warfare pertaining to the
rights of neutrals resulting from the Gulf War.

1671. Samuels, Marwyn S. Contest for the South China Sea. New York and London: Metheun, 1982.

1672. Schachte, Captain William L., Jr. "National Security Interests in the Central and Western Pacific." John P. Craven, Jan Schneider and Carol Stimson, eds. The International Implications of Extended Maritime Jurisdiction in the Pacific. Honolulu: The Law of the Sea Institute, University of Hawaii, 1989, pp. 388-401.

1673. Seth, S. P. "The Indian Ocean and Indo-American Relations." Asian Survey. vol. xv, no. 8, August 1975, pp. 645-653.

Discusses the facilities at Diego Garcia and the U.S.-Indian relationship in terms of global interests and Indian sensitivities.

1674. Shilling, David. "A Reassessment of Japan's Naval Defense Needs." Asian Survey. vol. xvi, no. 3, March 1976, pp. 216-229.

1675. Shyam, Manjula R. "The U. N. Convention on the Law of the Sea and Military Interests in the Indian Ocean." Ocean Development and International Law. vol. 15, no. 2, 1985, pp. 147-170.

1676. Silverstein, Harvey B. "Ocean Surveillance Technologies and International Payoffs." Ocean Development and International Law. vol. 10, nos. 1-2, 1980, pp. 187-198.

1677. Sinor, Morris. "National Security and Resource Management and Development." Jon M. Van Dyke, Lewis M. Alexander and Joseph R. Morgan, eds. International Navigation: Rocks and Shoals Ahead? Honolulu: The Law of the Sea Institute, University of Hawaii, 1988, pp. 333-336.

1678. Song, Yann-huei (Billy). "China and the Military Use of the Ocean." Ocean Development and International Law. vol. 21, no. 2, 1990, pp. 213-236.

This article discusses the importance of military use of the oceans in the development of China's marine policy. At the negotiations for the Third UN Conference on the Law of the Sea China went on record in favor of the superpowers' right of warship passage and insisted on a requirement for prior notification.

1679. "The Soviet Naval Forces." Oceanus. vol. 28, no. 2, Summer 1985, pp. 74-76.

An excerpt from the U.S. Department of Defense assessment of Soviet military power.

1680. Spindel, Robert C. "Anti-submarine Warfare." Oceanus. vol. 28, no. 2, Summer 1985, pp. 31-37.

Discusses the modern nuclear submarine and its strategic
mission; provides an analysis of anti-submarine warfare
(ASW) in its four phases of action: detection, identifi-
cation, localization and destruction.

1681. Sterner, Michael. "The Strategic Importance of the Red
Sea: A View from Washington." Abdel Majid Farid, ed.
The Red Sea: Prospects for Stability. New York: St.
Martin's Press, 1984, pp. 116-122.

1682. Telfer, Grant Richard. "Maritime Insurgency and the
Law of the Sea: An Analysis Using the Doctrine of Dis-
tress." San Diego Law Review. vol. 20, no. 3, April
1983, pp. 625-657.

1683. Thakur, Ramesh. "A Nuclear-Weapon-Free South Pacific:
A New Zealand Perspective." Pacific Affairs. vol. 58,
no. 2, Summer 1985, pp. 216-238.

Analyzes New Zealand's position in the South Pacific nuclear
free zone controversy.

1684. Thorpe, Capt. A. G. Y. "Mine Warfare at Sea: Some
Legal Aspects of the Future." Ocean Development and
International Law. vol. 18, no. 2, 1987, pp. 255-278.

The paper discusses the problems that new weapon technology
at sea are posing to traditional international law concepts.
This is illustrated by mine warfare at sea. Since wars are
no longer declared, the use of mines at sea raises questions
about the legality of their use as a weapon.

1685. Traavik, Kim and Willy Ostreng. "Security and Ocean
Law: Norway and the Soviet Union in the Barents Sea."
Ocean Development and International Law. vol. 4, no.
4, 1977, pp. 343-368.

1686. "Treaty on the Prohibition of the Emplacement of
Nuclear Weapons and Other Weapons of Mass Destruction
on the Seabed and Ocean Floor and in the Subsoil
Thereof: Appendix 15." George A. Doumani, ed. Ocean
Wealth: Policy and Potential. Rochelle Park, NJ:
Hayden Book Publishing Company, Inc., 1973, pp. 223-
229.

1687. Tsarev, V. F. "Peaceful Uses of the Seas: Principles
and Complexities." Marine Policy. vol. 12, no. 1,
April 1988, pp. 153-159.

1688. "U. S.-Soviet Incident in the Mediterranean." Oceans
Policy News. September-October 1989, p. 2.

1689. Vivekanandan, B. "The Indian Ocean as a Zone of Peace:
Problems and Prospects." Asian Survey. vol. xxi, no.
12, December 1981, pp. 1237-1249.

As the Indian Ocean region that includes the Persian Gulf is
a major source of oil for the world, an Indian scholar

argues the need to prevent any single naval power dominating the region.

1690. Vlahos, Michael. "Maritime Strategy versus Continental Commitment? ORBIS. vol. 26, no. 3, Fall 1982, pp. 583-590.

1691. Walker, George K. "Sea Power and the Law of the Sea: The Need for a Contextual Approach." Ocean Development and International Law. vol. 7, nos. 3-4, 1979, pp. 299-362.

1692. Wallace, Michele. "The Right of Warships to Operate in the Exclusive Economic Zone as Perceived by Delegates to the Third United Nations Law of the Sea Convention." Jon M. Van Dyke, Lewis M. Alexander and Joseph R. Morgan, eds. International Navigation: Rocks and Shoals Ahead? Honolulu: The Law of the Sea Institute, University of Hawaii, 1988, pp. 345-351.

1693. "The War beneath the Seas." Newsweek, 10 June 1985, pp. 36-38.

A very informative essay with illustrations on war or hide-and-seek technology at and beneath the sea.

1694. Weeks, Welford F. and Frank D. Carsey. "Remote Sensing of the Arctic Seas." Oceanus. vol. 29, no. 1, September 1986, pp. 59-65.

1695. Westing, Arthur H. "Military Impact on Ocean Ecology." Elisabeth Mann Borgese and Norton Ginsburg, eds. Ocean Yearbook 1. Chicago and London: University of Chicago Press, 1978, pp. 436-466.

1696. Wilkes, Owen. "Ocean-based Nuclear Deterrent Forces and Anti-submarine Warfare." Elisabeth Mann Borgese and Norton Ginsburg, eds. Ocean Yearbook 2. Chicago and London: University of Chicago Press, 1980, pp. 226-249.

1697. Winokur, Robert S. and Rene E. Gonzalez, Jr. "Ocean Science and Military Use of the Ocean." Oceanus. vol. 25, no. 4, Winter 1982-83, pp. 58-62.

Discusses the naval mission of power and control of the sea as basic functions.

1698. Young, Elizabeth. "Arms Control in the Oceans: Active and Passive." Elisabeth Mann Borgese and David Krieger, eds. The Tides of Change: Peace, Pollution and Potential of the Oceans. New York: Mason/Charter, 1975, pp. 110-120.

1699. _____. "To Guard the Sea." Foreign Affairs. vol. 50, no. 1, October 1971, pp. 136-147.

1700. Zedalis, Rex J. "Military Uses of Ocean Space and the Developing International Law of the Sea: An Analysis in the Context of Peacetime ASW." <u>San Diego Law Review</u>. vol. 16, no. 3, April 1979, pp. 575-664.

1701. Zeni, Capt. L. E. "Defense Needs in Accommodations among Ocean Users." Lewis M. Alexander, ed. <u>The Law of the Sea: International Rules and Organization for the Sea</u>. Kingston, RI: University of Rhode Island, March 1969, pp. 334-339.

Navigation, Communication
and Shipping

1702. Abrahamsson, Bernhard J. "International Shipping: Developments, Prospects and Policy Issues." Elisabeth Mann Borgese, Norton Ginsburg and Joseph R. Morgan, eds. <u>Ocean Yearbook 8</u>. Chicago and London: The University of Chicago Press, 1989, pp. 158-175.

The article gives an overview of the current situation, future trends and policy issues in the international shipping situation. World shipping issues involve ownership tonnage distribution, access to cargoes, competition as governed by the Convention on Registration Conditions for Ships, and safety and environment concerns.

1703. _____. "Commercial Sea Lanes of Communication." Jon M. Van Dyke, Lewis M. Alexander and Joseph R. Morgan, eds. <u>International Navigation: Rocks and Shoals Ahead?</u> Honolulu: The Law of the Sea Institute, University of Hawaii, 1988, pp. 39-52.

Discusses trade flows and sea lanes of communication (SLOC) and the implications of navigation as coastal states have extended their jurisdictions under the new Law of the Sea Convention.

1704. _____. "Economics of Regulation in Shipping." Douglas M. Johnston and Norman G. Letalik, eds. <u>The Law of the Sea and Ocean Industry: New Opportunities and Restraints</u>. Honolulu: The Law of the Sea Institute, University of Hawaii, 1983, pp. 130-140.

1705. _____. "Merchant Shipping in Transition: An Overview." Elisabeth Mann Borgese and Norton Ginsburg, eds. <u>Ocean Yearbook 4</u>. Chicago and London: University of Chicago Press, 1983, pp. 121-139.

1706. Ademuni, Odeke. <u>Protectionism and the Future of International Shipping</u>. The Hague, Netherlands: Martinus Nijhoff, and London: Graham & Trotman, Ltd., 1984.

This is a book on the following shipping topics as they relate to international law: world shipping, shipping policies of nations and major shipping groups (traditional maritime nations and developing nations), and implementation of shipping policies via protectionism and subsidy.

1707. Akaha, Tsuneo. "Internalizing International Law: Japan and the Regime of Navigation under the UN Convention on the Law of the Sea." Ocean Development and International Law. vol. 20, no. 2, 1989, pp. 113-140.

1708. _____. "Japan's Response to Threats of Shipping Disruptions in Southeast Asia and the Middle East." Pacific Affairs. vol. 59, no. 2, Summer 1986, pp. 255-277.

1709. Alexander, Lewis M. "Geographical Perspective on International Navigation." Jon M. Van Dyke, Lewis M. Alexander and Joseph R. Morgan, eds. International Navigation: Rocks and Shoals Ahead?" Honolulu: Law of the Sea Institute, University of Hawaii, 1988, pp. 73-82.

Points to the differences between perspectives held by geographers and lawyers on issues of international navigation.

1710. _____. "Uncertainties in the Implementation Process: The Case for Navigational Freedoms." Thomas A. Clingan, Jr., ed. The Law of the Sea: What Lies Ahead? Honolulu: The Law of the Sea Institute, University of Hawaii, 1988, pp. 545-550.

1711. _____. "Uncertainties in the Aftermath of UNCLOS III: The Case for Navigational Freedoms." Ocean Development and International Law. vol. 8, no. 3, 1987, pp. 333-342.

This paper discusses the types of actions states can adopt which are not in conformity with the 1982 Law of the Sea Convention and the problems relating to navigation and overflight in the aftermath of the signing of the 1982 Law of the Sea Convention.

1712. _____. Navigational Restrictions within the New LOS Context: Geographical Implications for the United States. Peace Dale, RI: Offshore Consultants, 1986.

This is an expert analysis of the effects of the UN Convention on the Law of the Sea on ocean navigation routes and international waterways which are of concern to the United States.

1713. _____. "Coastal State Competence to Regulate Traffic in Straits and Other Areas near Their Coast versus World Community Needs to Maximize Vessel Mobility." Thomas A. Clingan, Jr. and Lewis M. Alexander, eds. Hazards of Maritime Transit. Cambridge, MA: Ballinger Publishing Company, 1973, pp. 19-28.

1714. American Bar Association. "Synopsis of ABA Law of the Sea Workshop on Neutral Shipping." Law of the Sea Committee Newsletter. vol. 2, no. 2, May 1988.

1715. Anderson, Andres W. "In the Wake of the Dauntless the Background and Development of Maritime Interdiction Operations." Thomas A. Clingan, Jr., ed. The Law of the Sea: What Lies Ahead? Honolulu: The Law of the Sea Institute, University of Hawaii, 1988, pp. 11-40.

1716. Anderson, Thomas D. "Geographic Limitations in the Movement of Deep-Draft Tankers between the Indian and Pacific Oceans." Ocean Development and International Law. vol. 10, nos. 1-2, 1981, pp. 113-130.

1717. Ariyoshi, Yoshiya. "Marine Transportation and the Security of the West." Edward L. Miles and Scott Allen, eds. The Law of the Sea and Ocean Development Issues in the Pacific Basin. Honolulu: The Law of the Sea Institute, University of Hawaii, 1983, pp. 451-465

Provides a survey report on shipping industry of the West including topics such as liner code, bulk cargo, and open registry of shipping.

1718. el-Badri, Hassam. "Local Conflicts in the Red Sea and Their Implications over the Last Two Decades." Abdel Majid Farid, ed. The Red Sea: Prospects for Stability. New York: St. Martins Press, 1984, pp. 66-68, 72-82.

1719. Bates, Charles C. and Capt. Paul Yost. "Where Trends the Flow of Merchant Ships?" John King Gamble, Jr. and Giulio Pontecorvo, eds. Law of the Sea: The Emerging Regime of the Oceans. Cambridge, MA: Ballinger Publishing Company, 1974, pp. 249-276.

1720. el-Bazzaz, Hassan. "The Red Sea and the Arabian Gulf: Strategic and Economic Links (2)." Abdel Majid Farid, ed. The Red Sea: Prospects for Stability. New York, St. Martins Press, 1984, pp. 95-103.

1721. Bernhardt, J. Peter A. "Straightjacking Straight Baselines." Jon M. Van Dyke, Lewis M. Alexander and Joseph R. Morgan, eds. International Navigation: Rocks and Shoals Ahead? Honolulu: The Law of the Sea Institute, University of Hawaii, 1988, pp. 85-99.

Points out that straight baseline practice is the single most potential harmful threat to high seas freedoms.

1722. Bettink, H. W. Wefers. "Ocean Registry, the Genuine Link and Its 1986 Convention on Registration Conditions for Ships." Netherlands Yearbook of International Law. vol. xviii, 1987, pp. 69-120.

1723. Biggs, Robert B. "Offshore Industrial Port Islands." Oceanus. vol. 19, no. 1, Fall 1975, pp. 56-66.

Discusses a new concept for multipurpose industrial port
islands suitable for construction off the Atlantic and Gulf
coasts.

1724. Blake, Gerald. "The Red Sea and the Arabian Gulf:
Strategic and Economic Links (1)." Abdel Majid Farid,
cd3. The Red Sea: Prospects for Stability. New York:
St. Martins Press, 1984, pp. 87-89.

1725. Brigham, Lawson W. "Emerging Polar Ship Technology: An
Introduction." Marine Technology Society Journal.
vol. 3, no. 3, 1988, pp. 3-5.

1726. Brittin, Burdick H. International Law for Seagoing
Officers. 5th ed. Annapolis, MD: Naval Institute
Press, 1986.

Deals with international law issues facing naval commanders
and other seagoing officers who must be knowledgeable about
their legal rights and obligations in this age of instant
electronic communication on the high seas, in foreign waters
or in foreign ports.

1727. Burke, William T. "Contemporary Developments Affecting
Navigation Rights in the Law of the Sea." Thomas A.
Clingan, Jr., ed. The Law of the Sea: What Lies
Ahead? Honolulu: The Law of the Sea Institute, Uni-
versity of Hawaii, 1988, ppp. 141-149.

1728. _____. "Changes Made in the Rules of Navigation
and Maritime Trade by the 1982 Convention on the Law
of the Sea." Robert B. Krueger and Stefan A. Riesenfeld, eds. The Developing Order of the Oceans. Honolulu: The Law of the Sea Institute, University of
Hawaii, 1985, pp. 662-677.

1729. _____. "Exclusive Fisheries Zones and Freedom of
Navigation." San Diego Law Review. vol. 20, no.3,
April 1983, pp. 595-623.

The expansion of the 200 nautical mile exclusive fishing and
economic zones by coastal states, has revolutionized the law
of the sea. Burke points out the need for balancing coastal
states' rights to exclusive fishing against the rights of
navigation. He argues that limited coastal states' rights
affecting navigation be recognized and that they be reserved
for developing states which must depend on the exploitation
of fisheries.

1730. _____. Contemporary Law of the Sea: Transportation, Communication and Flight. Honolulu: The Law of
the Sea Institute, University of Hawaii, 1975.

This is considered to be a basic study on contemporary law
of the sea pertaining to navigation by ships and aircraft
on, over and under the oceans. It also discusses state
claims over navigation rights and policy alternatives in
dealing with conflicting claims.

1731. Busha, Thomas S. "Monitoring and Surveillance: Navigation." Elisabeth Mann Borgese and Norton Ginsburg,
eds. Ocean Yearbook 3. Chicago and London: University of Chicago Press, 1982, pp. 118-125.

1732. _____ and James Dawson. "A Safe Voyage to a New
World." Elisabeth Mann Borgese and Norton Ginsburg,
ed. Ocean Yearbook 1. Chicago and London: University
of Chicago Press, 1978, pp. 217-239.

1733. Butler, William E. Law of the Sea and International
Shipping. Dobbs Ferry, NY: Oceana Publications, Inc.,
1985.

1734. Cafruny, Alan W. Ruling the Waves: The Political
Economy of International Shipping. Berkeley, CA: University of California Press, 1987.

1735. Campbell, Douglas, II. "Navigation." David L. Larson,
ed. Major Issues of the Law of the Sea. Durham, NH:
The University of New Hampshire, 1976, pp. 125-139.

1736. Carlisle, Rodney. "Liberia's Flag of Convenience:
Rough Water Ahead." ORBIS. vol. 24, no. 4, Winter
1981, pp. 881-892.

1737. Chadwin, Mark Lincoln. "From Wharf Rat to Lord of the
Docks." Oceanus. vol. 32, no. 3, Fall 1989, pp. 51-58.

1738. Conant, Melvin A. "Strategic Aspects of Pacific Petro-
leum Trade." Edward L. Miles and Scott Allen, eds. The
Law of the Sea and Ocean Development Issues in the
Pacific Basin. Honolulu: The Law of the Sea Institute,
University of Hawaii, 1983, pp. 413-427.

1739. "Convention on Ship Security Adopted in Rome." IMO
News. no. 2, 1988.

1740. "Convention on the International Maritime Satellite
Organization (INMARSAT)." Elisabeth Mann Borgese and
Norton Ginsburg, eds. Ocean Yearbook 1. Chicago and
London: University of Chicago Press, 1978, pp. 734-755

1741. Couper, A. D. "Future International Maritime Transport
Developments and the Law of the Sea." Elisabeth Mann
Borgese and Norton Ginsburg, eds. Ocean Yearbook 6.
Chicago and London: University of Chicago Press, 1986,
pp. 97-106

1742. Craven, John P. "Freedom of Navigation for War, Commerce and Piracy." Jon M. Van Dyke, Lewis M. Alexander
and Joseph R. Morgan, eds. International Navigation:
Rocks and Shoals Ahead? Honolulu: The Law of the Sea
Institute, University of Hawaii, 1988, pp. 31-38.

Discusses the scope and limitation of "freedom of navigation" as new technology develops and brings with it new
interpretations for the control of the sea.

1743. "Draft Report to the Maritime Safety Committee." Sub-committee on Safety of Navigation, IMO.   January 17, 1989.

1744. Egiyan, G. S. "'Flag of Convenience' or 'Open Regis-tration' of Ships?" Marine Policy. vol. 14, no. 2, March 1990, pp. 106 111.

1745. Flory, John F. "Oil Ports on the Continental Shelf." Oceanus. vol. 19, no. 1, Fall 1975, pp. 45-55.

Discusses recent techniques on offshore sites to serve Very Large Crude Carriers (VLCCs) and the Single Anchor Leg Mooring (SALM) for loading very large tankers.

1746. Frankel, Ernst G. "Shipping and Role in Economic Development." Marine Policy. vol. 13, no. 1, January 1989, pp. 22-42.

1747. _____. "Choice of Technology: Problems in the World Shipping Industry." Douglas M. Johnston and Norman G. Letalik, eds. The Law of the Sea and Ocean Industry: New Opportunities and Restraints. Honolulu: The Law of the Sea Institute, University of Hawaii, 1984, pp. 207-225.

By providing the history of marine shipping technology, discusses the choices in shipping as an increasingly complex issue.

1748. _____. "Present and Future Approaches to the Creation of Systems for Reducing Risks through Improvements in Technology and Regulation." Thomas A. Clingan, Jr. and Lewis M. Alexander, eds. Hazards of Maritime Transit. Cambridge, MA: Ballinger Publishing Company, 1973, pp. 49-65.

1749. Friedheim, Amy. "Puerto Quetzal, Guatemala: Container Cranes or Stevedores." Oceanus. vol. 32, no. 3, Fall 1989, pp. 75-78.

1750. Gao, Zhiguo. "China's Navigation Policy in Its Terri-torial Sea." Thomas A. Clingan, Jr., ed. The Law of the Sea: What Lies Ahead? Honolulu: The Law of the Sea Institute, University of Hawaii, 1988, pp. 161-163.

1751. Gibbs, Stephen and David H. Teeter. "Management of Marine Transportation in the North Pacific." Ocean Development and International Law. vol. 6, no. 3, 1978, pp. 103-162.

1752. Gilmore, William C. "Narcotics Interdiction at Sea: UK-US Cooperation." Marine Policy. vol. 13, no. 3, July 1989, pp. 218-230.

1753. Gold, Edgar. "International Shipping and the New Law of the Sea: New Directions for a Traditional Use?"

Ocean Development and International Law. vol. 20, no. 5, 1989, pp. 433-444.

This study describes and analyzes the changes in the shipping industry in terms of technical development, economic infrastructure and operation procedures. In many important ways these changes will continue into the 1990s.

1754. _____. "The Future of Maritime Transit." Jon M. Van Dyke, Lewis M.Alexander and Joseph R. Morgan, eds. International Navigation: Rocks and Shoals Ahead? Honolulu: The Law of the Sea Institute, University of Hawaii, 1988, pp. 394-400.

Discusses the future of strategic maritime interests and commercial navigation in the context of the new Law of the Sea Convention.

1755. _____. "Ocean Shipping and the New Law of the Sea: Toward a More Regulatory Regime." Elisabeth Mann Borgese and Norton Ginsburg, eds. Ocean Yearbook 6. Chicago and London: University of Chicago Press, 1986, pp. 85-106.

1756. _____. "The Surveillance and Control of Navigation in the New Law of the Sea: A Comment." Elisabeth Mann Borgese and Norton Ginsburg, eds. Ocean Yearbook 3. Chicago and London: University of Chicago Press, 1982, pp. 126-134.

1757. _____. "The 'Freedom' of Ocean Shipping and Commercial Viability: Myths and Realities in the Aftermath of UNCLOS III." John King Gamble, Jr., ed. Law of the Sea: Neglected Issues. Honolulu: The Law of the Sea Institute, University of Hawaii, 1979, pp. 248-261

1758. Heishman, Marc J. "Port Concept often Adrift in Waterfront Revitalization." Oceanus. vol. 32, no. 3, Fall 1989, pp. 89-91.

1759. Hodgson, Robert and Terry V. McIntyre. "Maritime Commerce in Selected Areas of High Concentration." Thomas A. Clingan, Jr. and Lewis M.Alexander, eds. Hazards of Maritime Transit. Cambridge, MA: Ballinger Publishing Company, 1973, pp. 1-18.

1760. Hunt, Christopher. "Shipping Lines in Asia Warned about U. S. Law." Asian Wall Street Journal. 17-18 January 1989, pp. A-1, A-6.

1761. "IMO: Convention and Protocol from the International Conference on the Suppression of Unlawful Acts against the Safety of Navigation (done at Rome, 10 March 1988)." International Legal Materials. vol. xvii, no. 3, May 1988, pp. 668-690.

1762. "IMO: Convention on Salvage." Oceans Policy News. June 1989, p. 6.

1763. Jaafar, Abu Bakar. "The Changing Legal Status of the Malacca and Singapore Straits." Jon M. Van Dyke, ed. Consensus and Confrontation: The United States and the Law of the Sea Convention. Honolulu: The Law of the Sea Institute, University of Hawaii, 1985, pp. 284-291

1764. Jackson, David C. World Shipping Laws. Dobbs Ferry, NY: Oceana Publications, 1979.

1765. Kanter, Richard S. "The Japan-United States Treaty of Friendship, Commerce and Navigation: Lawyers as Treaty Traders." University of Hawaii Law Review. vol. 8, no. 2, Summer 1986, pp. 339-390.

1766. Kasoulides, George C. "The 1986 United Nations Convention on the Conditions for Registration of Vessels and the Question of Open Registry." Ocean Development and International Law. vol. 20, no. 6, 1989, pp. 543-576.

This paper discusses the implications of the 1986 Convention on Conditions for Registry of Ships by providing an analysis of the origin and evolution of open registries.

1767. Kim, Dalchoong. "Ocean Transportation and Sea Lanes of Communication of Korea: An Overview." Choon-ho Park and Jae Kyu Park, eds. The Law of the Sea: Problems from the East Asian Perspective. Honolulu: The Law of the Sea Institute, Univ. of Hawaii, 1987, pp. 52-69.

1768. Knight, H. Gary. "International Legal Problems in the Construction and Operation of Offshore Deep Draft Port Facilities." Thomas A. Clingan, Jr. and Lewis M. Alexander, eds. Hazards of Maritime Transit. Cambridge, MA: Ballinger Publishing company, 1973, pp.91-136.

1769. Lamson, Cynthia and Daviud L. Vander Zwaag, eds. Transit Management in the Northwest Passage: Problems and Prospects. Cambridge (UK): Cambridge University Press, Studies in Polar Research, 1988.

This is a collection of essays on the transit of Canada's Arctic waters. These essays argue for a single, comprehensive system of management for the use of the passage in those waters by vessels.

1770. Laurila, Simon H. Islands Rise from the Sea: Essays on Exploration, Navigation and Mapping in Hawaii. New York: Vintage Press, 1989.

1771. Levikov, George A. "Multimodal Container Transport Tariff Rules: Impact on Developing Countries." Elisabeth Mann Borgese and Norton Ginsburg, eds. Ocean Yearbook 6. Chicago and London: University of Chicago Press, 1986, pp. 149-159.

1772. _____. "Soviet Shipowners and International Shipping." Elisabeth Mann Borgese and Norton Ginsburg, eds. _Ocean Yearbook 2_.   Chicago and London: University of Chicago Press, 1980, pp. 117-122.

1773. Mahmoudi, Said.   "Customary International Law and Transit Passage." _Ocean Development and International Law_. vol. 20, no. 2, 1989, pp. 157-174.

1774. Marcus, Henry S.   "In Search of National Maritime Policies." Edward L. Miles and Scott Allen, eds. _The Law of the Sea and Ocean Development Issues in the Pacific Basin_. Honolulu: The Law of the Sea Institute, University of Hawaii, 1983, pp. 429-450.

1775. Molodtsov, Stepan V.   "The Exclusive Economic Zone: Legal Status and Regime of Navigation." Elisabeth Mann Borgese and Norton Ginsburg, eds. _Ocean Yearbook 6_. Chicago and London: University of Chicago Press, 1986, pp. 203-216.

1776. Morgan, Joseph R. "Strategic Lines of Communication: A Military View."   Jon M. Van Dyke, Lewis M. Alexander and Joseph R. Morgan, eds. _International Navigation: Rocks and Shoals Ahead?_ Honolulu: The Law of the Sea Institute, University of Hawaii, 1988, pp. 54-68.

Makes an important argument that trade   routes have become strategic lines of communication in time of crisis.   Thus, the protection of one's own sea lanes of communication has been a principal mission of navies.

1777. Muhjiddin, Atje Misbach. "Some Aspects that Should Be Considered in Designating Indonesia's Sea Lanes."   Jon M. Van Dyke, Lewis M. Alexander and Joseph R. Morgan, eds. _International Navigation: Rocks and Shoals Ahead?_ Honolulu: The Law of the Sea Institute, University of Hawaii, 1988, pp. 212-219.

Provides background on Indonesia's interests in designating sea lanes.

1778. Murphy, Don.   "Shipping Regulation: The Canadian Approach." Douglas M. Johnston and Norman G. Letalik, eds. _The Law of the Sea and Ocean Industry: New Opportunities and Restraints_. Honolulu: The Law of the Sea Institute, University of Hawaii, 1984, pp. 173-182.

A lawyer's view of problems of Canadian shipping regulation upon entry into the regulated industry and level of service, rates and licensing of carriers.

1779. Nailor, Peter.   "International Shipping."   R. P. Barston and Patricia Birnie, eds. _The Maritime Dimension_. London: George Allen and Unwin, 1980, pp. 142-158.

1780. "Navigation: Law of the Sea Institute's 23rd Annual Meeting." _Oceans Policy News_. June 1989, pp. 1-3.

1781. Negroponte, John D. "Who Will Protect the Freedom of the Seas?" Thomas A. Clingan, Jr., ed. The Law of the Sea: What Lies Ahead? Honolulu: The Law of the Sea Institute, University of Hawaii, 1988, pp. 126-131.

1782. Nweihed, Kaldone G. "The International Maritime Organization. A Venezuelan Perspective." Elisabeth Mann Borgese and Norton Ginsburg, eds. Ocean Yearbook 6. Chicago and London: University of Chicago Press, 1986, pp. 171-196.

1783. Oda, Masao. "Transportation of Japanese Seaborne Trade and Related Law and Regulations." Ocean Development and International Law. vol. 6, no. 5, 1979, pp. 237-304.

1784. Okere, B. Obinna. "Nigeria's Exclusive Economic Zone and Freedoms of Navigation." Ocean Development and International Law. vol. 13, no. 4, 1983, pp. 535-538.

1785. Osieke, Ebere. "Flags of Convenience Vessels: Recent Developments." American Journal of International Law. vol. 73, no. 4, October 1979, pp. 604-627.

1786. Oxman, Bernard H. "Dispute Settlement with and among Non-Parties to the Law of the Sea Convention: Navigation and Pollution." Thomas A. Clingan, Jr., ed. The Law of the Sea: What Lies Ahead? Honolulu: The Law of the Sea Institute, University of Hawaii, 1988, pp. 479-493.

1787. _____. "Navigation, Pollution and Compulsory Settlement of EEZ Disputes." Oceanus. vol. 27, no. 4, Winter 1984-85, pp. 52-56.

1788. Payne, Lachlan. "Customers, Transport and Ports: Bringing Them Together." Maritime Studies. vol. 37, November-December 1987.

1789. Parker, C. J. "A View from the Bridge." Douglas M. Johnston and Norman G. Letalik, eds. The Law of the Sea and Ocean Industry: New Oportunities and Restraints. Honolulu: The Law of the Sea Institute, University of Hawaii, 1984, pp. 226-231.

A working sea captain's view of the technical problems of crew sizes and officer training, as well as the problems of surveying and policing large ocean spaces, and design for bulk carriers in the trade.

1790. Pisani, John M. "Port Development in the U. S.: Status and Outlook." Oceanus. vol. 32, no. 3, Fall 1989, pp. 37-54.

1791. Plant, G. "International Legal Aspects of Vessel Traffic Services." Marine Policy. vol. 14, no. 1, January 1989, pp. 71-81.

1792. "Protection of Submarine Cables: Convention and Additional Article Signed at Paris, 14 March 1884."
Charles I. Bevans, ed. <u>Treaties and Other International Agreements of the United States of America
1776-1949</u>. vol. 1. Washington, DC: Department of
State, 1968, pp. 89-96.

1793. Ramsay, R. A. "The Organization of Shipping." Elisa-
beth Mann Borgese and Norton Ginsburg, eds. <u>Ocean
Yearbook 1</u>. Chicago and London: University of Chicago
Press, 1978, pp. 211-216.

1794. Richardson, Elliot L. "Law of the Sea: Navigation and
Other Traditional National Security Considerations."
<u>San Diego Law Review</u>. vol. 19, no. 3, April 1982, pp.
553-576.

Written by a chief United States negotiator at the Law of
the Sea Conference, the article discusses the navigational
and national security concerns in the the law of the sea
draft.

1795. Ricklefs, John. "Many Storms in a Port." <u>Oceanus</u>.
vol. 32, no. 3, Fall 1989, pp. 47-50.

1796. Riesenfeld, Stefan A.   "High Seas and Navigational
Rights: What Are They and Who May Assert Them in U. S.
Courts?" Thomas A. Clingan, Jr., ed. <u>The Law of the
Sea: What Lies Ahead?</u> Honolulu: The Law of the Sea
Institute, University of Hawaii, 1988, pp. 41-50.

1797. Robertson, Myles. "Morflot and Economically Account-
able Socialism: Developments in Soviet Pacific
Shipping." <u>Maritime Studies</u>. no. 40, May-June 1988.

1798. Shah, M. J. "Maritime Law and the Developing Countries: Attitude and Trends." Elisabeth Mann Borgese
and Norton Ginsburg, eds. <u>Ocean Yearbook 6</u>. Chicago
and London: University of Chicago Press, 1986, pp.
107-138.

1799. _____.   "Modern Maritime Legislation for Developing Countries: The UNCTAD Experience."   Elisabeth
Mann Borgese and Norton Ginsburg, eds. <u>Ocean Yearbook 4</u>. Chicago and London: University of Chicago
Press, 1983, pp. 140-149.

1800. _____. "The UN Liner Code Revisited." Douglas M.
Johnston and Norman G. Letalik, eds. <u>The Law of the
Sea and Ocean Industry: New Opportunities and
Restraints</u>. Honolulu: The Law of the Sea Institute,
University of Hawaii, 1983, pp. 152-172.

1801. Shearer, I. A.   "Problems of Jurisdiction and Law
Enforcement against Delinquent Vessels." <u>International
and Comparative Law Quarterly</u>. vol. 35, pt. 2, April
1986, pp. 320-343.

1802. "Shipping Issues at the GATT." Oceans Policy News. July 1989, p. 3.

1803. Silva, Maynard and William Westermeyer. "The Law of the Sea and the U. S. Exclusive Economic Zone: Perspectives on Marine Transportation and Fisheries." Ocean Development and International Law. vol. 15, nos. 3-4, 1985, pp. 321-354.

1804. Slot, P. J. "The International Legal Regime for Navigation." Ocean Development and International Law. vol. 15, no. 1, 1985, pp. 89-98.

This paper discusses the rules of navigation under international law which involve complex questions of jurisdiction as to which state should decide which rules of navigation, and how rules are to be enforced at sea.

1805. Sohn, Louis B.. "International Navigation: Interests Related to National Security." Jon M. Van Dyke, Lewis M. Alexander and Joseph R. Morgan, eds. International Navigation: Rocks and Shoals Ahead? Honolulu: The Law of the Sea Institute, University of Hawaii, 1988, pp. 307-323.

Points out that the new Law of the Sea Convention provisions on navigation represent a balance between coastal states' interests and those of traditional and new users of the oceans.

1806. Speranskaya, L. V. "Marine Environmental Protection and Freedom of Navigation in International Law." Elisabeth Mann Borgese and Norton Ginsburg, eds. Ocean Yearbook 6. Chicago and London: University of Chicago Press, 1986, pp. 197-202.

1807. Spindel, Robert C. "Acoustic Navigation." Oceanus. vol. 20, no. 2, Spring 1977, pp. 22-38.

This is a technical study of modern electronic navigation using sound waves instead of radio waves. There are technical illustrations of acoustic navigation. The study shows the appropriate use of acoustic navigation for precision navigation at sea and for long-range tracking and navigation of submerged objects.

1808. Stewart, Robert J. "Tankers in U. S. Waters." Oceanus. vol. 20, no. 4, Fall 1977, pp. 74-85.

1809. Stozky, Irwin P. "Interdiction at Sea and the Fourth Amendment." Thomas A. Clingan, Jr., ed. The Law of the Sea: What Lies Ahead? Honolulu: The Law of the Sea Institute, University of Hawaii, 1988, pp. 72-109.

1810. Strange, Susan and Christopher Cragg. "International Marine Insurance." Elisabeth Mann Borgese and Norton Ginsburg, eds. Ocean Yearbook 2. Chicago and London: University of Chicago Press, 1980, pp. 94-116.

1811. Talwani, Manik. "Position at Sea by Satellite Navigation." Lewis M. Alexander, ed. The Law of the Sea: International Rules and Organization for the Sea. Kingston, RI: University of Rhode Island, March 1969, pp. 189-193.

1812. Thomas, Stephen D. "The Sons of Palulap: Navigation without Instruments in Oceania." Oceanus. vol. 28, no. 1, Spring 1985, pp. 52-58.

1813. Todd, P. Contracts for the Carriage of Goods by Sea. Palo Alto, CA: Blackwell Scientific Publications, 1988.

1814. Topping, Thomas S. R. "International Action against Maritime Fraud." Elisabeth Mann Borgese and Norton Ginsburg, eds. Ocean Yearbook 5. Chicago and London: University of Chicago Press, 1985, pp. 102-116.

1815. United Nations. The Law of the Sea: Navigation on the High Seas. United Nations Pulbications, 1989.

Provides a needed legislative history for those Convention provisions--Part VIII, Section 1--which deal with navigation on the high seas.

1816. Valenzuela, Mario. "IMO: Public International Law and Regulation." Douglas M. Johnston and Norman G. Letalik, eds. The Law of the Sea and Ocean Industry: New Opportunities and Restraints. Honolulu: The Law of the Sea Institute, University of Hawaii, 1983, pp. 141-151.

1817. Van Dyke, Jon M., Lewis M. Alexander and Joseph R. Morgan, eds. International Navigation: Rocks and Shoals Ahead? Honolulu: The Law of the Sea Institute, University of Hawaii, 1988.

This is a very illuminating collection of panel papers and discussions presented at the 1986 annual meeting of the Law of the Sea Institute. Topics covered include: some basic views about freedom of navigation, geographic perspectives on international navigation; straight baselines, innocent passage, international straits and transit passage, archipelagic and sea lane passage, environmental issues of vessel-source pollution, and national security in relation to international navigation.

1818. Vitzthun, Wolfgang Graf. "The Baltic Straits." Choonho Park, ed. The Law of the Sea in the 1980s. Honolulu: The Law of the Sea Institute, University of Hawaii, 1983, pp. 537-607.

1819. Vogel, R. "Multimodal Transport: Impact on Developing Countries." Elisabeth Mann Borgese and Norton Ginsburg, eds. Ocean Yearbook 6. Chicago and London: University of Chicago Press, 1986, pp. 139-148.

1820. Volosov, M. E., A. L. Kolodkin and Y. M. Kolosov. "International Maritime Satellite-Communication System: History and Principles Governing Its Functioning." Elisabeth Mann Borgese and Norton Ginsburg, eds. Ocean Yearbook 1. Chicago and London: University of Chicago Press, 1978, pp. 240-270.

1821. Voskuil, C. C. A. and J. A. Wade. Carriage of Goods by Sea, Maritime Collisions, Maritime Oil Pollution, Commercial Arbitration. The Hague, Netherlands: Martinus Nijhoff, and London: Graham & Trotman, Ltd., 1980.

1822. Vrevich, Barry. "Treating a Vessel Like a Home for Purposes of Conducting a Search." San Diego Law Review. vol. 21, no. 3, June 1984, pp. 751-768.

1823. Wisnumurti, Nugroho. "Archipelagic Waters and Archipelagic Sea Lanes." Jon M. Van Dyke, Lewis M. Alexander and Joseph R. Morgan, eds. International Navigation: Rocks and Shoals Ahead? Honolulu: The Law of the Sea Institute, University of Hawaii, 1988, pp. 198-209.

1824. Wiswall, F. L., Jr. "The IMO: Private International Law and Regulation." Douglas M. Johnston and Norman G. Letalik, eds. The Law of the Sea and Ocean Industry: New Opportunities and Restraints. Honolulu: The Law of the Sea Institute, University of Hawaii, 1983, pp. 183-189.

1825. "Zone of Cooperation Proposed for Timor Gap." Marine Studies. no. 42, September-October 1988.

Marine Scientific Research
and Technological Transfer

1826. Adams, C. M. G. "Marine Science Research: Operating the Consent Regime." E. D. Brown and R. R. Churchill, eds. The UN Convention on the Law of the Sea: Impact and Implementation. Honolulu: The Law of the Sea Institute, University of Hawaii, 1987, pp. 383-386.

1827. Adelman, William J. "Trends in Neurobiology Using Marine Model." Oceanus. vol. 26, no. 2, Summer 1983, pp. 46-54.

Scientific study of nerve cells of squid, lobsters and sea worms may provide clues to human nerve disorders such as Alzheimer's Disease.

1828. Alexander, Lewis M. "Organizational Responses to New Ocean Science and Technology Developments." Ocean Development and International Law. vol. 9, nos. 3-4, 1981, pp. 241-268.

1829. Allen, S. and L.C. Hanson, ed. New Developments in Marine Science and Technology: Economic, Legal and Political Aspects of Change. Honolulu: The Law of the Sea Institute, University of Hawaii, 1989.

1830. Alverson, Dayton L. "The Concept of PICES in Relation to Fisheries in the Pacific." Edward L. Miles and Scott Allen, eds. The Law of the Sea and Ocean Development Issues in the Pacific Basin. Honolulu: The Law of the Sea Institute, University of Hawaii, 1983, pp. 581-584.

Presents pertinent background information on the Pacific International Council for the Exploration of the Sea, a forum by scientists for the North Pacific.

1831. "Arctic Research for an Arctic Nation." Report of the U.S. Arctic Research Commission to the President and the Congress of the United States for the period of 1 October 1987 - 30 September 1988. U. S. Arctic Research Commission. 31 January 1989.

1832. Baker, F. W. G.   "Cooperation among Non-governmental Organizations in Fostering Oceanic Research." Jacques G. Richardson, ed. Managing the Oceans: Resources, Research, Law. Mt. Airy, MD: Lomond Publications, Inc., 1985, pp. 213-222.

1833. Ballard, Robert D., Christopher Von Alt and William J. Hersey, III. "Live Deep-Sea Expedition Video Coverage Planned for Scientists Ashore, Educational Institutions." Oceanus. vol. 30, Fall, 1987, pp. 11-15.

1834. Bernard, H. Russell.   "Restrictions on Oceanic Research: An Anthropologist's View." Lewis M. Alexander, ed. The Law of the Sea: Needs and Interests of Developing Countries.   Kingston, RI: University of Rhode Island, 1973, pp. 206-210.

1835. _____ and Peter D. Killworth. "Scientists as Others See Them." Ocean Development and International Law. vol. 4, no. 3, 1977, pp. 261-268.

1836. Boczek, Boleslaw A.   "Transfer of Technology and UNCLOS III Draft Convention." Douglas M. Johnston and Norman G. Letalik, eds. The Law of the Sea and Ocean Industry: New Opportunities and Restraints. Honolulu: The Law of the Sea Institute, University of Hawaii, 1984, pp. 494-517.

Discusses the concepts of "technology" and "transfer." Provides an analysis of the special problems in the transfer of marine technology and the intent of the provisions in the draft Law of the Sea Convention on technology transfer.

1837. _____ .   The Transfer of Marine Technology to Developing Nations in International Law. Honolulu: The Law of the Sea Institute, University of Hawaii, 1982.

This paper is devoted to a discussion of the influence of marine technology on Western ascendancy and power. The developing nations' thirst for maritime technology remains a continued quest after the breakup of European world empires.

1838. Boxer, Baruch. "Marine Science in China: Development and Prospects."   Elisabeth Mann Borgese and Norton Ginsburg, ed. Ocean Yearbook 6. Chicago and London: University of Chicago Press, 1986, pp. 217-240.

1839. _____ .   "Marine Science and Society in China." Oceanus. vol. 27, no. 1, Spring 1984, pp. 47-49.

1840. Bradley, Michael D.   "Institutional Arrangements for Facilitating Access." Warren S. Wooster, ed. Freedom of Oceanic Research. New York: Crane, Russak, 1973, pp. 201-217.

1841. Brewer, Garry.   "An Ocean Sciences Agenda for the

1990s." Seattle: Institute for Marine Studies, University of Washington, February 1988.

1842. Brigham, Lawson W. "New Soviet Antarctic Research Ship Akademik Fedoror." Marine Technology Society Journal. vol. 21, no. 3, 1981, pp. 88-91.

1843. Burger, W.   "Treaty Provisions concerning Marine Science Research."   Ocean Development and International Law. vol. 1, no. 2, Summer 1973, pp. 159-184.

1844. Burke, William T. Scientific Research Articles in the Law of the Sea Informal Single Negotiating Text. Honolulu: The Law of the Sea Institute, University of Hawaii, 1975.

1845. _____. "Research Needs on Ocean Issues: Part Two." Lewis M. Alexander, ed. The Law of the Sea: A New Geneva Conference. Kingston, RI: University of Rhode Island, 1972, pp. 145-147.

1846. _____. Marine Science Research and International Law. Honolulu: The Law of the Sea Institute, University of Hawaii, 1970.

The paper discusses the impediments to scientific research imposed by the ocean enclosure movement under which coastal states have made expanded claims over the ocean space.

1847. _____. Law, Science and the Ocean. Honolulu: The Law of the Sea Institute, University of Hawaii, 1969.

For a background of scientific research in relation to the law of the seas, this paper by Burke, published in 1969, is instructive, for there are useful comments on the development of restrictive regulations over ocean activities and their consequences for marine scientific research.

1848. Campbell, Neil J. "Marine Science Programs of the Intergovernmental Oceanographic Commission in the Pacific." Edward L. Miles and Scott Allen, eds. The Law of the Sea and Ocean Development Issues in the Pacific Basin. Honolulu: The Law of the Sea Institute, University of Hawaii, 1983, pp. 591-596.

Discusses the history of the Scientific Committee on Ocean Research (SCOR) and its many major activities.

1849. _____, J. D. Bradford and G. L. Holland. "Implementation of the Scientific Provisions of the Revised Single Negotiating Text." Edward L. Miles and John King Gamble, Jr., eds. Law of the Sea: Conference Outcomes and Problems of Implementation. Cambridge, MA: Ballinger Publishing Company, 1977, pp. 295-303.

1850. Champ, Michael A. and Ned A. Ostenso. "Future Uses and Research Needs in the EEZ." Oceanus. vol. 27, no. 4, Winter 1984-85, pp. 62-68.

1851. Charney, Jonathan I. "Technology and International Negotiations." <u>American Journal of International Law</u>. vol. 76, no. 1, January 1982, pp. 78-118.

1852. Cheek, Conrad H. "Law of the Sea: Effects of Varying Coastal State Controls on Marine Research." <u>Ocean Development and International Law</u>. vol. 1, no. 2, Summer 1973, pp. 209-220.

1853. Cheever, Daniel S. "International Organizations for Marine Science: An Eclectic Model." Lewis M. Alexander, ed. <u>The Law of the Sea: National Policy Recommendations</u>. Kingston, RI: University of Rhode Island, 1970, pp. 377-390.

1854. Christy, Francis T., Jr. "Research Needs on Ocean Issues: Part One." Lewis M. Alexander, ed. <u>The Law of the Sea: A New Geneva Conference</u>. Kingston, RI: University of Rhode Island, 1972, pp. 143-144.

1855. Colwell, Rita R. and Jack R. Greer. "Biotechnology and the Sea." <u>Ocean Development and International Law</u>. vol. 17, nos. 1-3, 1986, pp. 163-190.

1856. Creech, Heather. "In Search of an Ocean Information Policy." Elisabeth Mann Borgese and Norton Ginsburg, eds. <u>Ocean Yearbook 6</u>. Chicago and London: University of Chicago Press, 1986, pp. 15-28.

1857. Dar, Vinod and Marcia Levis. "Effective Communication in Technology Sharing." <u>Ocean Development and International Law</u>. vol. 2, no. 4, Winter, 1974, pp. 379-402

1858. Dawson, Christine L. "A Comparison of National Resources Available for Fishery Research." <u>Ocean Development and International Law</u>. vol. 5, no. 1, 1979, pp. 1-22.

1859. Drewry, David J. "The Challenge of Antarctic Science." <u>Oceanus</u>. vol. 31, no. 2, Summer 1988, pp. 5-10.

1860. Flemming, N. C. "The Law of the Sea and the Exchange of Scientific Information and Data." E. D. Brown and R. R. Churchill, eds. <u>The UN Convention on the Law of the Sea: Impact and Implementation</u>. Honolulu: The Law of the Sea Institute, University of Hawaii, 1987, pp. 398-408.

1861. Franssen, Herman T. "Understanding the Ocean Science Debate." <u>Ocean Development and International Law</u>. vol. 2, no. 2, Summer 1974, pp. 187-202.

1862. _____. "Developing Country Views of Sea Law and Marine Science." Warren S. Wooster, ed. <u>Freedom of Oceanic Research</u>. New York: Crane, Russak, 1973, pp. 137-177.

1863. Fye, Paul M. "Commentary: Marine Scientific Research." Choon-ho Park, ed. <u>The Law of the Sea in the 1980s</u>.

Honolulu: The Law of the Sea Institute, University of Hawaii, 1983, pp. 313-317.

1864. Ginsburg, Norton.   "On the Nature of a Model Global Maritime Research Organization."   Elisabeth Mann Borgese and Norton Ginsburg, eds. Ocean Yearbook 5. Chicago and London: University of Chicago Press, 1985, pp. 109-116.

1865. "Global Change, Marine Scientific Research and the Law of the Sea." LOS Lieder. vol. 3, no. 2. Honolulu: The Law of the Sea Institute, University of Hawaii, October 1989, pp. 5-6.

1866. Gold, Edgar. "International Maritime Law in Transi- tion: New Challenges for Education and Training." Marine Policy. vol. 13, no. 3, July 1989, pp. 178-192

1867. Gonsalves, Maria Edward. "Science, Technology and the New Convention on the Law of the Sea."   Jacques G. Richardson, ed. Managing the Ocean: Resources, Re- search, Law. Mt. Airy, MD: Lomond Publications, Inc., 1985, pp. 239-248.

1868. Gulland, J. A. "Problems and Priorities in Providing Research Input to Fishery Decisions." Ocean Develop- ment and International Law. vol. 4, no. 1, 1977, pp. 27-38.

1869. Hafner, Gerard. "Commentary: The Regulation of Marine Scientific Research Activities of Landlocked and Geo- graphically Disadvantaged States in the Draft Conven- tion on the Law of the Sea.: Choon-ho Park, ed. The Law of the Sea in the 1980s. Honolulu: The Law of the Sea Institute, University of Hawaii, 1983, pp. 342-360

1870. Hanson, Lynne Carter and Sylvia A. Earle. "Submers- ibles for Scientists." Oceanus. vol. 30, no. 3, Fall 1987, pp. 31-39.

1871. Harrison, Craig S. "Costs to the United States in Environmental Protection and Marine Scientific Re- search by not Joining the Law of the Sea Convention." Jon M. Van Dyke, ed. Consensus and Confrontation: The United States and the Law of the Sea Convention. Hono- lulu: The Law of the Sea Institute, University of Hawaii, 1985, pp. 425-437.

1872. Helsley, Charles and Loren Kroenke. "Scientific Coop- eration in the Pacific Basin: Do Science and Politics Mix?" Edward L. Miles and Scott Allen, eds. The Law of the Sea and Ocean Development Issues in the Pacific Basin. Honolulu: The Law of the Sea Institute, Uni- versity of Hawaii, 1983, pp. 585-590.

Discusses the ad hoc arrangements between marine scientists and political entities--a cumbersome procedure in dealing with scientific programs--and the techniques used.

1873. Hollick, Ann L.   "National Ocean Institute: Research Needs." Ocean Development and International Law. vol. 3, no. 2, 1975, pp. 155-170.

1874. Hotta, Hiroshi.   "Deep Sea Research around Japan." Oceanus. vol. 30, no. 1, Spring 1987, pp. 32-34.

1875. _____.   "Recovery of Uranium from Seawater." Oceanus. vol. 30, no. 1, Spring 1987, pp. 44-47.

1876. International Oceanographic Commission (of UNESCO). "Ocean Science for the Year 2000."   Elisabeth Mann Borgese and Norton Ginsburg, eds. Ocean Yearbook 4. Chicago and London: University of Chicago Press, 1983, pp. 176-259.

1877. Jacobson, Jon L.   "Marine Scientific Research under Emerging Ocean Law."   Ocean Development and International Law. vol. 9, nos. 3-4, 1981, pp. 187-200.

1878. Kaczynski, Vlad M.   "In Search of Self-Reliance; Problems of Marine Technology Transfer to the Developing Countries: The Case of West Africa." Ocean Development and International Law. vol. 20, no. 6, 1989, pp. 623-641.

1879. Kay, David.   "International Transfer of Marine Technology: The Transfer Process and International Organization."   Ocean Development and International Law. vol. 2, no. 4, Winter 1974, pp. 351-378.

1880. Kesteven, G. L.   "The Flow of Information and Transfer of Knowledge."   Jacques G. Richardson, ed. Managing the Ocean: Resources, Research, Law.   Mt. Airy, MD: Lomond Publications, Inc., 1985, pp. 231-238.

1881. Kildow, Judith A. Tegger.   "Nature of Present Restrictions on Oceanic Research."   Warren S. Wooster, ed. Freedom of Oceanic Research. New York: Crane, Russak, 1973, pp. 5-28.

1882. King, Lauriston R.   "Introduction: Science, Technology and the Marine Resource System." Ocean Development and International Law. vol. 17, nos. 1-3, 1986, pp. 1-8.

1883. Knauss, John A.   "Marine Research: A Casualty of the Law of the Sea?" Seattle: Washington Sea Grant Program and the Institute for Marine Studies, University of Washington, 12 May 1987.

1884. _____.   "Present Status of the Marine Science Negotiations." Edward Miles and John King Gamble, Jr., eds. Law of the Sea: Conference Outcomes and Problems of Implementation. Cambridge, MA: Ballinger Publishing Company, 1977, pp. 287-303.

1885. _____.   "Developing the Freedom of Scientific Research Issue of the Law of the Sea Conference." Ocean

Development and International Law.   vol. 1, no. 1, Spring 1973, pp. 93-120.

1886. _____ and Mary Hope Katsouras. "Recent Experience of the United States in Conducting Marine Scientific Research in Coastal State Exclusive Economic Zones." Thomas A. Clingan, Jr., ed. _The Law of the Sea: What Lies Ahead?_ Honolulu: The Law of the Sea Institute, University of Hawaii, 1988, pp. 297-309.

This paper discusses the 1982 Law of the Sea Convention provisions for marine scientific research, state practices as observed in the United States, and the extent of conformity with the Law of the Sea Convention provisions.

1887. _____ and Mary Hope Katsouros. "The Effect of the Law of the Sea on Marine Scientific Research in the United States: Recent Trends." E. D. Brown and R. R. Churchill, eds. _The UN Convention on the Law of the Sea: Impact and Implementation_. Honolulu: The Law of the Sea Institute, University of Hawaii, 1987, pp. 373-382.

1888. "Landlocked States and Marine Scientific Research." _LOS Lieder_. vol. 3, no. 2. Honolulu: The Law of the Sea Institute, Univ. of Hawaii, October 1989, p. 5.

1889. Laughton, A. S. "The Future of Oceanographic Research in the Light of the UN Convention." E. D. Brown and R. R. Churchill, eds. _The UN Convention on the Law of the Sea: Impact and Implementation_. Honolulu: The Law of the Sea Institute, University of Hawaii, 1987, pp. 387-392.

1890. Lawson, Rowena. "Fisheries Research and the Law of the Sea." E. D. Brown and R. R. Churchill, eds. _The UN Convention and the Law of the Sea: Impact and Implementation_. Honolulu: The Law of the Sea Institute, University of Hawaii, 1987, pp. 392-397.

1891. Lee, Roy S. "Commentary: Marine Scientific Research in the International Seabed Area." Choon-ho Park, ed. _The Law of the Sea in the 1980s_. Honolulu: The Law of the Sea Institute, University of Hawaii, 1983, pp. 336-341

1892. "Logistic Support of Arctic Research: Findings and Recommendations of the US Arctic Research Commission." _Ocean Science News_. no. 1, July 1988.

1893. Mangone, Gerard J. "The Effect of Extended Coastal State Jurisdiction over the Seas and Seabed upon Marine Science Research." Choon-ho Park, ed. _The Law of the Sea in the 1980s_. Honolulu: The Law of the Sea Institute, University of Hawaii, 1983, pp. 294-312.

1894. _____. "The Effect of Extended Coastal State Jurisdiction over the Seas and Seabed upon Marine Science Research." _Ocean Development and International Law_. vol. 9, no.s 3-4, 1981, pp. 201-218.

This paper discusses the decline in freedom to conduct marine science research under contemporary political and legal settings and under claims by coastal states over the ocean space and the seabed.

1895. "Marine Scientific Research: The Law of the Sea Institute's 23rd Annual Meeting." Oceans Policy News, June 1989, p. 4.

1896. "Marine Scientific Research and Ocean Services; Law of the Sea Debate in the United Nations General Assembly." Oceans Policy News. December 1989, pp. 4-5.

1897. Mayama, Takashi. "The Japanese Marine Science and Technology Center." Oceanus. vol. 30, no. 1, Spring 1987, pp. 27-28.

1898. Miyazaki, Takeaki. "Wave Power Generator." Oceanus. vol. 30, no. 1, Spring 1987, pp. 43-44.

1899. Muench, Robin D. "Mizex: The Marginal Ice Zone Experiment." Oceanus. vol. 26, no. 2, Summer 1983, pp. 55-60

Studies by scientists on the dynamics of polar sea, ice and atmospheric interactions can provide vital information on climate, offshore oil development and fishery management.

1900. Munier, Richard. "The Politics of Marine Science: Crisis and Compromise." Lewis M. Alexander, ed. The Law of the Sea: Needs and Interests of Developing Countries. Kingston, RI: University of Rhode Island, 1973, pp. 219-223.

1901. Nemoto, Takahisa. "Japan's Ocean Research Institute." Oceanus. vol. 30, no. 1, Spring 1987, pp. 48-54.

1902. Osteno, Ned A. "Introduction: U.S.-China Collaboration in Oceanography." Oceanus. vol. 26, no. 4, Winter 1983-84, pp. 9-12.

U.S.-China collaboration provides China with the needed contemporary technology in ocean research.

1903. Palacio, Francisco J. "The Development of Marine Science in Latin America." Oceanus. vol. 23, no. 2, Summer 1980, pp. 39-49.

1904. Patel, Surendra J. "Technological Dependence of Developing Countries: A Survey of Issues and Lines of Action." John King Gamble, Jr. and Giulio Pontecorvo, eds. Law of the Sea: The Emerging Regime of the Oceans. Cambridge, MA: Ballinger Publishing Company, 1974, pp. 55-71.

1905. "Permits for U.S. Researchers in U. S. EEZ." Ocean Science News. vol. 30, no. 13, May 5, 1988.

1906. Peterson, M. N. A. and F. C. MacTernan. "A Ship for

Scientific Drilling." Oceanus. vol. 25, no. 1, Spring 1982, pp. 72-78.

1907. Pinto, M. C. W.. "Transfer of Technology under the UN Convention on the Law of the Sea." Elisabeth Mann Borgese and Norton Ginsburg, eds. Ocean Yearbook 6. Chicago and London: University of Chicago Press, 1986, pp. 241-270.

1908. _____. "Preface to a Proposed Indian Ocean Scientific Conference." Elisabeth Mann Borgese and Norton Ginsburg, eds. Ocean Yearbook 5. Chicago and London: University of Chicago Press, 1985, pp. 285-291.

1909. Pontecorvo, Giulio. "Ocean Science and Mutual Assistance: An Uneasy Alliance." Ocean Development and International Law. vol. 1, no. 1, Spring 1973, pp. 51-64.

1910. _____ and Maurice Wilkinson. "An Economic Analysis of the International Transfer of Marine Technology." Ocean Development and International Law. vol. 2, no. 3, Fall 1974, pp. 255-284.

1911. Pravdic, Velimir. "International Cooperation in Marine Sciences: The Nongovernmental Framework and the Individual Scientist." Elisabeth Mann Borgese and Norton Ginsburg, eds. Ocean Yearbook 5. Chicago and London: University of Chicago Press, 1985, pp. 117-129.

1912. Raleigh, C. Barry. "Commentary: The Internationalism of Ocean Science vs. International Politics." Marine Technology Society Journal. vol. 23, no. 1, March 1989, pp. 44-47.

1913. "Recommendations Made for Marine Science Education Guidelines in the Year 2000." IMS Newsletter. no. 51, 1989.

1914. Revelle, Roger. "The Need for International Cooperation in Marine Science and Technology." Elisabeth Mann Borgese and Norton Ginsburg, eds. Ocean Yearbook 5. Chicago and London: University of Chciago Press, 1985, pp. 130-149.

1915. Ridgway, Sam H. "Diving Mammals and Biomedical Research." Oceanus. vol. 19,no. 2, Winter 1976, pp. 49-55.

1916. Ringcard, Gisele. "Scientific Research: From Freedom to Deontology." Ocean Development and International Law. vol. 1, no. 2, Summer 1973, pp. 121-136.

1917. Ritchie-Calder, Lord. "Perspectives on the Sciences of the Sea." Elisabeth Mann Borgese and Norton Ginsburg, eds. Ocean Yearbook 1. Chicago and London: University of Chicago Press, 1978.

1918. Ross, David A. "Sea Grant: A National Investment for the Future." <u>Oceanus</u>. vol. 31, no. 3, Fall 1988, pp. 6-11.

1919. _____. "Ocean Science: Its Place in the New Order of the Oceans." Giulio Pontecorvo, ed. <u>The New Order of the Oceans: The Advent of a Managed Environment</u>. New York: Columbia University Press, 1986, pp. 65-84.

1920. _____. "Commentary: Marine Scientific Research." Choon-ho Park, ed. <u>The Law of the Sea in the 1980s</u>. Honolulu: The Law of the Sea Institute, University of Hawaii, 1983, pp. 317-320.

1921. _____ and Judith Fenwick. "Marine Scientific Research: U.S. Perspective on Jurisdiction and International Cooperation." <u>Proceedings</u>: The Law of the Sea Institute Annual Conference, University of Rhode Island, June 1988, pp. 128-137.

1922. _____ and Judith Fenwick. "U. S. Marine Scientific Research and Access to Foreign Waters." <u>Oceanography</u>. vol. 1, no. 2, November 1988.

1923. _____ and Michael C. Healey. "International Marine Science: An Opportunity for the Future." <u>Oceanus</u>. vol. 25, no. 4, Winter 1982-83, pp. 13-19.

1924. _____ and Leah J. Smith. "Training and Technical Assistance in Marine Science: A Viable Transfer Product." <u>Ocean Development and International Law</u>. vol. 2, no. 3, Fall 1974, pp. 219-254.

1925. Schaefer, Milner B. "The Changing Law of the Sea: Effects on the Freedom of Scientific Investigation." Lewis M. Alexander, ed. <u>The Law of the Sea: The Future of the Sea's Resources</u>. Kingston, RI: University of Rhode Island, 1968, pp. 113-117.

1926. Scharfe, J. "Interrelations between Fishing Technology and the Coming International Fishery Regime." Francis T. Christy, Jr., Thomas a. Clingan, Jr., John King Gamble, Jr., H. Gary Knight and Edward Miles ed. <u>Law of the Sea: Caracas and Beyond</u>. Cambridge, MA: Ballinger Publishing company, 1975, pp. 259-264.

1927. "Science to Support the Management of Southern Ocean Marine Living Resources." <u>Maritime Studies</u>. no. 44, January-February 1989.

1928. Silva, Ivan J. "The Transfer of Technology and the Role of the Indian Ocean Fishery Survey and Development Programme." John King Gamble, Jr. and Giulio Pontecorvo, eds. <u>Law of the Sea: The Emerging Regime of the Oceans</u>. Cambridge, MA: Ballinger Publishing Company, 1974, pp. 113-121.

1929. Silverstein, Harvey. "The Technique of Technology Assessment: A Comment." Douglas M. Johnston and Norman

G. Letalik, eds. The Law of the Sea and Ocean Industry: New Opportunities and Restraints. Honolulu: The Law of the Sea Institute, University of Hawaii, 1984, pp. 232-235.

1930. Song, Yann-huei. "Marine Scientific Research and Marine Pollution in China." Ocean Development and International Law. vol. 20, no. 6, 1989, pp. 601-622.

Examines China's attitude toward the legal regimes of marine pollution and scientific research.

1931. Soons, Alfred H. A. Marine Scientific Research and the Law of the Sea. Antwerp and Boston: Kluwer Law and Taxation Publishers, 1988.

This is a comprehensive analysis, article by article, of the origin, legislative history and implication of those provisions in the 1982 Law of the Sea Convention dealing with marine scientific research.

1932. _____. "Marine Scientific Research Provision in the Convention on the Law of the Sea: Issues of Interpretation." E. D. Brown and R. R. Churchill, eds. The UN Convention on the Law of the Sea: Impact and Implementation. Honolulu: The Law of the Sea Institute, University of Hawaii, 1987, pp. 365-372.

1933. _____. "Commentary: Some Comments on the New Regime for Marine Scientific Research." Choon-ho Park, ed. The Law of the Sea in the 1980s. Honolulu: The Law of the Sea Institute, University of Hawaii, 1983, pp. 361-380.

1934. Speiss, Fred N. "Commentary: Up Periscope! Observations on Ocean Research Policy and Administration." Marine Technology Society Journal. vol. 23, no. 2, June 1989, pp. 40-49.

1935. Stavridis, Lt. Cmdr. James. "Marine Technology Transfer and the Law of the Sea." Naval War College Review. vol. xxxvi, no. 4, sequence 298, July-August, 1983, pp. 38-49.

The paper discusses the controversial issue of technology transfer, one of the reasons for the United States refusal to sign the 1982 Law of the Sea Convention. It points out the strategic importance of technology in future marine development, as well as its impact on standard of living and economic welfare of many nations.

1936. Sullivan, William L., Jr. "Freedom of Scientific Inquiry." Lewis M. Alexander, ed. The Law of the Sea: National Policy Recommendations. Kingston, RI: University of Rhode Island, March 1970, pp. 364-376.

1937. Suman, Daniel O. "Marine Science in Cuba." Oceanus. vol. 28, no. 3, Fall 1985, pp. 43-49.

1938. Tiler, Christine and John Yates. "Marine Science and Technology in the Federal Republic of Germany: A Policy for Non-living Resource Utilization." _Marine Policy_. vol. 12, no. 4, October 1988, pp. 15-26.

1939. Toyota, Takayoshi and Toshimitsu Nakashima. "Using Deep Seawater for Biological Production." _Oceanus_. vol. 30, no. 1, Spring 1987, pp. 39-42.

1940. "U.S.-USSR Scientific Research Agreement." _Oceans Policy News_. May 1989, p. 2.

1941. Van Dyke, Jon M. and David L. Teichman. "Transfer of Seabed Mining Technology: A Stumbling Block to U. S. Ratification of the Convention on the Law of the Sea." Douglas M. Johnston and Norman G. Letalik, eds. _The Law of the Sea and Ocean Industry: New Opportunities and Restraints_. Honolulu: The Law of the Sea Institute, University of Hawaii, 1984, pp. 518-550.

1942. Vargas, Jorge. "Marine Scientific Research and the Transfer of Technology." Jon M. Van Dyke, ed. _Consensus and Confrontation: The United States and the Law of the Sea Convention_. Honolulu: The Law of the Sea Institute, University of Hawaii, 1985, pp. 453-456.

This short discussion traces development of the issue of marine scientific research in the 1982 Law of the Sea Convention. It points out that the new multi-national convention does establish freedom of marine scientific research on the high seas as additional to the traditionally accepted freedoms contained in Article 2 of the 1958 High Seas Convention.

1943. _____. _Normative Aspects of Scientific Research in the Oceans: The Case of Mexico_. Honolulu: The Law of the Sea Institute, University of Hawaii, 1974.

Examines the rules and regulations by Mexico on marine scientific research in its territorial sea.

1944. Verlaan, Philomene. "Marine Archaeology: A Trojan (Sea) Horse?" Elisabeth Mann Borgese, Norton Ginsburg and Joseph R. Morgan, eds. _Ocean Yearbook 8_. Chicago and London: University of Chicago Press, 1989, pp. 231-253.

1945. Vine, Allyn C. "Frontiers of Oceanography." Thomas A. Clingan, Jr., ed. _The Law of the Sea: What Lies Ahead?_ Honolulu: The Law of the Sea Institute, University of Hawaii, 1988, pp. 236-238.

1946. _____. "The Case for Semi-submerged Research Ships." _Oceanus_. vol. 25, no. 1, Spring 1982, pp. 15-17.

1947. von Welk, Stephan F. "Commentary: Marine Scientific Research." Choon-ho Park, ed. _The Law of the Sea in_ the 1980s.   Honolulu: The Law of the Sea Institute, University of Hawaii, 1983, pp. 326-335.

1948. Vorbach, Joseph E. "The Law of the Sea Regime and Ocean Law Enforcement: New Challenges for Technology." Ocean Development and International Law. vol. 9, nos. 3-4, 1981, pp. 323-343.

1949. Wecker, Miranda. "Developments in Marine Science and Technology." Paper presented at the 22nd Annual Conference of the Law of the Sea Institute, University of Rhode Island, 12-16 June 1988.

1950. Weiss, Charles. "Technology Transfer and the Oceans." John King Gamble, Jr. and Giulio Pontecorvo, eds. Law of the Sea: The Emerging Regime of the Oceans. Cambridge, MA: Ballinger Publishing Company, 1974, pp. 81-85.

1951. Wilkes, Daniel S. "Key Pitfalls in Thinking about New Rules for Science in the Oceans." Lewis M. Alexander, ed. The Law of the Sea: National Policy Recommendations. Kingston, RI: University of Rhode Island, March 1970, pp. 360-363.

1952. Winner, Russ. "Science, Sovereignty and the Third Law of the Sea Conference." Ocean Development and International Law. vol. 4, no. 3, 1977, pp. 297-342.

1953. Wolfrum, Ruediger.   "Commentary: Marine Scientific Research." Choon-ho Park, ed. The Law of the Sea in the 1980s. Honolulu: The Law of the Sea Institute, University of Hawaii, 1983, pp. 321-326.

1954. Wooster, Warren S. "Research in Troubled Waters: U. S. Research Vessel Clearance Experience, 1972-1978." Ocean Development and International Law. vol. 9, nos. 3-4, 1981, pp. 219-240.

1955. _____. "The Endless Quest." Oceanus. vol. 23, no. 1, Spring 1980, pp. 68-72.

1956. _____.   "International Cooperation in Marine Science." Elisabeth Mann Borgese and Norton Ginsburg, eds. Ocean Yearbook 2. Chicago and London: University of Chicago Press, 1980, pp. 123-136.

1957. _____. "Possible Action by U. S. Oceanographic Institutions to Facilitate Their Conduct of Marine Scientific Research in Distant Waters." Edward Miles and John King Gamble, Jr., eds. Law of the Sea: Conference Outcomes and Problems of Implementation. Cambridge, MA: Ballinger Publishing Company, 1977, pp. 307-310.

1958. _____. "Some Implications of Ocean Research." Ocean Development and International Law. vol. 4, no. 1, 1977, pp. 39-50.

1959. _____. "Conditions for Ocean Research." Elisabeth Mann Borgese and David Krieger, eds. The Tides of Change: Peace, Pollution and Potential of the Oceans. New York: Mason/Charter, 1975, pp. 310-317.

1960. _____, ed. Freedom of Oceanic Research. New York: Crane, Russak, 1973.

1961. _____. "Scientific Aspects of Maritime Sovereignty Claims." Ocean Development and International Law. vol. 1, no. 1, Spring 1973, pp. 13-20.

1962. _____. "Pollution: Scientific Research." Lewis M. Alexander, ed. The Law of the Sea: A New Geneva Conference. Kingston, RI: University of Rhode Island, 1972, pp. 130-134.

1963. _____. "International Organization for Science." Lewis M. Alexander, ed. The Law of the Sea: International Rules and Organization for the Sea. Kingston, RI: University of Rhode Island, May 1969, pp. 420-422.

1964. _____ and Michael D. Bradley. "Access Requirements of Oceanic Research: The Scientists' Perspective." Warren S. Wooster, ed. Freedom of Oceanic Research. New York: Crane, Russak, 1973, pp. 29-39.

1965. _____ and Michael Redfield. "Consequences of Regulating Oceanic Research." Warren S. Wooster, ed. Freedom of Oceanic Research. New York: Crane, Russak, 1973, pp. 219-234.

1966. Wyrtki, Klaus. "The North Pacific Experiment and Climate Variations." Edward L. Miles and Scott Allen, eds. The Law of the Sea and Ocean Development Industries in the Pacific Basin. Honolulu: The Law of the Sea Institute, University of Hawaii, 1983, pp. 597-601

Brief description of the Pacific experiment known as NORPAX, the project funded by the National Science Foundation.

1967. Yankov, Alexander. "A General Review of the New Convention on the Law of the Sea: Marine Science and Its Application." Elisabeth Mann Borgese and Norton Ginsburg, eds. Ocean Yearbook 4. Chicago and London: University of Chicago Press, 1983, pp. 150-175.

1968. Yuru, Luo. "Amassing Scientific Knowledge to Preserve the Marine Environment." Jacques G. Richardson, ed. Managing the Ocean: Resources, Research, Law. Mt. Airy, MD: Lomond Publications, Inc., 1985, pp. 125-129

Major Players at UNCLOS III:
Summary of Positions
on Selected Issues

1969. Adede, A. O. "Developing Countries' Expectations from the Responses to the Seabed Mining Regimes Proposed by the Law of the Sea Conference." Judith T. Kildow, ed. Deepsea Mining. Cambridge, MA: The MIT Press, 1980, pp. 193-215.

1970. _____. "The Group of 77 and the Establishment of the International Seabed Authority." Ocean Development and International Law. vol. 7, nos. 1-2, 1979, pp. 31-64.

1971. Akaha, Tsuneo. Japan in Global Ocean Politics. Honolulu: The Law of the Sea Institute, University of Hawaii, 1985.

This is a book which provides a detailed study of Japan's domestic politics in relation to ocean politics. It reviews of Japan's position, as influenced by domestic and bureaucratic politics, in the 1958, 1960 and 1974-1982 United Nations Law of the Sea Conferences.

1972. Ake-uru, Chalermpon. "Thailand and the Law of the Sea." Choon-ho Park and Jae Kyu Park, eds. The Law of the Sea: Problems from the East Asian Perspective. Honolulu: The Law of the Sea Institute, University of Hawaii, 1987, pp. 414-418.

1973. Alexander, Lewis M. "How Will the New Law of the Sea Affect International Organizations: The Case for Living Marine Resources." Choon-ho Park, ed. The Law of the Sea in the 1980s. Honolulu: The Law of the Sea Institute, University of Hawaii, 1983, pp. 446-460.

1974. _____. "Indices of National Interest in the Oceans." Ocean Development and International Law. vol. 1, no. 1, Spring 1973, pp. 21-50.

1975. Allison, Anthony P. "The Soviet Union and the UNCLOS III: Pragmatism and Policy Evolution." Ocean Development and International Law. vol. 16, no. 2, 1986, pp. 109-136.

1976. Allott, Philip. "Power Sharing in the Law of the Sea." American Journal of International Law. vol. 77, no. 1, January 1983, pp. 1-30.

1977. Amador, F. W. Garcia. Latin America and the Law of the Sea. Honolulu: The Law of the Sea Institute, University of Hawaii, 1972.

This study focuses on development of the 200 nautical mile claims, as well as the exclusive fishery enclosure and other delimitation of the ocean area for conservation purposes, by Latin American nations.

1978. Anand, R. P. "Odd Man Out: The United States and the UN Convention on the Law of the Sea." Jon M. Van Dyke, ed. Consensus and Confrontation: The United States and the Law of the Sea Convention. Honolulu: The Law of the Sea Institute, University of Hawaii, 1985, pp. 73-124.

1979. Belsky, Martin H. "The Ecosystem Model Mandate for a Comprehensive United States Ocean Policy and the Law of the Sea." San Diego Law Review. vol. 26, no. 3, August-September 1989, pp. 417-496.

1980. Bobrow, Davis B. "International Politics and High Level Decision Making: Context for Ocean Policy." Ocean Development and International Law. vol. 3, no. 2, 1975, pp. 171-180.

1981. Brunn, Stanley D. "Voting Patterns in the UN General Assembly on Uses of the Seas." Elisabeth Mann Borgese, Norton Ginsburg and Joseph R. Morgan, eds. Ocean Yearbook 7. Chicago and London: University of Chicago Press, 1988, pp. 42-64.

1982. Buhl, Johannes Fons. "The European Economic Community and the Law of the Sea." Ocean Development and International Law. vol. 11, nos. 3-4, 1982, pp. 181-200.

1983. Burke, William T. "Chinese Perceptions of the Law of the Sea." Thomas A. Clingan, Jr., ed. The Law of the Sea: What Lies Ahead? Honolulu: The Law of the Sea Institute, University of Hawaii, 1988, pp. 160.

1984. Buzan, Barry G. "Canada and the Law of the Sea." Ocean Development and International Law. vol. 11, nos. 3-4, 1982, pp. 149-180.

1985. _____. Seabed Politics. New York: Praeger Publishers, Inc., 1976.

For positions of the various player groups during the UN General Assembly seabed debate--Latin America, landlocked, the Group of 77, and many other nations--this is the most comprehensive study. (This is a repeat entry.)

1986. _____ and Barbara Johnson. <u>Canada at the Third Law of the Sea Conference: Policy, Role and Prospects.</u> Kingston, RI: University of Rhode Island, December 1975.

1987. Caron, David D. and Charles D. Buderi. <u>Perspectives on U. S. Policy toward the Law of the Sea.</u> Honolulu: The Law of the Sea Institute, University of Hawaii, 1982.

1988. Center for Ocean Management Studies, University of Rhode Island. <u>Comparative Marine Policy: Perspectives from Europe, Scandinavia, Canada and the United States.</u> Brooklyn, NY: J. F. Bergin Publishers, Inc., 1981.

1989. Chao, Kuo-Tsi. "The Republic of China and the Law of the Sea." Choon-ho Park and Jaw Kyu Park, eds. <u>The Law of the Sea: Problems from the East Asian Perspective.</u> Honolulu: The Law of the Sea Institute, University of Hawaii, 1987, pp. 336-347.

1990. Chee, Choung Il. "The Republic of Korea and the Law of the Sea." Choon-ho Park and Jae Kyu Park, eds. <u>The Law of the Sea: Problems from the East Asian Perspective.</u> Honolulu: The Law of the Sea Institute, University of Hawaii, 1987, pp. 174-194.

1991. Child, Terrin. "Enforcement of 200-Mile Exclusive Economic Zone Claims over Living Marine Resources in Southeast Asia." Thomas A. Clingan, Jr., ed. <u>Law of the Sea: State Practice in Zones of Special Jurisdiction.</u> Honolulu: The Law of the Sea Institute, University of Hawaii, 1982, pp. 438-464.

1992. Churgin, James. "The Structure of Oceanography in China." <u>Oceanus.</u> vol. 26, no. 4, Winter 1983-84, pp. 13-19.

1993. Clingan, Thomas A., Jr. "United States Ocean Policy and East Asia." Choon-ho Park and Jae Kyu Park, eds. <u>The Law of the Sea: Problems from the East Asian Perspective.</u> Honolulu: The Law of the Sea Institute, University of Hawaii, 1987, pp. 582-590.

1994. Coll, Alberto R. "Functionalism and the Balance of Interests in the Law of the Sea: Cuba's Role." <u>American Journal of International Law.</u> vol. 79, no. 4, October 1985, pp. 891-911.

1995. Colson, David A. "The United States, The Law of the Sea, and the Pacific." Jon M. Van Dyke, ed. <u>Consensus and Confrontation: The United States and the Law of the Sea Convention.</u> Honolulu: The Law of the Sea Institute, University of Hawaii, 1985, pp. 36-49.

1996. Cottrell, Alvin J. and R. M. Burrell, eds. <u>The Indian Ocean: Its Political, Economic and Military Importance.</u> New York: Praeger Publishers, 1972.

1997. Craven, John P. "The United States Position on the Law of the Sea." Douglas M. Johnston and Norman G. Letalik, eds. The Law of the Sea and Ocean Industry: New Opportunities and Restraints. Honolulu: The Law of the Sea Institute, University of Hawaii, 1984, pp. 103-126.

1998. Darman, Richard G. "U. S. Deepsea Mining Policy: The Pattern and the Prospects." Judith T. Kildow, ed. Deep-sea Mining. Cambridge, MA: The MIT Press, 1980, pp. 159-192.

1999. Darwin, H. G. "The Law of the Sea and the UN Convention of 1982: A United Kingdomn View." E. D. Brown and R. R. Churchill, eds. The UN Convention on the Law of the Sea: Impact and Implementation. Honolulu: The Law of the Sea Institute, University of Hawaii, 1987, pp. 129-134.

2000. "Debate on U. S. Policy on the LOS Treaty: Seminar of Center for Ocean Law and Policy, University of Virginia." Oceans Policy News. April 1989, p. 4.

2001. Dibb, Tracey. "Do Land-Locked States and the Third World Get a Look In?" Sea Changes. no. 6, 1987, pp. 50-79.

2002. Djalal, Hasjim. "A Southeast Asian Perspective." Giulio Pontecorvo, ed. The New Order of the Oceans: The Advent of a Managed Environment. New York: Columbia University Press, 1986, pp. 199-216.

2003. Dore, Isaak I. and Luke T. Lee. "The Law of the Sea Convention and Third States." American Journal of International Law. vol. 77, no. 3, July 1983, pp. 541-568.

2004. Drigot, Diane C. "Oil Interests and the Law of the Sea: The Case of the Philippines." Ocean Development and International Law. vol. 12, nos. 1-2, 1982, pp. 23-70.

2005. Eskin, Otho E. "U. S. Administrtion Views on the Law of the Sea." Edward L. Miles and Scott Allen, eds. The Law of the Sea and Ocean Development Issues in the Pacific Basin. Honolulu: The Law of the Sea Institute, University of Hawaii, 1983, pp. 277-281.

2006. Ferreira, Penelope Simoes. "The Role of African States in the Development of the Law of the Sea at the Third UN Conference." Ocean Development and International Law. vol. 7, nos. 1-2, 1979, pp. 89-130.

2007. Fieldhouse, Richard and Shunji Taoka. Superpowers at Sea: An Assessment of the Naval Arms Race. London: Oxford University Press, 1989.

2008. Friedheim, Robert. "Arvid Pardo, the Law of the Sea Conference and the Future of the Oceans." Robert L.

Friedheim, ed. Managing Ocean Resources: a Primer. Boulder, CO: Westview Press, 1979, pp. 149-161.

2009. _____, George O. Totten III, and Haruhiro Fukui, et. al., eds. Japan and the New Ocean Regime. Boulder, CO: Westview Press, Inc., 1984.

This is a collection of 10 essays contributed by mostly Japanese experts on Japan's role at the Third UN Conference on the Law of the Sea.

2010. Friedman, Alan G. and Cynthia A. Williams. "The Group of 77 at the United Nations: An Emergent Force in the Law of the Sea." San Diego Law Review. vol. 16, no. 3, April 1979, pp. 555-574.

The article traces the origin and development of the Group of 77, leading players at the Law of the Sea Conference. After a short historical overview of the group's formation, the article illustrates their activities and positions on ocean issues at the UN Third Conference on the Law of the Sea.

2011. Friedman, Norman. The U.S. Maritime Strategy. London: Jane's Publishing Company, Limited, 1988.

2012. Glassner, M. I., ed. Bibliography on Land-Locked States. 2nd rev. and enl. ed. London: Graham & Trotman, Ltd., 1986.

2013. Gulland, John. "Developing Countries and the New Law of the Sea." Oceanus. vol. 22, no. 1, Spring 1979, pp. 36-42.

2014. Hahm, Ryong-Choo. "A Korean Perspective on the Law of the Sea: A Private View." Choon-ho Park and Jae Kyu Park, eds. The Law of the Sea: Problems from the East Asian Perspective. Honolulu: The Law of the Sea Institute, University of Hawaii, 1987, pp. 138-147.

2015. Hamzah, B. A. "Malaysia and the Law of the Sea: Post-UNCLOS III Issues." Choon-ho Park and Jae Kyu Park, eds. The Law of the Sea: Problems from the East Asian Perspective. Honolulu: The Law of the Sea Institute, University of Hawaii, 1987, pp. 356-364.

2016. Han, Mukang, Shusong Zhao and Luiquing Ge. "China's Coastal Environment, Utilization and Management." Elisabeth Mann Borgese, Norton Ginsburg and Joseph R. Morgan, eds. Ocean Yearbook 7. Chicago and London: University of Chicago Press, 1988, pp. 223-240.

2017. Hayashi, Moritaka. "Japan and Deep Seabed Mining." Ocean Development and International Law. vol. 17, no. 4, 1986, pp. 351-365.

Identifies four factors that influence and shape Japan's ocean policy: uses of the ocean under a stable legal order, Japan's dependence on mineral imports, cooperation with

Western industrialized nations, and traditional ties between government and private industry.

2018. Hollick, Ann L. U. S. Foreign Policy and the Law of the Sea. Princeton, NJ: Princeton University Press, 1981.

This is a repeat entry on the role of the United States in the evolution of the law of the seas dating from the Truman Proclamation of 1945 to the UN Third Conference on the Law of the Sea. It is a comprehensive record of the development of United States foreign policy concerning the law of the sea.

2019. Ilid, Keisuke. "Third World Solidarity: The Group of 77 in the United Nations General Assembly." International Organization. vol. 42, no. 2, Spring 1988, pp. 375-395.

2020. Janis, M. W. and D. C. F. Daniel. The USSR: Ocean Use and Ocean Law. Honolulu: The Law of the Sea Institute, University of Hawaii, 1974.

This is a good reference to rely on for Soviet attitudes on law of the sea issues in the early stages of negotiations at the Third United Nations Conference on the Law of the Sea. It is one of the detailed records of the USSR in the seabed debate.

2021. Johnson, Barbara and Frank Langdon. "The Impact of the Law of the Sea Conference upon the Pacific Region: Part I." Pacific Affairs. vol. 51, no. 1, Spring 1978, pp. 5-23.

2022. _____. "The Impact of the Law of the Sea Conference upon the Pacific Region: Part II." Pacific Affairs. vol. 51, no. 2, Summer 1978, pp. 216-229.

2023. Joyner, Christopher C. "Normative Evolution and Policy Process in the Law of the Sea." Ocean Development and International Law. vol. 15, no. 1, 1985, pp. 13-36.

2024. Juda, Laurence. "UNCLOS III and the New International Economic Order." Ocean Development and International Law. vol. 7, nos. 3-4, 1979, pp. 221-256.

2025. _____. Ocean Space Rights: Developing U. S. Policy. New York and London: Praeger Publishers, 1975.

2026. Kent, George. The Politics of Pacific Island Fisheries Boulder, CO: Westview Press, Inc., 1980.

2027. Kim, Jung-Gun. "Reflections on the Attitude of North Korea toward the Law of the Sea Treaty (UNCLOS III)." Choon-ho Park and Jaw Kyu Park, eds. The Law of the Sea; Problems from the East Asian Perspective. Honolulu: The Law of the Sea Institute, University of Hawaii, 1987, pp. 212-244.

2028. Koers, Albert W. "Participation of the European Economic Community in the New Law of the Sea Convention." American Journal of International Law. vol. 73, no. 3, July 1979, p. 426-44.

2029. Koh, Tommy T. B. "How Can the United States and Other Nations Promote Order for the Oceans?"   Jon M. Van Dyke, ed. Consensus and Confrontation: The United States and the Law of the Sea Convention. Honolulu: The Law of the Sea Institute, University of Hawaii, 1985, pp. 537-539.

2030. Kolb, Kenneth H. "Congress and the Ocean Policy Process." Ocean Development and International Law. vol. 3, no. 3, 1976, pp. 261-286.

2031. Kolodkin, Antol and Anatoly Zakharov. "Some Aspects of Soviet State Practice on the Development of Ocean Resources." Jon M. Van Dyke, ed. Consensus and Confrontation: The United States and the Law of the Sea Convention. Honolulu: The Law of the Sea Institute, University of Hawaii, 1985, pp. 213-217.

2032. Kuribayashi, Tadao. "The United Nations Convention on the Law of the Sea and the Japanese Municipal Laws." Choon-ho Park and Jae Kyu Park, eds. The Law of the Sea: Problems from the East Asian Perspective. Honolulu: The Law of the Sea Institute, University of Hawaii, 1987, pp. 316-322.

Explains the relationship between the Law of the Sea Convention and Japanese municipal laws.

2033. _____. "The New Ocean Regime and Japan." Ocean Development and International Law. vol. 11, nos. 1-2, 1982, pp. 95-124.

2034. Larson, David L. "Deep Seabed Mining: American and Indian Perspectives." Ocean Development and International Law. vol. 14, no. 2, 1984, pp. 193-200.

A review of Kurt Michael Shusterich's book on deep seabed mining and Manjula R. Shyam's work on prospects for India in mining nodules.

2035. _____. "The Reagan Administration and the Law of the Sea." Ocean Development and International Law. vol. 11, nos. 3-4, 1982, pp. 297-320.

2036. McDorman, Ted L. "Implementation of the LOS Convention: Options, Impediments and the ASEAN States." Ocean Development and International Law. vol. 18, no. 3, 1987, pp. 535-580.

2037. Malone, James L. "Who Needs the Sea Treaty?"   Foreign Affairs. vol. 54, Spring 1984, pp. 44-63.

The author was President Ronald Reagan's special representative to the Law of the Sea Conference at the time the United

States decided not to become a party to the 1982 Law of the Sea Convention. The article is a defense of why the decision was made and justification for the decision.

2038. _____. "Law of the Sea and Ocean Policy." Department of State Bulletin. October 1982, pp. 48-50.

2039. Manansala, Mario C. "The Philippines and the Law of the Sea." Choon-ho Park and Jae Kyu Park, eds. The Law of the Sea: Problems from the East Asian Perspective. Honolulu: The Law of the Sea Institute, University of Hawaii, 1987, pp. 430-434.

2040. Miles, Edward L. "On the Roles of International Organizations in the New Ocean Regime." Choon-ho Park, ed. The Law of the Sea in the 1980s. Honolulu: The Law of the Sea Institute, University of Hawaii, 1983, pp. 383-445.

2041. Morris, Michael A. "Influence and Innovation in the Law of the Sea: Latin America and Africa; Introduction." Ocean Development and International Law. vol. 7, nos. 1-2, 1979, pp. 1-8.

2042. _____. "The Domestic Context of Brazilian Maritime Policy." Ocean Development and International Law. vol. 4, no. 2, 1977, pp. 143-170.

2043. Mullin, James. "Implications of the New Law of the Sea: An International Development Agency Perspective." Douglas M. Johnston and Norman G. Letalik, eds. The Law of the Sea and Ocean Industry: New Opportunities and Restraints. Honolulu: The Law of the Sea Institute, University of Hawaii, 1984, pp. 569-573.

2044. Nakauchi, Kiyofumi.   "Japan's Ocean Affairs: Ocean Regime, Policy and Development." Japanese-English Ocean Affairs Dictionary. Honolulu: The Law of the Sea Institute of Japan, 1989.

2045. Nasu, Noriyuki.   "Introduction: Japan and the Sea." Oceanus. vol. 30, no. 1, Spring 1987, pp. 2-8.

2046. Negroponte, John D. "Current Developments in the U.S. Oceans Policy." Department of State Bulletin, September 1986, pp. 84-87.

Outlines the official U.S. position on the Law of the Sea Convention and programs that the U.S. enacted to achieve law of the sea policy.

2047. Nordquist, Myron H. and Choon-ho Park. The Reports of the United States Delegation to the Third United Nations Conference on the Law of the Sea. Honolulu: The Law of the Sea Institute, University of Hawaii, 1983.

This large volume contains the unclassified reports of the United States delegation to the 1973 UN Seabed Committee and the 2nd through 11th (1981-1982) sessions of the Third UN Conference on the Law of the Sea.

2048. Ostreng, Willy. "Norway's Law of the Sea Policy in the 1970s." Ocean Development and International Law. vol. 11, nos. 1-2, 1982, pp. 69-94.

2049. Ouchi, Kazuomi. "A Perspective on Japan's Struggle for Its Traditional Rights on the Oceans." Ocean Development and International Law. vol. 5, no. 1, 1978, pp. 107-134.

2050. Park, Choon-ho. East Asia and the Law of the Sea. 2nd ed. Seoul, Korea: Seoul National University Press, 1985.

2051. Park, Choon-ho and Jae Kyu Park, eds. The Law of the Sea: Problems from the East Asian Perspective. Honolulu: The Law of the Sea Institute, University of Hawaii, 1987.

This volume contains the papers presented at two workshops (1981 and 1984) sponsored by the Law of the Sea Institute on relevant problems from the East Asian perspective.

2052. Piscatori, James P. "Saudi Arabia and the Law of the Sea." Richard B. Lillich and John Norton Moore, eds. U. S. Naval War College International Law Studies, Readings in International Law from Naval War College Review 1974-1977. vol. 61. Newport, RI: U. S. Naval War College, 1980, pp. 633-648.

2053. Pohl, Reynaldo Galindo. "Latin American Contribution to UNCLOS III: A Reflection." Elisabeth Mann Borgese and Norton Ginsburg, eds. Ocean Yearbook 4. Chicago and London: University of Chicago Press, 1983, pp. 390-410.

2054. _____. "Latin's Influence and Role in the Third Conference on the Law of the Sea." Ocean Development and International Law. vol. 7, nos. 1-2, 1979, pp. 65-88.

2055. Post, Alexandra. "United Nations Involvement in Ocean Mining." Ocean Development and International Law. vol. 10, nos. 3-4, 1982, pp. 275-313.

This study provides some background understanding on the debate at the Third UN Conference on the Law of the Sea over United Nations involvement in ocean mining, insisted upon by the Group of 77, representing developing nations.

2056. Prescott, J. R. V. "Existing and Potential Maritime Claims in the Southwest Pacific Ocean." Elisabeth Mann Borgese and Norton Ginsburg, eds. Ocean Yearbook 2. Chicago and London: University of Chicago Press, 1980, pp. 317-345.

2057. Redgwell, Catherine. "Current Developments: UK Practice in International Law of the Sea." Marine Policy. vol. 13, no. 3, July 1989, p. 266.

2058. Rembe, N. S. Africa and the International Law of the Sea: A Study of the Contribution of the African States to the Third United Nations Conference on the Law of the Sea. The Hague, Netherlands: Martinus Nijhoff, and London: Graham & Trotman, Ltd., 1980.

2059. Reynolds, Clark G. History and the Sea: Essays on Maritime Strategies. Columbia, SC: University of South Carolina Press, 1989.

2060. Samuels, Marwyn S. Contest for the South China Sea. New York and London: Methuen, 1982.

2061. Sauwant, Karl. Group of 77. Dobbs Ferry, NY: Oceana Publications, Inc., 1981.

2062. Sayed, H. El. Maritime Regulations in Saudi Arabia. London: Graham & Trotman, Ltd., 1987.

This is a first comprehensive study in English on the Saudi Arabian development of maritime law and regulations.

2063. Schneider, Claudine. "What Is the Future of the Oceans in the Absence of a U. S. National Ocean Policy?" Woods Hole, MA: Woods Hole Oceanographic Institution, 20 March 1987.

2064. Shulman, Marshall D. "The Soviet Turn to the Sea." Edmund A. Gullion, ed. Uses of the Seas. Englewood Cliffs, NJ: Prentice-Hall, 1968, pp. 138-162.

2065. Shyam, Manjula R. "Deep Seabed Mining: An Indian Perspective." Ocean Development and International Law. vol. 17, no. 4, 1986, pp. 325-349.

Since India is one of the "pioneer investors" registered by the Preparatory Commission to engage in deep seabed mining in the Indian Ocean area, this is a useful study of the Indian perspective on deep seabed mining.

2066. Sinjela, A. Mpazi A. "Land-Locked States Rights in the Exclusive Economic Zone from the Perspective of the UN Convention on the Law of the Sea." Ocean Development and International Law. vol. 20, no. 1, 1989, pp. 63-82

2067. _____. Land-locked States and the UNCLOS Regime. Dobbs Ferry, NY: Oceana Publications, Inc., 1988.

Examines the claims and rights of land-locked states in terms of transit through straits, freedom of the high seas, and resources in the territorial seas.

2068. Song, Yann-huei Billy. "China's Ocean Policy: EEZ and Marine Fisheries." Asian Survey. vol. xxix, no. 10, October 1989, pp. 983-999.

This article examines China's ocean policy dealing with marine fisheries and the exclusive economic zone. A detailed discussion is given on China's decision not to declare its own EEZ.

2069. Sulikowski, Terese. "Soviet Ocean Policy." Ocean Development and International Law. vol. 3, no. 1, 1975, pp. 69-74.

2070. Szekely, Alberto. Latin America and the Development of the Law of the Sea: Regional Documents, National Legislation. Dobbs Ferry, NY: Oceana Publications, Inc., 1976.

2071. "Third United Nations Conference on the Law of the Sea; Committee II: Report of United Nations Special Committee on Geographical Disadvantage, Comparative Proposal for Accommodation of Geographically Disad-vantaged Countries." Ocean Development and International Law. vol. 3, no. 1, 1975, pp. 181-186.

2072. Tin, Chao Hick. "Singapore and the Law of the Sea." Choon-ho Park and Jae Kyu Park, eds. The Law of the Sea: Problems from the East Asian Perspective. Hono-lulu: The Law of the Sea Institute, University of Hawaii, 1987, pp. 376-383.

2073. Touret, Denis G. "The French Deep-Sea Mining Legis-lation of 1981." Ocean Development and International Law. vol. 13, no. 1, 1983, pp. 115-120.

This article discusses the purpose and main provisions of the Deep Seabed Mineral Resources Exploration and Mining Act, enacted by the French Parliament on November 24, 1981.

2074. Treves, Tullio. "The EEC and the Law of the Sea: How Close to One Voice?" Ocean Development and International Law. vol. 12, nos. 3-4, 1982, pp. 173-190.

2075. U. S. Department of State. "President's Statement, 29 January 1982; and Ambassador Malone's Statement, 23 February 1982." Current Policy No. 371. Washington, DC, January-February 1982.

President Reagan's statement concerning changes needed to correct the unacceptable deep seabed mining elements in the Law of the Sea Convention.

2076. Van Syl, Uys. "Access to the Sea for Land-Locked States." Sea Changes. no. 6, 1987, pp. 112-133.

2077. Wang, Tie-ya. "China and the Law of the Sea." Douglas M. Johnston and Norman G. Letalik, eds. The Law of the Sea and Ocean Industry: New Opportunities and Restraints. Honolulu: The Law of the Sea Institute, University of Hawaii, 1984, pp. 581-589.

2078. Wells, Linton, III. "Japan and the United Nations Conference on the Law of the Sea." Ocean Development

and International Law.   vol. 2,   no. 1, Spring 1974,
pp. 65-91.

2079. Wisnomoerti, Noegroho.   "Indonesia and the Law of the
Sea." Choon-ho Park and Jae Kyu Park, eds.   The Law of
the Sea: Problems from the East Asian Perspective.
Honolulu: The Law of the Sea Institute, University of
Hawaii, 1987, pp. 392-403.

2080. Yuan, Paul C. "The New Convention on the Law of the
Sea from the Chinese Perspective." Jon M. Van Dyke,
ed. Consensus and Confrontation: The United States and
the Law of the Sea Convention. Honolulu: The Law of
the Sea Institute, University of Hawaii, 1985, pp.
184-204.

2081. Zivetz, Herman.   "The Peoples' Republic of China and
the Law of the Sea: Caracas 1974 and Geneva 1975."
Richard B. Lillich and John Norton Moore, eds. U.S.
Naval War College International Law Studies, Readings
in International Law from Naval War College Review
1974-1977. vol. 61.   Newport, RI: U. S. Naval War
College, 1980, pp. 616-632.

Author Index

The reference numbers used in this index are the numbers for the bibliographic entries. Next to the alphabetized authors' names for each subject chapter are the appropriate entry numbers.

Abbadi, Abdelkader K., 1526
Abir, Mordechai, 1527
Abrahamsson, Bernard J.,
   1702, 1703, 1704, 1705
Adams, C. M. G., 1826
Adede, A. C., 1969, 1970
Adede, A. O., 978, 979, 980
Adelman, William J., 1827
Ademuni, Odeke, 1706
Agrait, Luis E., 70
Akaha, Tsuneo, 1573, 1707,
   1708, 1971
Ake-uru, Chalermpon, 1972
Albers, John P., 841
Alexander, Lewis, 23, 193,
   194, 195, 196, 197, 198,
   199, 548, 549, 1442, 1443,
   1529, 1709, 1710, 1711,
   1712, 1713, 1817, 1828,
   1973, 1974
Alexander, Vera, 1153
Alexanderson, G., 200
Allen, Craig H., 192
Allen, K. Radway, 547
Allen, S., 982, 1492, 1529,
   1829
Amador, F. W. Garcia, 1977
Amerasinghe, C. F., 203
American Bar Association,
   1714
Amsbaugh, J. K., 983
Anand, R. P., 71, 204, 205,
   206, 207, 984, 1978
Anderson, A. T., 2
Anderson, Andres W., 1715

Anderson, Lee G., 555
Anderson, Richard, 1271
Anderson, Susan M., 1154
Anderson, Thomas D., 1716
Andrassy, Jurai, 985
Andreev, Anatoly, 1444
Andresen, Steinar, 554, 1445
Andrew, Andrew W., 61
Andriana, V. I., 1155
Antrim, Lance N., 986
Archer, Clive, 5
Archer, Jack H., 557, 630,
   1157
Ariyoshi, Yoshiya, 1717
Arkin, William M., 1531
Armi, Laurence, 6
Arnold, Frederick, 987
Arrow, Dennis W., 988
Asante, Samuel K. B., 843
Ashmore, Edward, 213
Attard, David Joseph, 214
Atema, Jelle, 1158
Atwood, Donald K., 1446
Auburn, F. M., 844, 989
Aune, Bjorn, 215, 1532

Baba, N., 1159, 1439, 1440
el-Badri, Hassam, 1718
Badurina, Berislav, 1534
Bailey, Bruce C., 1341
Baird, Irene M., 845
Baker, F. W. G., 1832
Ball, Milner S., 72
Ballard, Robert D., 1833

Busha, Thomas S., 1184, 1185, 1451, 1554, 1731, 1732
Butler, Michael J. A., 582
Butler, W. E., 244, 245, 1733
Buzan, Barry, 82, 83, 1555, 1984, 1985, 1986

Caflisch, Lucius C., 69, 545, 1012
Cafruny, Alan W., 1734
Caminos, Hugo, 246
Campbell, Douglas II, 247, 248, 249, 1186, 1735
Campbell, Neil J., 1848, 1849
Capuzzo, Judith M., 1187, 1226, 1421
Carlisle, Rodney, 1736
Carlson, Cynthia E., 583, 584, 585
Caron, David D., 459, 1013, 1987
Carroz, J. E., 586
Carsey, Frank D., 1694
Cate, R. P., 1431
Cates, Melissa B., 1188
Chadwin, Marl Lincoln, 1737
Champ, M. A., 854, 1189, 1226, 1434, 1850
Chao, Kuo-tsi, 1989
Chapman, Douglas G., 587
Charlier, Roger H., 855, 856
Charney, Jonathan I., 252, 253, 254, 255, 256, 857, 1014, 1851
Chasis, Sarah, 1455
Chee, Choung Il, 257, 1990
Cheever, Daniel, 858, 1853
Chen, Zhizhong, 258
Child, Terrin, 1991
Chircop, Aldo, 74, 1456
Chiu, Hungdah, 259, 260
Chopra, Sudhir K., 27, 588
Christrup, Judy, 589
Christy, Francis T., Jr., 590, 591, 592, 593, 1854
Chung, Le Kim, 263
Churchill, R. R., 78, 264, 594, 595
Churgin, James. 1992
Cicin-Sain, Biliana, 265
Cipriano, Frank, 837
Clark, Allen, 905
Clark, Jennifer Cook, 522
Clark, Joel P., 1015
Clark, John, 859
Clark, R. P., 1191

Clay, Gerald S., 860
Clemons, John H., 84
Clingan, Thomas A., Jr., 85, 266, 267, 268, 1192, 1556, 1557, 1993
Coe, James M., 1193
Cohen, Lewis I., 1016
Cohen, Robert, 862
Coll, Alberto R., 1994
Colson, David A., 86, 269, 270, 764, 1995
Colwell, Rita R., 1855
Conant, Melvin A., 13, 863, 1738
Conforti, Benedetto, 271
Constans, Jacques, 864
Cook, B. A., 599
Cooper, John, 273, 320, 600
Copes, Parzival, 601, 602
Cordle, Frank, 1199
Corredor,Jorge E., 1200, 1446
Corwin, Edward, 1201
Costa, Daniel, 603
Cottrell, Alvin J., 1559, 1560, 1588, 1642, 1996
Coull, James R., 604
Council on Ocean Law, 274
Couper, A. D., 1461, 1741
Cousteau, Jacques Yves, 16
Cragg, Christopher, 1810
Craven, John P., 275, 276, 312, 605, 982, 1017, 1202, 1997
Creech, Heather, 1856
Crosby, Donald B., 87
Cross, F. A., 1434
Cross, Melvin L., 606
Cruickshank, Michael, 866
Cunho, Derek da, 1562
Curtis, Clifton E., 1203, 1204, 1205, 1206
Cushing, D. H., 607
Cutting, Richard, 645
Cuyvers, Luc, 17, 277, 278

Dahl, Christopher, 608
Dahmani, M., 609
Dallmeyer, Dorinda G., 279
Dalton, Harvey, 1563
D'Amato, Anthony, 88, 89, 90
Daniel,C. F., 2020
Daniel, Donald C., 1564
Danzig, Aaron L., 280
Dar, Vinod, 1857
Darby, Joseph J., 281, 1565
Darwin, H. G., 1998
Davidson, Lynn, 1463
Davin, E. M., 1018

Subject Index

The reference numbers used in this subject index are the numbers for the bibliographic entries arranged under subject chapters. The entries are numbered consecutively from the first subject chapter to the end of the bibliography.

About the Author

JAMES C. F. WANG, Professor of Political Science, University of Hawaii at Hilo, is the author of *Handbook on Ocean Politics and Law* (Greenwood Press, forthcoming, 1992), and *Contemporary Chinese Politics* (1989), among other works.